*A Story of Boxing, Betrayal, Homophobia,
and the First Latino Champion*

BLACK INK

JOSE CORPAS

Win By KO Publications
Iowa City

Black Ink
Jose Corpas

(ISBN-978–0–9903703–8-3):

(softcover: 50# acid-free alkaline paper)
Includes bibliography, appendix, and index.

© 2016 by Jose Corpas. All Rights Reserved.

No part of this book may be reproduced, or transmitted in any form or by any means, graphic, electronic or mechanical, including photocopying, recording, taping, or by any information storage retrieval system without the written permission of Jose Corpas.

Cover art and design by Lloyd Lelina © 2016.
Manufactured in the United States of America.

Back cover- Paris- October 1928. Photo by Meurisse from author's personal collection.

Win By KO Publications
Iowa City, Iowa
winbykopublications.com

ACKNOWLEDGEMENTS

My phone rang one chilly afternoon. It was Springs Toledo. We got to talking boxing when he asked if I finished the "Panama Al Brown book." Not only was I nowhere near done, the book was still without a title.

Like a great corner man who motivates a tired boxer with a seemingly simple phrase at the right moment, Springs Toledo said two words. "Cinderella Man."

That film about a contemporary of Brown served as a reminder that good stories have no expiration date. A special thanks goes to Mr. Toledo. And to my family and friends who were patient with me while my mind was lost somewhere in 1920s Paris.

Also to Zach Levin - the closest thing to a writing mentor I ever had. Thanks for the 2AM emails loaded with constructive criticism, corrections, and, sometimes - praise.

Thanks also to the helpful Deborah Green. And to the cover designer, Lloyd Lelina, who created a cover I think even Al Brown would have liked. Others who contributed anecdotes along with hard-to-find magazine and newspaper clippings without hesitation were historian Alister Scott Ottesen and the grandson of Dick Burke, Steve Barr. A huge thank you to both for their eagerness and to the many others since a book does not get written by one person.

"The reward of art is not fame or success but intoxication : that is why so many bad artists are unable to give it up."

Jean Cocteau

Table of Contents

Acknowledgements	III
Foreword by Springs Toledo	1
Introduction	5
1. Cólon	7
2. Canal Boxing	13
3. Kid Téofilo	22
4. Panama Al Brown	44
5. Pariah	60
6. Uncrowned Champion	74
7. World Champion	99
8. Exile	119
9. Betrayal	166
10. Redemption	199
11. Twilight Years	217
12. Final Round	227
13. References	229
14. Boxing Record	232
15. Index	240

"When a work appears to be ahead of its time, it is only the time that is behind the work"

Jean Cocteau

FOREWORD

by Springs Toledo

One late afternoon in June 1984, a dozen teenagers headed north on Washington Street in Boston's Combat Zone, trying hard to look hard like Robert De Niro or Clubber Lang, depending on their complexions. One of them, called "Snaz," was smiling. He popped a cassette into a banged-up boom box, hefted it up on his shoulder, and said "get to this."

We got to it all right. A five-beat percussion introduced a meandering rhythm broken up by congas and a whistle like the one we heard behind us when we robbed Filene's. The lyrics were a chant, an electric voice yearning for action. It was what we called a "jam."

Set it off on the left ya'll
Set it off on the right ya'll
Set it off
On the left (start it)
On the right (start it)
On the left I suggest while we're left

I never did figure out just how it was that Snaz got his hands on "Set It Off" and I-couldn't-count-how-many more like it. It wasn't as if he could do a Google search or download them to his iPhone, and many of them never aired on mainstream radio then and don't air on Sirius XM now. We'd put the squeeze on him sometimes but all we'd get was the runaround and that familiar smile. I overheard him on a payphone once. *Underground*, he said, which was obvious; and *New York,* which should have been obvious.

The New York underground. Years later, I heard that "Set It Off" was hard to find even there, that the record company was selling it out of the trunk of a car, that the DJs got it first and were spinning it all night at two clubs in Manhattan. At the Fun House, corner kids were under the same spell we were two hundred fourteen miles away. Larry Levan, a drag queen and one of the pioneers of what is now called House music, introduced it to gay sophisticates at the exclusive Paradise Garage. Two worlds embraced by a song, a jam.

From spark to flame
A little thinking
Desires burning
Live us this day

Back in the day, the word "jam" was an exclamation with two meanings. It also meant "to fight," and New York's underground circuit was the epicenter not only for jams but for *jams*.

Way back in the day, boxing gyms dotted the blocks of the five boroughs and beckoned swarms of poor and marginalized teenagers to learn a peculiar trade, an integrated trade, where the grandsons of slaves mingled their sweat and blood with the sons of European immigrants. Two worlds in a clinch.

In 1920, the New York State Legislature legalized boxing and escorted it out of the back rooms of men's clubs and into arenas. Other states caught on though it would be decades before they caught up. In 1925, more than half the champions in the ten divisions were New York fighters. They dominated one division particularly: the bantamweights. Ted Carroll, an African-American sports cartoonist and writer from Greenwich Village, remembered the Golden Twenties when "every hamlet had its bantamweight fighter and how the public loved them! The turnstiles clicked so merrily whenever they performed that they should have been called the Golden Bantams."

One among them stood head and shoulders above the rest like a black headmaster at a Hebrew school. Wicket thin with shoulders that would fill a zoot suit, he was five feet nine in a division where the average height was five four. Alfonso Teófilo Brown was already a fighter in Colón, Panama when he stowed away on a ship and headed to the big city of dreams in June 1923. He disembarked with nothing, knowing no one, squinting in the sun. I imagine him looking for a familiar or even a friendly face, finding none, wandering up beyond 110th Street where the words wouldn't be so confusing and the complexions matched his own. I see him standing on the banks of the Harlem River watching the horizon darken and brighten and darken again behind the High Bridge. Did his eyes burn with ambition? Was he afraid?

Six years later, "Panama" Al Brown would be crowned king of the Golden Bantams not four miles from the port where he arrived as an undocumented immigrant.

The old photographs show Brown with a springtime smile. But it was a disguise. It concealed more than anyone knew. In an era when lynchings were regular news items in the dailies, nativism was at its last raging peak, and homosexuality was locked in the crawl space under the house, never mind the closet — Brown was black, Panamanian, and as gay as Larry Levan.

The story of the first Latino champion in boxing history, the truth of him, is in good hands. Author Jose Corpas, a Latino American, is more than just another historian huddled over a microfilm reader in a public library until closing time. A former fighter, he is familiar with both the wallops and the whispers of the underground circuit. He got his start there, sweating and bleeding in similar clubs on similar streets in the same big city as Brown himself. Corpas has been researching the life of this boxing anomaly for more years than he spent in the professional ring. He spent hours talking to fighters born a half-century before him who knew Brown; who saw that springtime smile and what was behind it.

I was surprised to find out he was born only six months earlier than I was; that he's Brooklyn to my Boston and was a corner kid in the Eighties. I asked him if he remembered "Set It Off." He started singing it and I started to wince.

Give us this day
To show our gratitude

BLACK INK

To change our attitude
Come on we're many
With all that we feel
The time is ideal

Long before Strafe's electric voice formed a psychic bridge between discordant cultures, Panama Al Brown set it off in New York City. He was not accepted either as a man or as a champion during his lifetime, though something tells me he would have been celebrated in ours.

I see him standing on the banks of the Harlem River watching the horizon behind the High Bridge. It's brightening now.

SPRINGS TOLEDO
Boston-2016

Introduction

*B*lack Ink started out as a chapter in a book I was writing on the history of boxing in Latin America. After completing chapters on John Budinich and Luis Firpo, I came to the one on Panama Al Brown.

I first heard of him through my father right around the time Roberto Duran twice surprised Sugar Ray Leonard – first by winning, then by quitting. Those two, my father said, could hang with any fighter from the past. Having witnessed the excitement, and - in the rematch - the disappointment, Duran and Leonard created inside the smoke-filled closed-circuit theaters and back home on the block, I imagined what it might have been like to have many more *Sugar Rays* and *Robertos*. I had to find out more about this "past" my father talked about.

Through conversations, magazine articles, the "B" encyclopedia, VHS tapes, and a few silent 8mm reels, an image of the past formed in my mind. It was a time with more fighters, more fights, more gyms, more trainers, and fewer weight classes. As a result, it was harder for a boxer to reach the top. One who did was Brown.

When I joined some of the boxing gyms throughout New York City during the early 1980s, I met some of the trainers and boxers from the past. Some of them knew Panama Al Brown and repeated some of the same stories my father told me. He was blackballed they said and discriminated against because of his sexual preference. Brown was forced to travel to Europe to make a living. Financially he did well but met with the same hate- adored by some, mocked by others. They spat on him during his ring walks, screamed obscenities, and, after one fight, attacked him in the arena and beat him until the riot police arrived.

BLACK INK

Those were the stories I wrote when I started his chapter. When I thought I was finished, I went online and searched for final details such as dates and cities. Those details I found but not any of the stories I'd heard about him. His story, and many of the people who knew him, were gone.

I set out on a mission to re-tell his story.

The mission lasted five years and took me through the virtual libraries of Central America and Europe, and through newspaper archives in English, Spanish, French, and Italian. Enough lost pieces were found to put together not just a chapter, but a book. Some of the stories I was told by the likes of Pedro Montanez, Tony Pellone, and Syd Martin, proved difficult to support. The homophobia he encountered, for instance. There were however, enough questionable actions taken against him where the reasons given were dubious. Something about him drew the ire of many in the boxing establishment. Homophobia can't be ruled out. It still exists. As recently as November 2015, more than sixty years after his death and almost certainly by someone he never met, his Wikipedia page was altered and filled with homophobic slurs.

His life was a tragic one. And just as tragic, his life is nearly forgotten. That's why I decided to write his story. Because he deserves it and because his is a story that shouldn't be lost again.

Colón

"Al was a poem in black ink..." - Jean Cocteau

Al was a poem in black ink. Those are the words Jean Cocteau used to describe Panama Al Brown. What type of poem Cocteau didn't specify but if we are talking about his ability to float and sting in the ring long before anyone in Louisville did and will his way to victory while afflicted with disease, we can say he was a ballad. If we're describing his habit of buying a new hat every day or mailing his suits to London from Paris to be pressed, we can say he was a free verse. If we're talking about his life after he was found at death's door, passed out on a mattress of litter on Broadway and too weak to knock, we can say he was an epic.

His journey started just as the Thousand Days' War neared its end in a country known as the waist of the Americas. On Sixth Street in the coastal city of Colón in Panama where the street marker; painted on the corner house; reads "6ta." Alfonso Téofilo Brown was his given name and he was born on July 5th, 1902 though he often tried to pass himself off as younger even going as far as giving false dates on official travel documents. Like those of the *Ile de France*, next to his occupation (boxer) and place of birth (Panama), one can almost see him smiling playfully as he told the record keeper he was born in 1905 and, in a later voyage, 1908.

He grew up on the second floor of a weathered grey barracks-style wood home a few blocks from the piers. He slept in a small room with his three brothers on beds that were lined up side by side along the wall and behind mosquito screens.

Colón was a young city, not in its infancy - more like its awkward teens - when Brown was born. Originally called Navy Bay, later Aspinwall, it was a rugged place nature didn't intend for habitation by large populations of humans. Even the land-hungry sailor the area was named after, *Cristobal Colon,* or - in English - Christopher Columbus - took a good look at the hostile terrain and the hazy atmosphere and shook his head "no" before settling some fifty miles to the west.

The shoreline of *Manzanillo Island,* where Colón is located, was made up of equal parts mud, marsh and reptiles. A few yards behind that were mangroves so dense the native snakes that navigated through them were no wider than a rope. Looming in the background were deadly *Manzanilla* trees. Named after the tiny apples that decorated its branches, simply touching the fruit or the leaves, was enough to make you foam at the mouth and send your body into convulsions that continued even after you died.

Above it all, the skies were polluted with noxious fumes many believed were the source of yellow fever. Completing the poisonous atmosphere were disease ridden mosquitoes with felonious intentions that were so thick, Rear Admiral Thomas O. Selfridge Jr. witnessed one snuff out a lit candle with its body.

The thirst for gold was what brought the masses to this part of the world. Preferring to sail the rough seas rather than risk the treacherous, expensive, and crime-ridden cross-country wagon trails of America, gold-seekers looking for a shortcut to California made a right after the Bahamas and zigzagged through the Greater Antilles.

Compared to sailing around South America, past *Cabo de Hornos,* which is translated Cape Horn but literally means Cape of Ovens, past the snowcapped mountains of *Tierra de Fuegos* where according to Magellan, the waters turned frigid, the waves grew bigger and the land spewed fire, then sailing back north more than five thousand nautical miles to San Francisco, going through Panama was four months quicker.

Once there, they had to schlep through 47 miles of tropical jungle to reach the Pacific coast where another steam liner waited to sail to California. The route along the neglected *El Camino Real* path was a dangerous and unpredictable one with a timetable that depended as much on the weather as it did on how sprightly the mule you sat on was.

To make this easier, plans were drawn up for a railroad going north to south right down the middle of the country. Workers came from around Central and South America, the Caribbean, and Europe to convert this swamp into a city.

Among the workers were Brown's maternal ancestors. They came from Martinique and joined hundreds from the islands of the West Indies in search of jobs not gold. They found work as laborers and together with workers from America, China and Africa laid train tracks like you do floor tiles - one piece at a time - from the north while another crew worked their way up from the south.

Along with the influx of workers came doctors, home builders, hustlers, and pimps with their prostitutes. Prostitutes who gave more than happy endings to unsuspecting customers who found out right around the time they were sailing through the Tropic of Cancer on their way to Frisco.

Plumbing was limited. Potable water was scarce so most took to drinking cheap liquor for breakfast, lunch, and dinner. The empty bottles were tossed the same way smokers toss cigarette butts. The bottles and the litter became part of the landscape. They were bottles no one picked up since there wasn't yet a sanitation, or even a police department.

There were two seasons in Colón - very hot and - very hot and wet. The climate was a haven for mosquitoes and disease. When workers awoke in the middle of the night with muscle aches and chills, death was usually around the corner. The mere mention of the words Yellow Fever, or *Changres* Fever as they originally called it, was enough to send people rushing to the docks to board the next ship out.

After the Gold Rush ended and the First Transcontinental Railroad in America was completed, there was less reason to cross through Colón. Most left the city. The comparatively few who remained continued working for the railroad or at the shipping yards. Others operated small businesses and quite a few sat idly in the stifling heat among sunburned dogs and horses.

BLACK INK

The city was engulfed in a morale-sapping heat that over the years baked out any sense of urgency from its residents. It was a place where flies buzzed in your face and then dropped dead in midflight, too exhausted to make it to their destination, landing with a tiny thud on someone's table. *"Muerto,"* they'd say while brushing it onto the dirt floor where Tabasco-colored ants wasted no time in pouncing.

Plump vultures patrolled the skies like police choppers, diving down in unison at the scent of a corpse.

"Death was distilled in every breath of air," wrote Hubert Howe Bancroft in 1851.

Travelers passing through Colón were advised not to roam the dirty streets and to stay out of the rain, which was believed to be contaminated. Despite this, many more travelers, including Brown's father, were about to pack their bags and join his maternal ancestors in Panama.

With the announcement of the construction of the Panama Canal and the countless number of jobs it promised, a huge wave of people ignored odds that favored ending up two meters underground wrapped in a wooden overcoat, and made their way to Colón.

The project proved more difficult than the building of the railroad. Originally attempted by the French, workers were recruited from neighboring islands like Barbados and Jamaica. Concerns about the harsh conditions faced by the railroad workers were drowned out by the excitement caused by the promises of high pay. Ads circulated throughout the Caribbean of "The Colón Man" or, as he was known in Barbados, "The Panama Man."

Panama Man was presented as a regular Joe who found work in Colón and returned home sharply dressed with pockets full of gold. Once there, things were not nearly so easy - laborers found themselves in a struggle against the same homicidal nature that Columbus avoided. Close to 300 people per month died throughout the French construction. The fevers - yellow, malaria and dengue - claimed the lives of many.

If fevers didn't get them, something else probably did. Coral snakes and yellow beard vipers were a constant threat slithering in the trenches. Those who survived the poisonous fangs could be seen days later rubbing arms or legs that looked like burned logs.

Recruiting new workers was a difficult and costly assignment. It helped that some workers believed that no matter how bad the conditions were in Colón they could not possibly be worse than the conditions were where they came from.

Brown with trainer Bob Roberts (middle) and unnamed before the Angelmann fight in uncredited publicity photo.

Canal Boxing

Following the official end of the American Civil War, the Thirteenth Amendment was passed abolishing slavery. Gone were the shackles and throat collars though for many, freedom came with restrictions.

The freed slaves were free to be turned away from certain establishments and free to drink from water fountains as long as they were labeled "colored." They were free to attend inadequate schools and free to receive poor medical care. Free to clean homes their wages could not afford and free to tend the lawns of owners who pointed locked and loaded rifles at their children if they played too close to the grass.

Even those who rose above the poverty and inequality to become civic leaders and elected government officials lived under the constant threat of violence including death. About an hour's drive south of Nashville, a group of former Confederate soldiers formed a brotherhood of whites on Christmas Eve, called themselves the Ku Klux Klan, and aimed to restore white supremacy through acts of terrorism.

During the Colfax Massacre on Easter Sunday of 1873, dozens of blacks were killed by white Democrats who tried regaining control of the Colfax courthouse. That same year, the country would find itself in the early stage of the original Great Depression. In the ensuing years unemployment rose while wages and property values dropped. Anxious to leave all that behind with just the clothes on his slim but muscular shoulders was Al Brown's father.

Horace Brown was born on a tobacco and cotton plantation outside Nashville and for about the first five years of his life, he, his brothers, sisters, and parents "belonged" to somebody. As a free teen and young adult, he spent almost as much time looking for a job as he did watching out for lynch mobs. Thousands were hung, burned, and dismembered in front of cheering crowds sipping lemonade. When the opportunity to work on the Panama Canal presented itself, Horace, barred from schooling for much of his life, hesitated only slightly before trading the old slave codes for the fever infested city of Colón.

The city wasn't much improved from the railroad building days. As the population swelled, so did the number of murders. Cadavers in the gutter were as common as crack houses in 1980s Northeast Philadelphia. Unlike the trash - and the crack houses - the bodies disappeared quickly since the sale of unclaimed bodies to science was- like crack- good business.

Horace dug trenches by day and slept in unscreened barracks at night. Despite Dr. Carlos Finlay having linked the fevers to the mosquito years before in Cuba, the residents of the Canal Zone continued to place the legs of their beds in trays of water to keep the creepy crawlers away. It worked for most of the bugs though mosquitoes loved the trays enough to raise their families in them.

Increasing numbers of workers were kept awake by the chills, body aches, and urgent runs to a window to vomit dark blood. Some workers never returned after checking in to the French Hospital. As a result, many equated falling ill with death.

The sick ignored their back and knee aches and worked through the abdominal contractions to earn a few extra dollars to send home before their organs shut down. Some collapsed and died while pushing a wheelbarrow of dirt. Moments later a laborer would pass by, dump the dirt from the wheelbarrow he pushed moments before on top of them in an impromptu burial.

The French aborted their mission after they came to the realization that shoveling tropical dirt and clay was much more difficult than parting the sands of the Suez. They abandoned Panama and left behind debt, machinery, and an unused ditch in the middle of the country.

Horace, by then known as Horacio, began working as a fruit vendor. Before the roads were paved and vendors used the small wheeled carts called *carritos,* they placed their fruit in large trays that they carried on their heads.

Back and forth each day Horacio walked through the city and sold his fruits. Past the pimps on Bottle Alley where the prostitutes waited against the walls, legs spread and dresses hiked up so no one would confuse their intentions. Peeks were free, the pimps informed but, stares were not allowed.

Horacio walked past cantinas that were full by noon and the barber shops where you could get a clip, a shave, and a bottle of mercury ointment for genital chancres while a cadaver behind a curtain was being prepped since, back then, many barbers did double and triple duty as VD clinics and morticians.

Horacio was married by then to a local *Colónense* woman named Esther Dally. Together they bore six children including Al. Horacio spoke English to his children while Esther spoke Spanish and French with them.

Horacio often told his four boys and two girls stories of the racist ways of the American South and of the reasons he came to Panama. Those same racist ways he left behind would soon follow him there.

After toying with the idea of digging through Nicaragua, the United States decided to pick up where the French left off. Once the Thousand Days' War ended, the digging resumed. Contractors from the southern states brought with them the Jim Crow way of life. The gold and the silver payrolls were created. Officially, skilled engineers were paid in gold and laborers in silver. It soon became apparent that the gold rolls were reserved for the lighter complexions while the darker-skinned workers were placed on the silver rolls.

The gold people had bigger sleeping quarters and better-stocked dining halls which were designated gold only. Not even death could put an end to the separation. Cemeteries were divided into gold and silver plots for those gold people who couldn't bear the thought of their ivory-colored bones decaying alongside the ivory-colored bones of silver people.

Deaths continued at an alarming rate. The organizers worked hard to improve the conditions, prevent deaths, keep turnover low and, to attract additional workers. Oil was sprayed on the dirt roads to keep dust down and on mosquito breeding areas. Soon the flying pests were rarely seen but parts of the city were left smelling like a five-minute lube shop. Main roads were paved and improved sleeping quarters with screened windows and plumbing were built. Workers were encouraged to bring their families and housing and schools were built to accommodate them.

Entertainment became a priority. Restaurants, markets, theaters and social clubs catering to American interests sprang up throughout the area and gave the new residents places where they could congregate while the music of Irving Berlin and the Peerless Quartet played in the background.

The weekends were mainly reserved for sporting events. Bullfighting, baseball, and boxing were offered weekly with horse racing, dog racing, dog fights, and cock fights also drawing sizeable crowds and healthy betting action.

Brown and his siblings qualified for only two of the fifteen schools in Colón. Not because of their academic skills - because of the dark color of their skin. Schools were segregated and Brown had to attend one of the "blacks-only" schools despite there being two schools closer to his home.

Dressed in the required white shirts, they joined their classmates each morning and walked to school. They learned to read with third-hand books, some with missing pages, and played music with rusted instruments. Many of the classes were conducted in English, which made school harder for many of his friends.

Baseball was the most popular sport in the Canal Zone followed by what would become Brown's favorite sport. Though prohibited within the boundaries of the Canal Zone since September 4th, 1909, boxing thrived on the other side of the fence as well as the rest of Panama.

After school many of the boys gathered on the streets surrounding the skating rink and took part in simulated boxing matches without gloves. Some pretended to be heavyweight champion Jack Johnson or lightweight Joe Gans. When it was Brown's turn to put up his dukes, he pretended he was Kid Norfolk.

Norfolk was the uncrowned Panamanian Heavyweight Champion at the time, having defeated the infamous Abe "The Newsboy" Hollandersky, a holdover from the days when men boxed in tights or in shorts that would make a Hooters girl blush.

Originally from Baltimore, Kid Norfolk, real name William Ward, was 180 pounds of legitimate badass. Built like a modern day running back at about 5'9", he often challenged much larger boxers. Heavyweights such as Harry Wills, the challenger deemed too great a risk for the legendary Jack Dempsey to fight and who went on to score terrific victories over the likes of Sam Langford, Sam McVae, and Jeff Clark in Panama.

Norfolk had come to live in Colón with his manager, a construction contractor working on the canal. Though widely considered to be the best in Panama at that time, it was Jack Ortega and Abe Hollandersky who got the championship billing.

The cigar chomping Ortega came from California with his gloves and reputation. A cruiserweight by today's standards, he was a real life Jake Heke who backed up his hard man reputation several times in and out of the ring everywhere from the Eureka State to Mosquito Gulf.

Abe "The Newsboy" Hollandersky brought with him an empty brown leather traveling bag, 38 cents, and a fight record no one was able to keep up with. When he arrived in Colón from Jamaica he possessed a record of about 700 fights and the scars to prove it. Among those fights were about a hundred wrestling matches including one with a North American Black Bear, a match with a Judoka where no one told him choking was allowed, and a kick boxing match with a kangaroo.

Abe, who was given the title of official "Newsboy of the Navy" many years earlier when he sunk his pre-teen fist into the stomach of President Teddy Roosevelt, headed to Panama after he heard of all the betting action and the number of sailors there he could sell newspapers to. After a pit stop in Jamaica, where he picked up the 38 cents and the leather bag by beating a boxer who was petrified of

BLACK INK

Abe's crossed eyes and the voodoo he believed caused it, Abe boarded the steamer Joachim to the port in Cristobal, Panama.

Within hours of arriving, a challenge was made and bets were placed before the fight with Ortega was even finalized. It didn't matter that Ortega had a 35-pound weight advantage. The gambling money generated from 40,000 canal workers, hundreds of U.S. servicemen and a million plus Panama City locals for this matchup of champions was too great to pass up.

Much of the gambling took place in bars and barber shops where updated betting lines were written on the windows and mirrors. After the fights, boxers inched their way through the crowded bars and barbershops and shook hands with the winning gamblers who kicked back a few dollars from their wads.

Ortega had the size advantage. Abe had the edge in experience. Ortega was billed as the heavyweight champion of Panama and Central America. Abe was billed as champion of Jamaica and the Caribbean. Fighting in a crouch and still wearing the Hooters like shorts, Abe was able to withstand a fierce early assault and started to take control. Ortega, tiring and unable to ward off the surging Abe, lifted his leg and kneed The Newsboy in the groin.

Abe won by disqualification and was carried from the ring by his fans. Bets were settled around ringside and Abe's share was placed in a purse and handed to him. Talk of a rematch started before Abe even counted the money.

He expected his "purse," a term still used today, would reach four figures for the rematch. Abe boxed a pair of exhibitions and then returned home to Connecticut for personal matters. Before he left, he assured the locals he would return to box Ortega.

Meanwhile, Ortega went back to the drawing board and Kid Norfolk, recently returned from a visit to Baltimore, was whipping himself back into condition.

Filling the void left by Abe as the hot newcomer was a middleweight from Pittsburgh with just one loss in fifty fights against top notch foes like Leo Houck, Jack Dillon, and George Chip. Buck Crouse quickly scored a string of knockouts in Panama including one over Al Goodrich, who had recently beaten Norfolk. Crouse was being groomed for a match against Ortega, who first wanted to avenge his loss to Abe in a rematch.

The return match was set in Panama City once Abe returned. Ortega still considered this to be his town and just as in the first fight, pulled out all the stops to try to win. He planted spies in the form of sparring partners in Abe's camp and sent beautiful women to lure him away from the gym. Abe was admittedly caught off guard by some of the tricks and also by the influence Ortega wielded. Inside the ring it was a different story. With the experience of hundreds of fights under his belt, Abe was always on guard.

The rematch was similar to the first fight only more vicious. Ortega took the early lead. Both boxers bled profusely midway through. Then, in round 18, Abe landed a combination and Ortega stumbled backwards until his back leaned on the ropes. As the cross-eyed Abe moved in for the finish, throwing hooks to the heart, Ortega stuck out his leg and kicked Abe in the stomach. Once again he was disqualified.

Despite the ending, the fight was an action-packed one and Ortega remained an attraction. He became the fighter the fans loved to hate and was matched up against Buck Crouse. The bigger news for Brown and his friends was that Abe was coming back to Colón to fight Kid Norfolk.

Norfolk, originally going back and forth from Baltimore to Colón, was a full-time resident of Panama by the time he fought Abe. Still only 17, he walked the same dusty streets as Brown and felt the same drops of water on his head from the clothes drying on the second floor porches. He passed the same bars with the green labeled Three Dagger Rum bottles in the window, shopped in the same crowded markets, knew the same people, and sometimes hung out with Brown's older brothers.

Even with the experience gained from hundreds of fights, Abe was no match for the teen who was rapidly approaching Hall of Fame level skills. Abe managed to win only about three of the 25 rounds. After the fight a small crowd awaited Norfolk outside the skating rink where he and Abe fought. To them, and many more from Front to Balboa Avenues, Norfolk was the champion. Officially he may have been as well if the championship hadn't become dormant following a scandalous match a few months earlier.

One way or another, Jack Ortega was informed that Buck Crouse planned to take a dive. This troubled Ortega greatly because, so was he. It became a race between two fighters trying to lose. Crouse pawed with a harmless left jab that brushed his opponent's chin. Ortega reacted as if he had just been smashed by a Mike Tyson uppercut and dropped flat. Crouse rushed over to Ortega and stood above him like Muhammad did against Sonny and implored him to get up. Ortega didn't budge. At the count of eight, Crouse kicked him in the ribs. The referee was left with no alternative but to disqualify Crouse.

A riot broke out while Ortega and Crouse argued over who lost. Crouse jumped over the top rope, out of the ring, and ran as fast as he could away from the police officer he had just struck. Both Ortega and Crouse were arrested and did time for their actions. When his time with the chain gang was up, Crouse returned to Pittsburgh. Ortega had a few more fights after he was released though never again at a high level.

The debacle jeopardized boxing in Panama. Already banned in the Canal Zone, the rest of Panama threatened to follow. Never mind the seedy element it attracted, boxing was primitive. The rings were canvas over plywood, no cushion. Injuries, and death, occurred when heads slammed on the floor after knockdowns. Broken noses were fixed by the guy carrying the spit bucket and orange peels were used as mouth shields to prevent the teeth from shredding the lips and leaving them looking like twisted pasta noodles. To prevent biting their tongues, boxers bit down on wooden match sticks during fights. Pre-fight and post-fight medicals consisted simply of the question, "How do you feel?"

The Panamanian National Assembly decided that boxing would continue only if promoters deposited into an escrow account a significant amount of gold. If the fight looked suspicious to the Assembly, the promoter would forfeit the bounty. That ruling restored much of the public's faith in the tainted sport.

Kid Téofilo

After overcoming landslides and a potent earthquake near Balboa, along with its dozens of aftershocks, the canal was completed well ahead of schedule. That summer the SS Cristobal made a practice run through the entire canal and shortly after, the SS Ancon officially opened it though President Wilson was unable to attend and would not formally announce the opening until years later.

The world was at war. A few weeks earlier, the Archduke of Austria, Franz Ferdinand, was assassinated. His death triggered the beginnings of World War I. A convoy of ships slated to pass through the canal on their way to the San Francisco World's Fair was called off because of submarine attacks and naval blockades throughout the oceans.

Many of the canal workers left, taking with them much of the fight racket's fan base. It took an unexpected boost from a Galveston, Texas man to keep the game afloat on the Isthmus.

A fugitive of the Mann Act, Jack Johnson found himself on the run from Europe to South America. His arrival, and later his campaign, in Latin America were widely covered in newspapers from Mexico to Chile.

Johnson was the first boxing champion Argentine fight fans saw in person. Although boxing was outlawed in Buenos Aires, the city council granted special permission to the visiting champion to engage in boxing matches. On January 10, 1915 he stepped into a ring in Palermo Stadium and faced three opponents. The first two were exhibitions against locals Segundo Guiralechea and Enrique Wilkinson, both of whom were dispatched of in a single round. Then, in what appeared to be an official bout, he stopped one of his sparring partners, Jack Murray, in three rounds.

When it was time for Johnson to make his next defense, there was some initial hope that it might be staged inside a Panama City bullring. It was short lived however, as the choice of host city came down to three options - Tijuana or Juarez in Mexico, and Havana in Cuba.

Long associated with gambling and violence, boxing was still banned in many Latin American countries. Cuba's boxing roots originated in Chile in the person of John Budinich. After starring as an amateur he then headlined the first professional card in Chile. He went to the United States to attend College and served as a sparring partner for champion Philadelphia Jack O'Brien. Budinich then wound up in Cuba where he opened what is believed to be the first ever boxing gym on the island.

By the time Jack Johnson arrived, the sport was banned in Havana. But the promise of tourist dollars persuaded Cuban officials to, according to the *NY Times*, lift "any ban that existed" and permit Jack Johnson to defend his championship against the latest of the Great White Hopes, Jess Willard.

Thousands of Americans arrived in steamships from New Orleans and Key West days before the fight. Among the early arrivals were reporters still stuck on black and white.

A *New York Times* sub header read, "Havana whites give boxer big ovation - Johnson in court."

In a reception compared to the arrival of Cuba's first president, Havana whites rallied around big, impressive-looking Jess while Johnson was detained by the police for stealing a man's bag. Newspapermen flocked to the station house for the details.

The bag belonged to "Tremaine," one of Johnson's assistants. Johnson was in possession of the bag as collateral for a loan he gave Tremaine. After much hassle, the case was dismissed but not before becoming international news.

Willard won the title after 26 rounds. Johnson was floored and rather than struggle to get up, he shielded his eyes from the sun. Debate swirled for many years regarding this act and controversy grew when Johnson later stated he lost on purpose after his wife received a box with $50,000 cash in it. His wife was indeed seen leaving the arena before the 26th round but most felt Johnson was simply too tired to get up.

BLACK INK

Willard simply shrugged his shoulders and said he would've appreciated it if Johnson had "tanked" much earlier in the fight because, it was "hotter than hell out there."

Willard returned home to out-of-control mobs of fans that tore down fences and pushed past police to see him. Johnson remained in exile. He sailed to Europe. Then to Mexico, where his presence helped kick off the sport in that country as well.

The buzz that surrounded the Willard-Johnson fight gave a much needed boost to the sport in Panama. Gyms were packed and boxers from the Caribbean made their way over to participate in the shows at the Ancon Theater in Panama City and to the Garden and American Theaters in Colón. They joined a crop of young locals hungry for some of the fame and money the sport seemed to promise. They boxed against each other and against American servicemen billed as *Sailor This* or *Sailor That*.

Canal Zone residents were still prohibited from participating under section 288 of the Laws of the Canal Zone. Participation was considered a felony with fines of "not less than $1,000 and not more than $5,000" and a possible prison bid of one to three years. Under section 289, anyone attending was guilty of a misdemeanor. Employees of the Canal Zone or the railroad were prohibited from participating as a judge, referee, promoter, trainer, second, backers, or manager. Enforcement was rare however and dozens of fights took place each month.

That summer Horacio collapsed at work in the bakery. Seconds later he died on the floor, clutching his chest. Without him, the family went from poor, to poorer than poor. Neighbors pitched in whenever they could. They gave Esther food for her family and let her sweep their floors for a few dollars.

Brown began to wear his father's caps and vented his anger through his fists. Name calling and jokes about his appearance were enough to trigger a bone-rattling combination from the skinny teen in the oversized cap. He was good with his hands. After each street fight, after the highlights of the fight were reenacted multiple times, someone would tell him he should go to the gym. Brown was too good a fighter for the streets.

When thirteen-year-old Brown walked into a boxing gym for the first time, he found it packed. He was greeted by the same, trapped stench that modern boxing gyms have. It's as if all the leather from the boxing gloves and punching bags died together days before a skunk lifted its tail and sprayed the room. New funk mingled with old funk and everyone's idea of fresh air was flapping a musky towel in your face. It's an almost traumatic odor yet, one that somehow smells just right.

With the rest of Colón smelling like smoke and burned wood, the gym stink was probably a welcome reprieve. April 1915 saw a large chunk of the city go up in flames. All that remained in the 22-block stretch the fire seared through was soot and ash covered by charred corrugated metal sheets that once were the roofs of homes.

And the noises of the gym, the jump ropes whipping the floor, the speed bags rattling like engine knock, and the shouts in Spanish, English and, Pidgin, provided a distraction Brown needed.

The 90-pound Brown, wearing his father's cap - tilted to the side - was immediately approached by anxious trainers who seemed to be waiting for him.

What's your weight and do you have experience are the first questions a prospect is asked. Then they asked to see your stance and made you throw a few jabs into the calloused palms of their hands. Only if interested did they bother asking your name. Brown, called Téofilo back then, soon shadowboxed in front of the same mirrors, ducked through the same ropes, tossed the same medicine balls, and punched the same scuffed bags as some of the best boxers in the world.

Located on the ground floor of a two-storey building off *Avenida Bolivar*, the Strand was the stomping grounds of Kid Norfolk and an 18-year-old Barbadian lightweight good enough to soon become a sparring partner of Jack Dempsey. Cyril Quinton Jr., better known as Panama Joe Gans, was just getting his start in Panama after beating the best in Barbados. Panama Joe trained at the Strand as did heavyweights Sam McVae and Jeff Clark when they were in town. Sam Langford, who fought at just about every weight, also made the Strand his headquarters when he was in the area.

While Colón rebuilt itself, Brown laid down the foundation of a Hall of Fame career. Pounding the bags with a dingy pair of Maynard boxing gloves, he found solace in a gym filled with red flags. Coin-sized brown spots, once red, dotted the ring floor. The "knockout seat," where dazed boxers went to gather their senses, was always occupied. Along with the jab and straight right, he picked up other habits. Cigarette butts were constantly being swept up and bottles of rum were everywhere. Despite all that, Brown considered what lurked outside to be worse.

Brown later described this period as one of *"pura miseria."* That's a Spanish saying for poverty. It's a condition words can only partially describe. I could tell you it's taking a bath with cold water and no soap but your heart won't skip beats like the person feeling the cold splashes. You might know that his mom often didn't eat so her children could but you won't be awakened at two in the morning from hunger pangs like she was. Miseria means no gifts on the holidays and no cake for your birthday. It means it's not your turn to eat the strips of beef. It's washing your shirt in the sink every day because it's the only one you have for school. Esther Dally struggled mightily to feed her six children. Though there were days some went hungry, they never starved. Though there were days they were angry and thought life wasn't fair, they kept their manners. They were taught to never talk back and always say thank you.

When Brown started competing, he developed a saying which he would repeat many times in his life. *"Si sabes pelear te pagan; Si no sabes te pegan."* The rhyme is lost in translation. Roughly, it says something along the lines of "If you can fight, you get cash; If you can't, you get bashed." It was hard-earned money.

Eyes were thumbed, kidneys were pounded, and laces were dragged across faces until blood flowed. There was no standing eight-count and holding and hitting was allowed. A coddled prospect being fed a steady diet of carefully selected stiffs on the way to a sparkling 20-0 record was virtually non-existent and impressed no one the few times it occurred. Fighters fought whoever was available.

Many of the trainers were holdovers from the bare knuckle, fight to the finish days. And some of the fighters, like Kid Norfolk, got their starts in the battle royals. Those battle royals were contests organized almost exclusively by white businessmen in the American south. At least six youngsters at a time waited inside the ring with a folded handkerchief wrapped over their eyes and knotted behind their little Afros.

When the bell rang, they all started swinging at the same time. It was a bell some didn't hear above the shouting of bets being placed, realizing the fighting started only after a fist smashed against their heads. With their cocked right hands ready to unleash fury as soon as the fingertips of their outstretched left arms touched a body, the kids beat each other bloody until only one was left standing. After the fight ended they had the honor of scrambling on their hands and knees trying to gather any coins the cheering, and laughing, ringsiders threw at them.

Around the time the Battle of Verdun started in France, Brown had his first amateur fights. Lighter than a flyweight, taller than a lightweight, blessing himself with the sign of the cross before each fight, and using the *nom de guerre* Kid Téofilo, he fought as often as three times a month, his passion fueled by poverty and grief. His mother wasn't fond of the fight game even though everyone told her he was very good. She worried, but relented, and found use in some of the prizes he brought home, like a can of evaporated milk.

He stayed in school and took up track. He did well enough that years later, while boxing champion, he expressed regret at giving it up. "You made the right choice," he was told by a track star in France. "You're getting paid in currency. Track stars are paid with medals."

He sparred with Hook Dawson and Young Mike Gibbons. The old timers, who fought bare fisted until only one man was standing, teased them about the six ounce "pillows" on their hands and laughed at the twenty round limits. Between jokes they shared tips. Remember the taste of your sweat they told each other. It was supposed to be salty and if one day it wasn't, you needed to drink more water and shouldn't spar.

Brown worked on his footwork and made sure to stay in his opponent's blind spot, where he punished them with combinations if they tried to change lanes. He boxed at a distance where his height and reach were advantages and took Norfolk's advice to avoid the trenches.

There was a playoff atmosphere in the city during May 1916. A heavyweight double header in Colón featuring Norfolk against Milton Durant in the main bout and Bill Tate against Kid Hudson in the co-feature was slated with the winners to meet the following month in Panama City for the heavyweight championship of Panama.

Norfolk stopped Durant in three and Tate scored an impressive first round knockout. Fans awaited the fight between Norfolk and the 6'6," or 6'7," depending on what time of the day they measured, Tate. Tate was coming off three impressive knockouts in Panama including a 12 rounder against Strand Gym's Jack Livingstone. A mobile, strong fighter, Tate outweighed Norfolk by forty pounds.

Norfolk overcame all of that and convincingly beat Tate over twenty rounds. The fight illustrated to Brown how a shorter fighter could turn his height disadvantage into an *advantage*. Norfolk once demonstrated to him the tricks and techniques he used to get close enough to make his opponent smell his dandruff. Tricks like moving in at the end of punches and taking bigger steps than the opponent to close the gap. Brown worked hard at keeping his opponent at the end of his punches and he backed up each time his foe's shoe laces were out of his view.

When they got too close, his favorite tactic was a right uppercut followed by a clinch. His right uppercut, thrown in a loop that went back before going forward, was the punch he relied on most during those three and six round amateur brawls. Until Sam McVae arrived in Colón in 1917 and showed them the benefits of attacking behind a straight left.

After President Valdez followed the United States by a day and declared war on Germany, many Americans left Panama. Much of the boxing fraternity including Norfolk and Gans soon followed. Both fighters ended up in New York's Harlem section where their new manager, Leo P. Flynn, waited.

Sam McVae stayed behind as did rival Jeff Clark. McVae was well versed in the long range "bombs away" style the majority of boxers used. He also had a quick left lead that he threw like an arrow. It was a punch Jack Livingstone had no defense for. After losing to McVae, Livingstone often demonstrated to the fighters at the Strand Gym how McVae threw his left. Unlike the probing, range finding lead lefts most of the fighters Livingstone faced threw, McVae's frequent left jab was thrown like a center punch.

Within a year Harry Wills and Sam Langford were in town headlining fights. Brown continued training, stopping occasionally when he spotted a newspaper. His eyes scanned the sports pages and looked for anything on Kid Norfolk. Once in a while at the gym, someone passed along the "hellos" and the "I'm doing fines" the fighters telegraphed.

After graduating high school, Brown worked for a while loading ships at the pier near Front Street then later got a job as a clerk for a lawyer. Almost all the money he made he gave to his mother. Some of it he gave to his younger sister. He kept just enough to be able to buy a few rounds at one of the Chinese owned pubs.

After the war ended, Colón was a different place. Dressing up was no longer just for Sundays or evenings. Many more cars, with two plates - Canal Zone and Panama - bustled about, forcing pedestrians off the street and on to the narrow sidewalks. Newspapers had English and Spanish sections. The fevers were a thing of the past and locals joked that if a fly or mosquito so much as buzzed, the U.S. Navy would be after it within seconds.

BLACK INK

While still a teenager, and still using the ring name Kid Téofilo, he won the national amateur championship. Thoughts of turning professional began to occupy his mind.

By the 1920s, boxing activity in Panama once again matched the pre-war levels. Brown often stated he had more professional fights than those documented in newspapers and record books. At least one American paper reported in 1930 that his record totaled 160 fights - twice the amount he was credited with at that time.

Boxing reports in the *Panama Star and Herald*, except those regarding then heavyweight champion Jack Dempsey, took a backseat to baseball and full page advertisements by BF Goodrich tires and Lucky Strike cigarettes. The reports that made it into print lacked details such as weights; and boxer's records, and sometimes appeared several days after the fights took place. Some reports made no mention of preliminary fights. It is possible, even likely, that some fights went unreported.

The record shows his professional career started with a six-round decision win over José Moreno on March 19th, 1922 with his boss serving as his advisor. Years later, in an interview with French sports writer Georges Peeters, he confirmed the Moreno fight was indeed his introduction into the pro game.

Following the Moreno fight, Brown scored five straight stoppages. He then wrapped up the year with a match against Sailor Patchett for the Panamanian Flyweight championship. Stationed on the minesweeper USS Quail in nearby Coco Solo, Patchett's first bout was coincidentally on the same day as Brown's debut. Patchett had held the Panamanian championship since the preceding September, which he won by outscoring Brown's stable-mate Young Mike Gibbons over 15 rounds.

Organized by Matty Nolan and held at the Colón Athletic Club on December 9th, the Patchett fight was a tough one. Brown, who blessed himself with the sign of the cross before the start, went on to floor the sailor in round three. Patchett chipped away at Brown's early lead with an attack to the body during the middle rounds. By the end of the fight, Brown was on the receiving end of a punishing barrage he was too tired to defend against. With the early rounds going to Brown, the middle rounds close, and the end going to Patchett, the fight was scored a draw after 15 rounds.

The two fighters took opposite paths after the fight. Patchett defended the flyweight championship in his next fight against a fighter with a difficult to spell last name while Brown struggled to land his best punches in a win by decision over Panamanian Pedro Troncoso in another rough brawl. Troncoso then won the flyweight title from Patchett in what was a nice round robin of action packed fights.

But more people plunked down their 25 cents at the Cecilia Theater to watch replays of the year-old Dempsey-Carpentier beatdown than they did to watch the local flyweights scuffle. Because of that, Brown made the calculated decision to follow the other Panamanian boxing stars to New York. The Troncoso fight was Brown's last fight in Panama until his return in the 1940s.

When he arrived in New York in 1923, he was billed as champion of Panama despite never winning that distinction as a professional. This fact didn't stop his promoters from pulling their marketing ploys out of the polluted air and soon everyone blindly followed along - much like they did in 1928 when the opposite transpired and a title he earned in the ring was taken away.

Brown had only a few dollars stashed under his mattress to show for his ring endeavors. Staying in Panama likely meant playing hot potato for the national title with the other five or six flyweights in town. Brown contemplated his future often. He did not want to lead the life his father led. Horacio, he later recollected, worked one honest job after the other, day in and day out, with no time or money for luxury or vacations. It was an honorable life but one Brown and his boss felt he didn't have to lead. His boss convinced him he had an ace in the hole. The ring earnings of the best boxers were greater than that of any lawyer in the banana republics. He had the ability to be a champion and earn large amounts, he was told. But it would have to be in American rings.

New York had become a hotbed of boxing that attracted fighters and trainers from the Southern and Midwestern states, Europe, and

BLACK INK

Latin America since the passing of the Walker Law in 1920. Reversing the steps Horacio made decades before, Brown hesitated only slightly when leaving behind the tooth-colored concrete streets of Colón for ones paved in gold.

He spent a lot of time at the docks the next few months. At times he worked as a stevedore. Mostly he paced back and forth along the dock and studied the routines of the ships the way he did his opponents in the ring. He looked for an opening where he might be able to slip in, not a jab, but his slim body and like a good pressure fighter, stay hidden long enough to feel the mooring lines loosened.

When the *Alvarado* passed through the canal on May 21st 1923 on its way to New York, Brown lined up on the docks with a crew loading food onto the ship. Wearing two shirts, two underwear and his father's cap pulled down over his eyes, he did what they did. He followed them in when they loaded the ship, his eyes scanning every corner inside. He followed them out and repeated the process. On the last trip, as they lifted the final boxes, they nodded silently to him and Brown took one last look in the direction of Sixth Street and, under his breath said, "Good bye Mom."

Each morning during the weeks leading up to that day Brown said goodbye to his family. A hug followed by a kiss on the cheek, just in case that day was the day. A few times he came close to leaving but the sound of boots here or a voice there prevented him from sailing to New York sooner. What would have been an omen to stop for some was an invitation to try again for Brown.

When the moment finally came, there wasn't time for goodbyes. Without anyone in charge noticing, he headed down towards the kitchen area and hid until after he felt the ship move. Once found, he told them he was 19 and his name was "Alberto." He was put to good use in the kitchen peeling potatoes. Seated in a trench with a carving knife in one hand and a potato in the other, he twisted and turned the potato while chalky foot long spirals of skin fell into and filled bucket after bucket. Once full, the buckets were dumped into the ocean along with other "wet" trash. Fish food they hoped, showing concern for the ocean only a brief moment before they resumed the process all over again.

His wage for working the kitchen, payable upon return to Panama after a two-day holdover in New York, was five dollars per week. On the surface it was a simple assignment. Peel the potatoes, toss the skins, wash the buckets. But it proved to be strenuous physically and demanding mentally. At the end of the long days his palms and fingers were white, shriveled, and rubbery. His skinny arms, bony shoulders, and slim neck ached. The table doubled as a bed. Five dollars per week was too little pay for the work but it wasn't about the pay. It was about getting to New York.

The Red Scare had made U.S. officials tighten the borders and develop policies to reduce immigration. The Chinese were already excluded from the country and groups from the Middle East, India, and Eastern Europe among other places were restricted to quotas based on previous census reports. For Brown, peeling potatoes on a ship was the only way to reach New York. And even if the wage were a good one, Brown had no intention of collecting.

The only moment of comfort he felt on the voyage was on the last day when the ship veered west alongside the beaches of Long Island and sliced through the Raritan Bay into New York waters. What he thought was the most beautiful sight in the world reached 100 yards into the sky above the heads of the kitchen workers who took turns poking their heads out of the portholes. Partially surrounded by stubby army barracks that formed a horseshoe around Bedloe's Island was the green patina statue of the Roman goddess Libertas.

He arrived in New York on June 29th, 1923. While the passengers disembarked, Brown and the rest of the crew cleaned their areas before being given their furlough. Brown, however, would not return to his quarters that night or any other. His goal was to get to Harlem and find kid Norfolk.

He tucked his shirt into his pants then threw on another over the first. "I wouldn't do that," one of the older crew members told him. "And don't bring any money or belongings." A few other crew members with the same intentions warned Brown of the vigilant border agents.

"I didn't want to tip anyone off," Brown recalled.

With just the clothes on his back, Brown headed down the ramp where the doctors, out of sight, triaged the passengers without their knowledge. The doctors studied their gaits, searched for weaknesses and singled out the infirm before the more thorough, though still brief, examinations that awaited at the end of the line.

Nervous sweat beaded on Brown's forehead and coated the palms of his hands as the doctors fixed their piercing eyes on him. He was ushered forward where a suspicious border agent awaited with a round of questions. Seated behind a large, elevated desk he rapidly fired one question after another and occasionally stopped to ruffle through the papers on his desk and fix his eyes on Brown. The young boxer kept his answers short and made sure they did not give away any of his intentions. It worked.

The agent found no reason to keep Brown from setting foot in New York City.

When Brown got off the ferry that took him into Manhattan, he stepped out into the sun drenched street, looked around and made sure no one was watching, inhaled deeply and, laughed for the first time in days.

"Which way to Harlem?" he asked, and a stranger's finger pointed north. It was about nine miles of brick and concrete from where he stood. With no money for cab or train, he pointed his toes uptown and began his hike, still smiling, under the shadow of the El. Follow the train tracks above he was told.

He soon found himself amid the rows of the not-quite-brown brownstones of Chelsea, the neighborhood named after the estate of The Night Before Christmas author Clement Clark Moore. When the shadows turned darker and the grime slicker, he was in Hell's Kitchen.

The neighborhood, if seen from above, forms the shape of a magazine clip from W 35th Street to W 59th Street between Eighth Avenue and the Hudson River piers. Its name dated back to before the

1880s and was considered by police to be the most crime ridden section of New York. It was an area cops walked through with guns drawn and on any given day directions to any place in *The Kitche*n could sound something like - make a left at the fist fight then turn right at the shootout, step over the dead body, go past the whore house and you're there.

Tilted hats that covered faces sat menacingly atop the heads of thugs who played with the revolvers concealed in their pockets, spinning the cylinders as if they were mini Ferris wheels. Brown avoided making eye contact with any of the angry faces he passed. That included those of the police who crept by in first gear on their motorcycles and cased those who were casing the joints.

Somewhere after 42nd Street, Brown- no longer smiling- was almost trampled by the evening crowd rushing home for the weekend. At an intersection, he stopped to gaze at the red light atop the granite and bronze tower. The pedestrians were held back by the light, like the waters of the canal were by the locks. Like the water, the crowd grew impatient until the light turned green and then, like the releasing of the locks, the people flooded the street.

Several bumps and maybe a "move it pal" interrupted his thoughts and had him stumbling for a moment like some of his ring foes.

As the street numbers got higher, an excited patter filled his chest. After 57th Street, the crowd thinned slightly and to his right, breaking up the sea of concrete, was the green forest of Central Park. He couldn't resist deviating from his path below the bi-level El and headed over one block to the right somewhere around 61st Street, where plans for building a playground for kids were met with strict opposition from various civic groups, including the League of Women Voters who contended that the park was built for taking strolls and resting on the grass and not for children to run around in.

When he reached 125th street, ten times the number of faces he had ever seen in Colón walked past him. None belonged to Kid Norfolk. What he did see was the "other" side of Harlem.

The Harlem he saw was a ghetto inhabited by thousands of people who struggled to make ends meet. There were street corner hustlers selling stolen watches with their accomplices a few feet away ready to steal them back from anyone foolish enough to buy. Housing demand drove rent to levels that necessitated rent parties and a boarder or three in order to avoid eviction. Too many heads under a roof meant sleeping was done in shifts.

It was fertile ground for anger, resentment, crime, and ultimately, hate. Racism thrived in that environment. Being black meant walking into a store and getting welcomed by leery eyes that judged you a thief. Shop keepers guarded one cent candies and suspiciously followed around the darker skinned patrons as though there were an epidemic of thefts of BB Bats chocolates.

Even amongst the blacks there was discrimination based on color. The yellows, the tans, and the paper-bag-browns considered themselves better looking. Those who yearned to be a lighter shade could turn to any number of products advertised in newspapers and pharmacy windows that promised to do just that.

Located in the northern section of Manhattan where the land takes the shape of a revolver aimed north, Harlem had been since the end of the Civil War a predominantly African American community. Nearly two million migrated to Harlem, mostly from southern states but also from the Caribbean, before the Great Depression. They came for the industrial jobs, better schools, and fewer lynching compared to the Delta.

Artists were also attracted to the area. Poets and novelists such as Wallace Thurman, Langston Hughes, and Zora Neal Hurston - who called themselves the *"Niggerati"* - settled alongside the playwrights and musicians and together helped shaped the Harlem Renaissance.

Harlem music, jazz in particular, rivaled anything heard in New Orleans or Kansas City. Still called "Jass" by some, the music of Wilbur Sweatman, Duke Ellington, and Fletcher Henderson, engulfed in a cloud of cigarette smoke, made its way out like a draft and resonated off the urban landscape everywhere from Harlem down to 49th Street. Clubs like the Bamboo Inn, Tillie's, and Small's Paradise attracted big crowds.

Once he had money in his pockets, Brown would be among the many who partied until the sun ruined the night. If there was liquor and music, he was likely there - except for those places he was barred from stepping into because of the color of his skin. The only ways a black, brown, cinnamon, or mulatto person could get into those clubs was if he were carrying a trumpet or a mop. Even then it was through the alleyway, past the trash bins, and in through the rear door.

One of the more famous of the clubs, the Cotton Club, was dubbed the Cotton Plantation. Originally called Club Deluxe and owned by heavyweight champion Jack Johnson, it was taken over by the illegal substance dealers of the day and turned into a place where whites went to be waited on plantation style and entertained by, according to their window signs, "sepia dancers," or "copper colored gals."

For those who danced and sang there over the years, like Ernestine Holly, who performed atop a large drum under the name Edna Mae and would later marry Sugar Ray Robinson, it was a good living. For those barred from entering, it was a reminder planted firmly in the epicenter of the neighborhood that the *Renaissance* wasn't for everyone.

Brown had snuck onto a ship and sailed more than two thousand nautical miles only to come face-to-face with the origins of the gold and silver payrolls.

While Brown had little idea of what to expect in Harlem, he was clueless of what awaited him in the boxing world. His dreams of being a boxing champion were filled with cheers, victories, and checks being cashed. Like the neighborhood he stepped into, the sport's dark side was the one that greeted him.

Much like today with multiple sanctioning bodies and Halls of Fame, boxing in the 1920s was a divided sport. The New York State Athletic Commission (NYSAC) was formed in 1920 and recognized thirteen weight divisions. Shortly after several other states questioned and challenged New York's control of the sport. Not satisfied with the answers they received, they formed the National Boxing Association (NBA) and recognized ten weight divisions. Both organizations recognized their own champions though at times, they recognized the same fighters.

Meanwhile, the International Boxing Union (IBU) regulated the European boxing scene again following a hiatus during World War I and they too designated their own champions. Though treated like a second-rate operation by the influential East Coast media, Europe had a vibrant boxing scene where boxers earned purses comparable to those in American rings. But the super fights, what would be pay-per-view events today, and the sport's most influential promoter, Tex Rickard, were based in New York.

In Rickard's stable were some of the biggest names in the sport and they were cashing some of the biggest checks. The reports Brown heard about ring earnings were correct. Though Brown would go on to reach the talent level of the best in the world, he lacked an important trait the best fighters in the world shared. In a time when white was right, being darker than his last name was wrong.

Though not officially segregated in all states, boxing operated like two leagues. Most black fighters in New York were relegated to off-Broadway status. They secured fights in smaller clubs against each other in non-title affairs for less money. Unable or unwilling to obtain title shots for any of the widely sought after titles, Tex Rickard awarded diamond-studded "Negro" championship belts to the dark-skinned boxers.

Harry Wills held the "Colored" heavyweight title; Kid Norfolk the colored light heavyweight title; Panama Joe Gans the colored middleweight title; and the colored welterweight title was vacant. In Harlem and almost exclusively in other predominantly black neighborhoods, Wills, Norfolk, and Gans were treated like every bit the champions their white counterparts were. Brown would become a part of this circuit some called the "chitlin circuit," but, as a flyweight, he did not have even a colored title to shoot for.

The memory of Jack Johnson was still fresh in the minds of the American officials. Born in Galveston Texas in 1876, he literally chased world champion Tommy Burns around the world, pleading and taunting Burns, for a shot at the title. Finally, in 1908, they fought in Australia in a match where Johnson agreed to just about every concession asked including the allowance of Burns's promoter, Hugh Macintosh, to serve as referee.

After 14 one-sided rounds, Johnson was the winner and a reign of dominance began that saw him turn back one Great White Hope after another.

After Johnson was dethroned, fights between blacks and whites were avoided if not outlawed. Louisiana prohibited fights, and public dancing, between blacks and whites. In the 1950s, boxer Joe Dorsey of New Orleans's Seventh Ward filed a suit settled in the U.S. Supreme Court lifting the ban on "mixed race" matches.

Before then, boxers Bernard Docusen and Ralph Dupas struggled to prove their "whiteness" in order to be able to participate in the higher paying matches that fights against whites provided. Docusen, the tan-skinned son of a Filipino father who later challenged Ray Robinson for the championship, had to present his white mother to the state commission in order to be permitted to box against whites.

Ralph Dupas endured a headline-grabbing court case complete with lifelong friends and neighbors testifying as to the blackness or whiteness of the Dupas family. He eventually proved his whiteness but not without accusations that his family members were imposters who were not white but mixed race and whose real name was Duplessis. Being half white was apparently good enough, as long as the other half wasn't black. Back then - in Louisiana, one was legally considered black if only 1/32 black.

In 1930, *New York Graphic* writer James W. Jennings wrote "Fair opportunities for Negroes in boxing are as rare as diamond soles on a pair of shoes as big as those of Primo Carnera."

Other sports were not exempt. When Moses Fleetwood Walker played his last game in the majors in 1884 for the Toledo Blue Stockings, baseball would go the next 62 seasons without an African American player.

BLACK INK

This sentiment extended beyond sports. Less than twenty years earlier, the Bronx Zoo in New York included Ota Benga, an Mbuti Pygmy *man* from Congo, in its *orangutan* exhibit.

While some in boxing probably felt only whites should be champions, others avoided the issue for safety reasons. Race riots were triggered by anything from sailors celebrating the 4th of July by beating up on dark skinned folk to children fighting over a rag doll. The riots that followed boxing matches were especially violent. As many as eight people died in the aftermath of the Jack Johnson-Jim Jeffries match.

The summer of 1919 was christened Red Summer because of all the blood spilled during more than two dozen race riots that spanned the country. Among them was a series of riots in Chicago triggered by a white man stoning a black child to death at a segregated beach because the child crossed into the "white" side of the water. When the police let the man go and instead arrested a black man, who had confronted the rock thrower, more than six days of rioting and looting followed.

When word got out that injured blacks were being treated at Provident Hospital, a mob of angry whites stormed the hospital and prevented doctors from providing them with medical attention. Thousands of National Guard troops were called in to help stop the hostilities that resulted in dozens of lost lives.

Following the Russian Revolution, members of the press and politicians expressed a concern that a similar revolt could occur in America. President Wilson feared that blacks, because of their views on equality and labor practices, would be supportive of a revolution. Amidst all this sentiment, membership in the revitalized Klu Klux Klan approached the millions and infiltrated politics - swaying the outcomes of elections in several states.

Making matters worse, America was reeling from the ongoing Teapot Dome scandal and the so-called Ohio Gang in President Harding's cabinet. Harding himself was ailing, and his death a few weeks after Brown's dusty shoes stepped on 125th Street, was mired in mystery. While Harding's coffin traveled cross country by train speculation surrounding the cause of death grew. Some said it was suicide. Others suspected murder with the First Lady topping the list of suspects.

But no cloud is completely dark. In March of 1923 New York hosted the George Godfrey-Jack Renault fight. It was the first mixed-race fight in years. Pancho Villa and Johnny Datto were among the first Filipinos to create a buzz in America. Luis Firpo of Argentina was becoming a featured attraction. Coming off a win over contender Bill Brennan, Firpo was in training for a July "Battle of the Giants" match against Jess Willard at Boyles Thirty Acres in Jersey City. 75,000 shoved their way onto the wooden bleacher seats of the arena, where Montgomery Street is today, and watched Firpo become the logical contender for Jack Dempsey's crown. Firpo would soon become the first boxer from Latin America to challenge for a world title.

The earliest of the Latin American boxers to make their presences felt internationally were from South America. Among the better fighters were hard hitting Uruguayan light heavyweight Angel Rodriguez and Chilean lightweight Stanislaus Loayza. But no star shines as brightly as a heavyweight star to the American press. At 6'3" tall and weighing 220 pounds, the self-managed Firpo was nearly fifty pounds heavier than Dempsey's previous challengers.

Firpo fought the way a big man was expected to. He came forward, no feints, no dips, and no tricks. His game plan was a simple one that many school children on their lunch breaks could devise. His fighting style suited his nickname, which was the "Wild Bull of the Pampas," though it sounds better - *El Toro Salvage*- in Spanish. The Savage Bull's intention was simply to kick his opponent's ass.

The epitome of America's idea of machismo - meaning virility and not the Spanish definition, which means chauvinist - Firpo became the first Latin American boxing star. Forget the turn-of-the-century "Mexican" warriors from the West Coast, but not because they weren't great.

The first of the three was featherweight Solomon Garcia Smith. Born in Los Angeles to an Irish father and a mother of Mexican and

BLACK INK

Native American descent, he fought as Solly Smith and became featherweight champion - a 120-pound limit back then- in 1897 by beating George Dixon.

Shortly after came another featherweight, Aurelio Herrera. Born in San Jose, California and raised about a four-hour drive away on I 5, in Bakersfield, Herrera might still rank among the ten hardest hitting featherweights ever. Herrera was called a "savage" and was slurred in print with names like "The Mexican Greaser." Herrera rumbled with Battling Nelson and Abe Attell and, fought Terry McGovern for the title - a fight he later claimed to have been drugged in by his own corner to make sure he didn't win.

The third fighter, also out of Los Angeles and coincidently also 5'4" only a bit thicker in the torso, was the lightweight with the unforgettable moniker of Mexican Joe Rivers. Ybarra was his real name and he probably should have been champion the night he boxed Ad Wolgast. They went down simultaneously - a double knockdown. Wolgast, out cold from a punch, landed on top of Rivers, who was doubled over in pain clutching his own crotch, claiming he was hit low. The referee ignored the calls for Wolgast's disqualification, pulled Wolgast off of Rivers, and counted out Mexican Joe while holding the still unaware Wolgast up. Billed as a Mexican from somewhere by the river, Rivers was in fact a fourth generation Californian, born and buried in Los Angeles.

You can forget those three because; contrary to popular contemporary belief, those "Mexicans" were Americans and none had thrown a punch in Mexico or any other country south of the Rio Grande. Firpo was the first Latin American boxing star and Al Brown, half Firpo's weight but twice as good, would become the first champion. But in June 1923, he was too preoccupied with more urgent matters than making history. He had to find Kid Norfolk.

Already weary and hungry, desperation increased as he walked back and forth through the streets looking for Norfolk, a boxing gym, or even someone who looked like he was a boxer. By the time he made a right on 125th Street, it was that time of the day when the sun gets dunked into the Hudson. In near-unison, shop-keepers turned off their lights, locked their doors and walked with a purpose past the lost out-of-towner. Darkness quickly covered all and as the trolley cars became less frequent and the streets less crowded, it was obvious that his first night would be spent on the streets.

Brown kept moving throughout the night, not knowing where to sleep and not really wanting to either.

"I went through a lot of pain and sorrow those days," he shared years later.

The following day was no different. He didn't eat, sleep, or find Norfolk. On his second night in America, he met another homeless man. The man didn't know where any gyms were and never heard of Norfolk. What he shared was advice on how to get by on the streets. Make some friends and in the summer sleep in Central Park he was told. Just as importantly, he told him where he might be able to find some work.

The next day Brown lined up to find work with other homeless men. His youthful looks made him a popular choice with those hiring help. He found work in the kitchen of a small restaurant during the lunch and dinner tours. Stacks of plates, bowls, dishes, and cups were brought to the kitchen where Brown would wipe them clean, sometimes nibbling on the untouched portions, before dipping them into a sink filled with soapy water.

Nights were spent walking around looking for a safe spot to doze off or huddled with others in a hobo circle listening to stories while his dry, wrinkled hands clutched a bottle of cheap booze. During one session, his second week in the city, Brown shared the story of his journey. When he finished, one of the guys told him, "I know who Norfolk is. He trains on the East Side."

The words were a blast of hope.

Panama Al Brown

Brown still didn't have an address. But for the first time since he stowed away on board the ocean liner, he had a lead. It's a small world except when looking for something. He spent his breaks between the lunch and dinner shifts walking through the East Side searching for the gym. Where exactly on the East Side he didn't know. Though East Harlem is only a few blocks squared, to Brown, those few blocks were an endless maze.

He passed through the growing Puerto Rican community that would soon be called Spanish Harlem. When he grew hungry, he stood in the sun because, as he often said, hunger is less noticeable in the light.

One humid afternoon in July, leaning against a brick wall and taking in the sun, he closed his eyes and thought about nothing in particular. He was interrupted when opportunity knocked in the form of a familiar voice.

"Téofilo is that you?"

It was Young Mike Gibbons. Boxing in New York under his real name of Bobby Risden, he wasted no time telling him that Norfolk was fighting out of town and that he too was managed by Leo P. Flynn. After Brown told him he was living in the streets, Risden immediately took him to the gym which was actually on the West Side- 252 W 116th Street.

When Al stepped onto the hardwood floors of the long, narrow Grupp's Gymnasium and Athletic Club, he felt for the first time in months, that he was where he belonged. Seated along the white walls were familiar faces. Panama Joe Gans, Sam McVae, Harry Wills, and Sam Langford were regulars at the gym along with Norfolk and Risden.

Grupp's was one of the top gyms in the area at the time. Stillman's Gymnasium, with the unintentional help of Grupp, was on its way to being, if not already, the premier gym in the city. Billy Grupp, a former middleweight from St. Louis who lost more than he won, paced back and forth in his gym, in a drunken state, blaming the Jews for the War, and the weather too according to Ray Arcel.

Benny Leonard, the outstanding lightweight who to this day is considered by some to be the best lightweight ever, took offense. It wasn't the first time Grupp had mouthed off. Leonard packed his gloves and left. To Stillman's he went and, like always a crowd - including many boxers - followed him. Stillman's remained the premier boxing gym in New York until 1959 when owner Lou "Stillman" Ingber closed it because felt there were "no more tough guys," no more slums, and the active fighters were all "pussies."

There was no shortage of boxers back then and enough of them sauntered through the frosted glass doors of Grupp's to keep it in business. Among the tutors giving lessons in hit-and-not-be-hit was David "Dai" Dollings. From Swansea in the boxing rich country of Wales, a country that has arguably produced more great fighters per square mile than any other, Dollings recognized the potential in Brown from day one.

Dollings himself was a standout battler in clandestine bare knuckle matches throughout Wales that were set up in the pubs and took place in hills that bore names like "Lovers Lane" and "Murder Valley."

An all-around fitness trainer, he helped prepare runners for marathons and swimmers for competitions. Dollings, who was Ray Arcel's mentor, made his mark as a boxing trainer by working at one time or another with Ted "Kid" Lewis, Jack Britton, Johnny Dundee, Matty Wells, Bombardier Billy Wells, Harry Wills and Al McCoy.

Dollings had Brown strip naked and step on the scales with his skinny arms raised above his head. 114 pounds was his weight that day and when they measured his height and his wingspan, an incredulous Dollings reportedly said, "A flyweight with the height and reach of Jack Dempsey!"

Brown was not quite the same height as Jack. He measured 5'9" barefoot and a tick under 5'11" in his Oxfords. Either way he was about half a foot taller than the average flyweight. An impromptu sparring session in front of boxing manager Leo P. Flynn was arranged. Matched up against featherweight Ansel Bell, a familiar face from Colón, Al held nothing back.

This was the moment he dreamed of. In his corner tying his gloves was one of the top three or four trainers in New York. Standing a few feet away was Flynn, manager of Kid Norfolk. The man in the opposite corner did not matter. Al's mind was on the future. This was his chance.

Those present say it was one of Al's greatest performances. Boxing on an empty stomach, his rusty punches were fueled by a desperate desire. Motivated by the memory of his father's death, his penniless mother, the long boat ride, and the sleepless nights roaming the streets of New York, Brown let out a fury of punches from long range that left the featherweight in a state necessitating rescue.

They saw enough.

"What's your name?"

"Kid Téofilo," answered Brown.

Flynn didn't like it. It was too ethnic he thought. Besides, the "Kid" part wouldn't fly with him being so much taller than his opponents. It took a few minutes before Flynn, citing Panama Joe, said from now on you will be "Panama Al Brown."

Brown preferred Kid Téofilo. It was the name he envisioned in bright lights and newspaper headlines. Aside from the name, his dream seemed to be coming true. Flynn had the largest stable of boxers of any American manager at the time and possibly in history. At any one time his stable consisted of as many as 40 boxers, many of whom he never met in person.

There was a story reported in several sources of a punch drunk former boxer who paced back and forth with a cup in front of the midtown building where Flynn kept an office. Whenever Flynn pulled up in his chauffeured Rolls Royce Silver Ghost, he'd toss a coin in the cup of the old pug. One day the pug commented to fellow onlookers about how nice the car was when one of them shook his head and told him something along the lines of glad you like it because the money he took from you helped pay for it.

Eventually the old pug found a lawyer who was willing to take Flynn to court. The astonished Flynn was flabbergasted that someone he never met before had the audacity to sue him. After looking into the case, Flynn's lawyer advised the disbelieving manager to settle out of court as soon as possible because yes indeed Flynn was his former manager and had dipped into the old pug's share of the purses.

Even with the fighters he met, Flynn was indifferent. Ray Arcel, who trained many of his boxers, recalled one fight when he and Flynn worked a corner together. The fighter was knocked flat on his back and remained still after the referee counted ten. Without a hint of emotion Flynn turned to Ray and instructed, "Go get him."

Flynn was also an expert manager. Along with Risden, Norfolk, and Panama Joe, he worked with Jack Dempsey and managed leading welterweight, middleweight, and light heavyweight contender Dave Shade. Without looking at the specifics of the contract, Brown signed a five-year contract with Flynn.

The next day Flynn helped Brown get situated. He set him up in a room in the same hotel as Norfolk and Risden. They sized him up for shoes, boots, and clothes. Pick out what you need he told him and when it came time to pay, Flynn took care of it and explained it was an advance against future earnings. Brown had yet to fight in New York and was already in debt. It was a cycle that took years to break.

The early training sessions saw Brown struggling to keep up with Dollings. Despite being over sixty, Dollings was as fit as any of his fighters. A vegetarian and an avid walker, he walked to and from his apartment, located to the right of Union Square on 14th Street, to the gym on 116th Street each day. Some joked it was because he was too cheap to spring for the nickel the trolley cost. While Grupp stressed defense, Dollings stressed the importance of being as energetic in the last round as the first.

Despite having boxed fifteen rounds in Panama, the months of inactivity coupled with the long trip and time on the streets left Brown out of shape. When the bell rang for his first fight in New

York, it was for a four rounder. In the weeks leading up to that match, Brown readily absorbed his gym lessons. Dollings had Brown boxing off the back foot and countering in a style reminiscent of Johnny Dundee and Jim Driscoll.

It was a style built around the left jab. At times it was a probing jab, one that possessed radar long before the military did. Dollings had him using the jab defensively, snapping his opponent's head back when the rest of his body wanted to come forward. Offensively he used it as a smoke screen, something to distract his opponent while the right waited to do the damage.

In contrast, his style in Panama revolved around the right hand. Every punch was programmed to inflict damage. It was a full on assault rather than the sneak attacks Dollings taught. Brown trusted his old trainer despite some outrageous claims he made. Like being the world's best doctor and having a cure for baldness. Although Brown had been in the company of very good fighters his entire life, he trusted the old man from Swansea because *he* had been in the company of champions.

Flynn booked Brown's American debut on the Pancho Villa-Charley Rosenberg undercard along with stable mate and sometimes sparring partner Tony Vaccarelli. Many undercards were filled by Flynn boxers. Flynn, through the use of his extensive stable of fighter, had saved many promotions from being cancelled. If a promoter had a fighter suddenly fall ill just as the doors opened, a call to Flynn would save the show. The only thing he needed to know was what sized "palooka" to send over.

He called all his fighters "pah-loo-ka!" because, he said, that was the sound their bodies made when they crashed onto the ring floor. Ham Fisher created the comic strip "Joe Palooka" in the 1920s but legend has it Flynn had been calling his fighters that since the Great War.

By the time of the weigh-in, main event boxer Charley Phil Rosenberg pulled out. Flynn reached into his file of flyweights and came up with Jack Feldman to take his place opposite Villa. It didn't matter that he was overmatched, the show was saved.

The undercard, aka preliminary, fighters were the first to weigh in. Undercard, incidentally, is a name held over from the days of illegal boxing. Since posters could not be used, promoters had cards small enough to fit inside the palm of a hand printed before their shows. Word on upcoming shows, which became known as "cards," was spread by men handing out the cards, concealed in a handshake, at train stations, pubs, and street corners. On the front, or top, of the cards were the headliners, the date, and location. On the flip side, or- "under" the card, appeared the names of the preliminary fighters.

During the weigh-in, Brown was the center of attention. With two flyweight bouts scheduled on the undercard, some in the room thought they were short a flyweight. A quick scan of the room counted three flyweights to their eyes. Some didn't believe Dollings when he pointed at Brown and told them he was the fourth. Taller than even the featherweights on the card, like Mike Ballerino and Vaccarelli, the onlookers were surprised enough to make Brown step on the scale twice. Both times he tipped the scales at 113 pounds.

Brown was a full head taller than his opponent, Johnny Breslin. Many in the room thought it was a physical mismatch. He was skinny though not in a puny way. "Don't go for the knockout," Dollings advised. The request left Brown confused.

Leo P. Flynn sometimes awarded his fighters bonuses whenever they scored a knockout. Brown wanted the bonus and the reputation that comes along with a knockout badly. Dollings leaned in closer to the befuddled face of Brown and whispered in his East Side Swansea accent, "We'll never get another fight if you do."

After the weigh-in, Dollings told him to get something light to eat. Brown didn't feel like it. Instead, he grabbed his gym bag, skipped lunch and headed to Central Park by himself. He sat on a bench by the Harlem Meer and let his mind drift. It was a bench he once slept on.

Inside his gym bag was a brand new pair of black leather boxing shoes and violet-colored satin trunks with a single black stripe on each leg. He sat on that bench until it was time to meet up with Dollings for the fight.

BLACK INK

Brown and his team arrived at the saucer-shaped arena around 6:30 that evening. Made entirely out of wood, the New York Velodrome might have been filled to capacity had Villa been fighting a competitive opponent. Instead of 16,000 fans, 4,000 made their way up to 225th Street and Broadway in the Bronx for the matches. Brown's fight, the second match of the night, was scheduled to go on at 8:15.

His opponent was Johnny Breslin, a short, red-headed tough guy - the type they don't make anymore. Built like a fire hydrant only a little bit taller Breslin warmed up just a few yards away from him. When Brown started shadowboxing, and unleashed rapid fire combinations in the air, his arms reached across the room. Everyone stared and wondered what to make of this sliced-down-the-middle heavyweight in their presence.

When Brown made his way into the ring with his new shoes, violet trunks, a rolled up white towel wrapped around his shoulders and an orange rind for a mouthpiece and took his place alongside Breslin for the introductions, it looked like a cruel practical joke. He was about seven inches taller and his arms seemed as long as Breslin's legs.

A second, and closer, look revealed that the joke may have been on Brown instead. Despite the wiry muscles that were tightly braided around his bones, the consensus among ringsiders was that he looked almost anorexic and appeared likely to cave in after a few body shots.

His opponent shared this sentiment. While Brown boxed under orders of holding back, Breslin bore in under Brown's occasional jabs with sweeping hooks, many of which landed below the belt. As it turned out, Breslin needed no favors. This he would go on to prove throughout his career, never being stopped in more than 50 bouts.

The bout turned into a toe-to-toe affair filled with roughhousing, occasional head-butts to Brown's chin and low blows. Brown had only his footwork and an occasional lifting of his leg at his disposal to shield his *cojones* when he boxed Breslin. Fighting with a governor on his engine against the aggressive Breslin nearly resulted in defeat. It took a last-round rally by the Panamanian to salvage a draw after four fast-paced rounds. Dollings was satisfied and Flynn, who acted as though he couldn't care less, paid Brown half of the negotiated $40 purse. A sore Brown didn't say a word.

The protective cups worn in those days were better suited for an errant ground ball than a strayed left hook. The boxing-specific protectors weren't invented until a few years later when an English stage actor with hair like Einstein's invented the early model. His role in an off-Broadway play called for a fencing match that ended with a stab to the groin. No props existed so he made one out of rubber and aluminum and tested his invention at local boxing gyms and baseball fields where he challenged the heaviest punchers and the cleanup hitters to take a swing.

Boxers threw their best hooks and baseball players swung for the fences and though he often ended up on the floor, and once through a dry-wall section in Madame Bey's camp, the cup worked.

He became known as Foul-Proof Taylor and back then the thespian from Manchester was credited with saving boxing in New York. In the late 1920s there was a string of suspicious endings resulting from low blows and as a result, public interest waned.

When the heavyweight championship match between Max Schmeling and Jack Sharkey ended with Max on the canvas pointing to his crotch and being carried to his corner before being declared the new champion, boxing adopted the foul proof cups and the public's trust was restored.

Before that happened, leading up to Brown's next fight, all anyone in boxing circles could think about was the upcoming Dempsey - Firpo clash. Hours before the fight started, 86,000 fans filled the streets around the Polo Grounds in lines that stretched for half a mile.

When the preliminaries ended and Firpo climbed into the ring in his checkered robe, the roar of the crowd was heard in some parts of the Bronx. When the champion made his way to the ring and climbed the steps with a white sweater tied around his shoulders, the crowd's rumble was not only heard - but felt as far away as Harlem. Once the posing for photos ended, announcer Joe Humphries introduced, without using a microphone, the fighters and shortly after that, the bell rang for what is still the wildest title fight ever.

At the bell Dempsey walked out of his corner and once he reached the center of the ring crouched, quickened his step, and attacked with both hands. Firpo, who was on par with Dempsey when it came to power, threw a short counter that buckled the champ's knees and made him sag to the canvas. On his way down, Dempsey clung onto the Wild Bull and shook off a series of clubbing rights to drop Firpo with a single shot of his own.

Firpo rose quickly and just as fast Dempsey sent him back down twice more. Dempsey landed hard to the body and to the jaw. The fourth knockdown suffered by Firpo was the most serious. He rolled onto his back and barely beat the count. As soon as he rose, Dempsey greeted him with a right that dropped him again and when he got up from that one, Dempsey dove in for the kill. Instead a Firpo right landed that made his gloves touch the canvas.

They wrestled in a corner where Dempsey dropped him twice more with hooks. Firpo rose and threw his right the way a catcher does when throwing out a base stealer. Dempsey covered up and Firpo rained down a series of clubbing shots that backed the champion into the ropes. Another right stiffened Dempsey and froze him in an upright position as though he had just been tasered.

Firpo landed another right square on the jaw that sent Dempsey through the ropes and out of the ring head first onto his back. He landed in press row where the newspaper writers graciously held up their hands to break the champ's fall. Before the referee reached the count of ten, the reporters had pushed Dempsey back into the ring clearly violating the rules that state a fighter must climb back into the ring unassisted.

When the action resumed Firpo pounced on Dempsey immediately. Dempsey dug down into that well only the greatest champions have and summoned the strength to trade toe-to-toe until the end of the round.

When round two started the fans were as tired as the fighters and the crowd that gathered outside of the Polo Grounds had doubled in size. Round two picked up where round one left off. Dempsey dropped Firpo for a five count. He rose slowly. A smashing right to the jaw sent him down again this time for the count.

Firpo became an international star and an idol in Latin America. Newspapers there lamented the poor officiating while at the same time praising Dempsey's remarkable recuperative powers. Large crowds gave him a champion's reception when he passed through Cuba, Panama, and Peru on his way back to Argentina. Neither fighter was the same after this fight. Dempsey never won another title fight and Firpo never beat another contender.

In Grupp's Gym, Brown and Risden fantasized about being champions and what that would mean for Panamanians. The Panamanian boxing contingent became a close-knit group. As outsiders to the world of boxing, and to black Harlem, they banded together in their quests for respect, acceptance, and success.

Considered a "lesser negro" by local blacks, many shared apartments, clothing, equipment, and information. They also shared a desire to show the world that Panama was more than just a bridge between two oceans.

Eight days after the Dempsey fight, Brown scored his first win on American soil. Dollings took the leash off for this fight and Brown responded with two knockdowns on his way to a first round knockout. It was a right hand thrown like a spear that was the winning blow. His opponent, Tommy Martin dropped suddenly like a dozen apples from the bottom of a torn bag. The fight lasted 29 seconds.

When Brown received the same $20 payment, he inquired about the "knockout" bonus. Take it up with the boss he was told. After some thought, Brown wondered how a poor black foreigner could confront a rich white "boss." Throw in the fact that the boss was the same person who took him off the streets and gave him the opportunity he left home for and it's not too hard to understand why Brown never "took it up with the boss."

Unlike the Breslin fight, less than one thousand filled the Commonwealth Sporting Club to watch local favorite Charlie Phil Rosenberg. Brown's impressive performance had many of the ringsiders saying he was only a few fights away from challenging the leading flyweights. Their predictions seemed on target the following year when Brown was rated in the top five. However, because of his color, and his lifestyle, those "few" fights ended up being close to 60 over six years before Brown found himself in a championship match.

Before the misery that waited for him in the coming years, Brown, in 1923, was living his dream. Kid Norfolk was back in town after a series of matches in Baltimore just in time to watch Brown go against Bernie Hyams on October 13TH. A week before that a last-minute match was needed to fill the card and Brown laced them up against his buddy Bobby Risden. Often, fights between friends are so violent it leaves everyone scratching their heads and wondering how they would treat their enemies. With Brown fighting the following week and Risden having fought two days earlier, no one was left scratching their heads after the tap fest between the two. They took turns landing soft punches, each one making sure not to throw more than the other. What was either a coincidence or a prearranged outcome, the match was scored a draw after six rounds.

It was a good night for all. It was easy money for the fighters, the promoter met his allotment of fights, and the fans came to see the main event fighters anyway. After the fight, Brown took his first of many forays into the Harlem nightlife. But not before walking the streets looking for the homeless crew that helped him get by. A bottle of liquor and a few dollars passed from Brown's hands to theirs in a ritual that became routine for a few months. After those visits, he'd head over to one of the watering holes where the dollars continued to pass from his skinny hands.

The following week, Hyams went out like Roberto Duran did against Tommy Hearns. The buzz in Harlem was loud enough that other promoters considered having Brown headline a card. In his next fight he was co-featured alongside Panama Joe Gans. While Gans fought against an opponent with no chance to win, Brown was matched tough. Willie Darcy was fighting for the 18th time that year. He was a bantamweight with two wins over Charlie Phil Rosenberg, a draw against Sammy Cohen, and was a few months removed from going the twelve-round distance against flyweight champion Pancho Villa.

Darcy, dubbed The Fighting Irishman from the Bronx, brought his A-Game to the Brown fight. Called a "glutton for punishment" by the Brooklyn Daily Eagle, Brown soon found out what Rosenberg, Villa and even Corporal Izzy Schwartz did during their fights with the hard-hitting Darcy. There was no quit in him and he was nearly impossible to hurt. Brown however, put on a display of fast, accurate combinations that had the fans coming out of their seats. Panama Al Brown had arrived.

Brown had become a headliner at the Commonwealth. Boxing in front of crowds that included the young poet Langston Hughes and members of the all-black "Commons" basketball team and their former power forward, Paul Robeson, Brown electrified the crowds with his nuclear punching power and artistic footwork. Each fist carried enough dynamite to crumble an opponent. And his sudden break aways in either direction had opponents thinking they were fighting a ghost.

He was also a regular of the Harlem party scene.

During this time he developed a friendship with Battling Siki. Coming off a loss to Kid Norfolk in a highly hyped match, the former French war hero frequently made his way uptown from Hell's Kitchen to spar and afterwards, to drink. After breaking his right hand in the Willie LaMorte fight, Brown found himself with a lot of free time. It was time he spent with Siki. During the four-month layoff Brown spent more time getting to know the hot spots and was often seen returning to his room in the early morning hours.

Siki had worn out his welcome in France following his upset victory over Georges Carpentier for the light heavyweight title. It was a fight he agreed to lose provided he did not get hurt. He played along willingly. Perhaps too willingly for the referee's taste. After Siki comically flopped to the canvas in a fashion that even a World Cup player would deem embarrassing, the referee refused to count.

Siki was ordered to stand and fight. At that point Carpentier began to throw hard punches. Siki went down again. Feeling betrayed, he rose with payback on his mind. The script was lost in the process and Siki walked out of the ring the winner and new champion of the world.

After losing the title in Ireland in his first defense, Siki left behind a wife and a pet lion he could not control and came to New York. A lot of the hype that came with him subsided after the loss to Norfolk. Still, he was an attraction and a favorite of the tabloids. A friendly sort willing to give the clothes off his back to a friend in need, he turned into a turbulent type after a few drinks.

Together they frequented a French bistro on 47th Street owned by a cycling champion from Marseilles who doubled as a part-time boxing trainer. It was a popular meeting spot for many in the fight game, especially among the visiting French fighters like Siki, Charles Raymond Gaston, and a flyweight with a popcorn-shaped ear named Robert Diamant - also known as Bobby Diamond.

The effervescent Siki was the pick-me-up Brown needed at that time. The LaMorte fight was a disaster. He broke his hand early and was unable to fend off his rival with only the left at his disposal. He suffered a knockdown and the consensus was that he lost. Officially it was No Decision. New Jersey still outlawed judges in boxing matches because their decisions were so suspect, or so incompetent, that announcing the decisions was an embarrassment to the sport and local commission. Gamblers quickly found a way around it by turning to, and often influencing, the newspaper write-ups for an unofficial verdict.

It was a difficult time for Brown. Winter was a new experience for him and the cold air left his teeth chattering worse than a one-two. His hand was healing slowly and until it did, he could not fight. He borrowed money from Flynn and found work as a bus boy in a beanery during the day and at night, he drank. Brown knew once your hand breaks, it will keep breaking.

While he nursed his injured weapon, Chilean boxers Quintin Romero-Rojas, a heavyweight, and lightweight Luis Vicentini were making their way up the Atlantic from Valparaiso aboard the *Teno* courtesy of Tex Rickard. Romero-Rojas, who held a knockout victory over Luis Firpo, was being groomed for a match against Harry Wills and his arrival in New York was being hailed as confirmation that Latin Americans had become a force in the world of boxing.

Writer Robert A. Martin, a frequent traveler of Latin America through his job as agent for W.R. Grace & Co., kept close tabs on the scene from Panama down to Argentina. He called the rise in boxing one of the "enlightening phases" of the "awakening" of the Latin American. The Latino boxers, he explained, were no longer the laughingstocks they were before World War I. The days of brave locals being bowled over by American servicemen were over. In 1924 he wrote that the development of the Latino boxer, in Panama particularly, had been "rapid and remarkable" with world-class fighters such as Norfolk, Gans and Midget Smith having developed there. Lack of training was their Achilles heel in the past because, he stated, there was "still a great deal more of the animal in these pugilists than in ours."

His personal determinations aside, Martin was correct that Latin American fighters were on the verge of making a mark on the international scene. In Panama City, where he spent most of his time, he felt the best of the locals were featherweight Jose Lombardo and a flyweight named Midget Toneta. He made no mention of the recuperating Al Brown.

When the four-month layoff ended, Brown returned with a first round knockout. Brown was back a week later at the Commonwealth fighting on a Tiger Flowers undercard. His opponent was a Brooklyn featherweight named Bobby Burns. Burns turned out to be a good club fighter which, back then, was something many aspired to. He went on to score good wins in his career over tough fighters like Phil McGraw and Mike Ballerino, and ended the career of Hall of Famer Kid Williams. Against Brown, he had no luck. Brown beat him to the punch every step of the way.

Dolling's fears were becoming realized. Few flyweights wanted to fight Brown. It was a relief when hard hitting contender Joe Colletti accepted a match. The first boxer to beat Frankie Genaro, Colletti, who performed cartwheels in the ring after each victory, came in at

109 pounds. The night he fought Brown there was no head-over-heels celebration in the ring. The much shorter Colletti could not overcome the physical disadvantages or the high skill level Brown fought at. Brown won all twelve rounds and took home a lopsided decision win.

One week later, Brown headlined again at the Commonwealth with Ansel Bell fighting in the co-feature. Matched up against LaMorte again, Brown, with two good hands, was too much for his old rival. The fight lasted two rounds.

After knocking out bantamweight Allie Kaufman in the opening round of his next fight, Brown spent the rest of the summer mixing it up with featherweights. On October 25th, 1924 Brown took on his highest ranked opponent.

Frankie Ash was coming off a draw against Corporal Izzy Schwartz three months prior. The month before the Schwartz fight, he lost a 15-round decision to champion Pancho Villa in a title fight. That fight was delayed twice due to weather and a temporary injunction after complaints of nuisance by the residents up and down Nostrand Avenue in Brooklyn. Eventually the fight was held and Villa had a hard time keeping up with the fleet-footed Englishman. Some felt Ash did well enough to earn a draw that night.

Against Brown, he didn't make it out of the first round. Ash, described by the *Brooklyn Daily Eagle* as being a replica, "a little brother" in appearance and skill - of Jimmy Wilde but without the big punch, crumbled under the force of a straight right that knocked him out of the ratings and sent him back to England where he proclaimed that Brown was the best he'd ever faced. The fight crowd back in Harlem liked Brown's chances against Pancho Villa.

Villa followed up a successful defense in New Orleans with a trip back to his homeland in the Philippines. A hero's welcome awaited him including a parade through Manila led by Senate-elected President Quezon. Villa was a *Negrense* from the Visayas region that was formerly known as *Buglas* before the Spanish Colonization renamed the island "Blacks" and called the residents "The Blacks." Raised by a single mother, Villa's real name was Francisco Guilledo. Like many named Francisco, he was called Paco or Pancho. At age 11, the slightly-taller-than-four-feet Villa sailed to Iloilo where he found work shining boots and shoes among the territorial bootblacks of Mango Avenue near the ferry terminals.

Pancho spent his days fighting off bigger shoe shiners who tried to take over his spot. In the evenings he defended whatever he earned that day from older teens and young men who figured it was easier to rob at night than work during the day.

That way of life continued for the maturing, though hardly growing, young man for several years. Until he made it up north to Manila and began boxing professionally. The one-time street urchin who, like Brown, didn't blow out candles on his birthdays when growing up, quickly rose to the top of the national boxing rankings. He became the best of a nation of hard-working victims of Spanish oppression who were forced to speak a new language and worship in a church their ancestors never did. A people so poor that, when they unwrapped the newspapers their fish came in, they complained not of the fish having ink, but of the newspaper coupons having fish.

Villa was regarded by his contemporaries as great. Still, Dollings felt Brown could beat him. With Villa planning to return to the United States after a defense in Manila, Brown was in an excellent position to get the next shot. If Villa decided to vacate the title and make a run for the bantamweight title, as some reported, Brown was likely in line for a chance at the vacant title. Either way, things were looking good.

Pariah

Then Flynn got sick. About the same time, Dollings returned to Wales following the death of his son. While Flynn recuperated in Hot Springs, he transferred the managerial responsibilities of many of his fighters to his associates. Some sources say it was Tom Fahy who booked fights for Brown during this spell. However, Eduardo Arroyo wrote in his book that it was Frankie Genaro's manager. Genaro, originally managed by Harry Garsh, was managed by Phil Bernstein at the time Flynn became ill. What happened next was a series of events that led to Brown once again being out on the streets.

Brown was banned from the gym. Without Flynn or Dollings around, no one stepped forward to intervene. Still in debt and living punch check to punch check, it took less than two weeks for Brown to be evicted from the hotel.

Some said he was banned from the gym because he was considered a threat to Genaro and his stake at the championship. Genaro, who wanted to be a jockey until being turned down by W.C. "Pa" Daly for being, at 102 pounds, "too fat," went on to win a gold medal in the 1920 Olympics before embarking on a Hall of Fame career. He was a high caliber boxer who didn't seem the type to lose sleep over an opponent. His manager, of course, might have disagreed. While boxers bask in all the glory, in reality, most are pawns in the careers of their *managers*. Financially, a loss to Brown may have been disastrous enough for Bernstein to want to avoid it at all costs.

Other believed there was another reason- he was banned from the gym because of his lifestyle.

The rumors spread like mange throughout Lenox and Saint Nicholas Avenues down to 125th Street where they made a left, a right, went up, down, and passed through every side street and eventually made their way into the boxing gyms.

Brown was gay the rumors said. He was "in the life" and patronized the same establishments as all the other so-called "sexual deviants." Harlem had plenty of places where homosexuals could gather to listen to music, share a drink, and talk. Places like the speakeasy on 126th Street and Seventh Avenue where the "rough queers" went according to writer Bruce Nugent. Or a few blocks up and to the right on Fifth and 132nd where Edmond's Cellar was *the* spot on Saturday nights for men to flaunt their sister's skirts and their mom's wigs.

Several performers such as singer Gladys Bentley and writers like Nugent were openly gay. Many concealed their preferences, able to be themselves only behind thicker closet doors than those of today. Brown fell somewhere in between; his closet door was somewhat ajar.

He came from a place where alcohol and prostitution were legal but consensual affections between same-sex adults was a crime. Homosexuality remained illegal, though unenforced, in Panama until 2008. The church he went to as a youth preached forgiveness, love, and instructed parishioners not to judge one another, but considered homosexuality an abomination with passages in Genesis and Leviticus referring to "upside-down-turned cities."

Many in the science and medical professions were against it too. Parents brought their gay children to doctors who would drill a 1/4-inch hole through their skull with a trephine or insert an ice pick through their eye sockets and perform a lobotomy because, science believed, something inside the brain needed fixing.

Toss in the anti-gay customs brought over from the Caribbean where homosexuality is still illegal in some areas and popular songs today contain lyrics like "all *bah-tee mon fi-dead*," (all gays must die) and it's not hard to fathom the animosity gays may have encountered in Colón. Being called gay, *maricón, fassy boy, cueco,* or *bulla,* was almost the same as being forced to stand on a public scaffold in a Puritan town wearing a blood red letter on the front of their shirts.

More than once Brown was told to "tone it down." At times, he spoke of a girlfriend and even of a wife. When he returned to Panama in 1929 as champion he released a statement about a girl awaiting his arrival. In the 1940s, he repeated to a Baltimore newspaper his "straight" story of being forced to leave behind a wife, a white one, and a daughter in France after the war broke out.

Those who knew him said the women never existed.

In Harlem boxing gyms, it was not uncommon for Brown to have the showers to himself. A 1980s article in *Boxing Illustrated* called him a "notorious homosexual," and said "no one dared bend over when he was in the shower."

Reading this today it seems exaggerated but 1920s America was not a place of tolerance. Immigrants anglicized their names and dropped their customs in the hopes of fitting in for the sake of their children since America was a cruel place for the ostracized. Cultural assimilation was expected as much to make life easier as it was because American ways were considered better.

Terms such as "metrosexual" didn't exist and politically correct was a phrase only students of Supreme Court cases had ever heard. In today's world, where men are taught that along with a feminine side, they have an inner lesbian as well, Brown may have been a role model like basketball player Jason Collins. A few months after publicly announcing his bedroom preference, Collins saw his jersey ranked among the best sellers and comparisons to Jackie Robinson flooded the news.

In boxing today, rather than being stripped of his championship status, he may have been catapulted to the top of the rankings. Orlando Cruz followed two consecutive losses and a drop in the ratings with his own announcement. Within six months, he appeared on the undercards of high profile cards and was in line for a title shot despite not having defeated any standout contenders. When he stepped into the ring proudly wearing boxing trunks emblazoned with a Puerto Rican flag with the red, white, and blue stripes changed to the green, yellow, and orange of the rainbow, he was valiant but overmatched.

Today a boxing promoter could announce that, after sixty-odd years of being male, he has decided to change his sex and become Kellie, who he said she was all along, and be met with support, encouragement, a spot on a reality show, and a public calling "him" a "her" and addressing her by her new name immediately.

In contrast the 1970s saw many Americans refuse to recognize Cassius Clay's name change to Muhammad Ali, instead calling him Cassius nearly a decade after he publicly stated that Clay, a slave name, meant "dirt" and that his new name meant "praiseworthy" and "Most High."

For the second time since boarding the ocean liner from Peru, Brown was homeless. Norfolk was out of town and Risden was living in Pennsylvania at the time. Siki was upstate preparing for a fight and Gans rented a tiny room in the crowded apartment of a Trinidadian family. Brown left the few belongings he had in the room of another boxer from Panama, Jimmy Brown, and told Jimmy he was going to stay with a friend.

Instead Brown wandered the cold streets. The other "tramps" and "hobos" he knew from his last stint on the streets weren't in their usual spots. Nor were the reefer men selling their ten cent "marahuana" cigarettes. It was November in New York and temperatures hovered around freezing with winds that pierced skin and flesh. He spent the first night with his hands buried in his coat pockets, his father's cap pulled down over his ears huddled in an alley he shared with a stray cat and an aluminum trash can that shielded him from the winds.

Eddie McMahon was the promoter and managing partner of the Commonwealth Sporting Club. He and his younger brother Jess were among the premier promoters in boxing, wrestling, and basketball. Jess, the grandfather of current WWE boss Vince Jr, was busy making matches downtown for Tex Rickard while Eddie booked most of his fights in Harlem. Like he did those June nights in 1923, the homeless Brown went looking for a member of the boxing fraternity.

It took a few days but when Brown finally met with Eddie McMahon and explained the situation, Eddie wasted no time contacting Flynn. A deal was struck that allowed McMahon to become

BLACK INK

Brown's manager immediately with 10% of Brown's future earnings going to Flynn until the fighter's debt to the former manager was paid off.

Eddie got Brown his room at the hotel again and when the fighter knocked on Jimmy's door to pick up his stuff, Jimmy told him he should have stayed with him.

"I've burdened you enough already. My problems should not become yours," Brown told Jimmy.

Training shifted to the Pioneer Gym under the expert tutelage of Bill Miller. The beret-wearing Miller, who told most people he was from "one of the islands," was actually from the U.S. Virgin Islands, though some thought he was from an island off the coast of Georgia. A former middleweight boxer who toured the British Isles fighting against all comers in a boxing booth owned by thousand-fight veteran Bobby Dobbs, Miller was one of Leo P. Flynn's go-to trainers.

When he took over the corner duties for Brown, he was best known for his work with middleweight champion Tiger Flowers. After his days with Brown ended, Miller cemented his status as one of the best trainers ever. He trained Primo Carnera and Beau Jack and even tried his hand at managing with Johnny Saxton and Coley Wallace. It was a short run as manager the Hall of Fame writer Dan Parker explained.

Parker listened intently as Miller detailed in an accent laced with "Virgin Island patois" how the mob worked their way in. "Blinky" Palermo, whose eyelashes never stopped batting, approached Miller in the gym and asked who was Miller's muscle.

"I'm doing this solo," Miller said.

"You need backing," he was told. Palermo offered his services for half the winnings. "You can get half of mine," Miller said, "but not half of the fighters take."

Palermo agreed and other than showing up after each fight for his cut, he did nothing. Just as Miller's contract with the two fighters was set to expire, Palermo decided he wanted total control of the well-schooled fighters. He whispered in the ears of Saxton and Wallace and soon after both stopped talking to Miller.

Miller also had a hand in the early development of numerous amateur champions when he worked out of the Salem Crescent Gym in Harlem. One of those amateurs was an eleven-year-old originally from Detroit. When seeing him for the first time, Brown said, "If he don't get too fly, he'll be a champion." That youngster, who they called "Smitty" and we call Sugar Ray Robinson, did become champion.

Miller's most infamous fighter might have been Thomas Reed, who made headlines for different reasons. Saint Thomas was Reed's disciple name in the church, some say cult, of Father Divine. A church where sex, unless Father Divine was the one doing the thrusting, was not allowed.

Because of an intimate relationship with a female disciple, Saint Thomas was expelled from the church. After he became an "overnight" contender by blasting out Gus Dorazio in four, he was invited back into the church and remained there until committing the apparent sin of losing to Melio Bettina in his next fight. Back to being Thomas Reed, he made headlines again after turning himself in for a string of robberies. The following week he was a free man because, the police said, none of the robberies he confessed to doing were reported.

Miller and Brown got off to a losing start together. Brown fought less than two weeks after hooking up with his new trainer. His opponent was Jimmy Russo. The fast punching Grand Rapids fighter, who fought out of the Brownsville section of Brooklyn and was sometimes billed out of New Orleans, had wins over contenders Davey Abad, Benny Schwartz, and amateur standout Nat Pincus to his credit.

Despite the obvious credentials of his opponents and the rust acquired while sleeping on cold concrete, Brown, strapped for cash, wagered his entire purse on himself.

Brown suffered his first official loss. Russo outworked him throughout the ten rounds for the decision. A rematch was scheduled for January 3rd, 1925. Training throughout the holidays, Brown reversed the result winning a clear-cut decision after ten rounds.

Two weeks later Tex Rickard released his top ten rankings in each of the nine weight divisions. Brown was ranked third among flyweights behind Villa and Genaro. But his days at flyweight were numbered.

He continued improving under Miller, who taught him how to control the pace and feint with his feet- the same moves he would later teach Robinson. On his toes, boxing from a distance while his left swung like a pendulum by his hip, Brown carried the right by his face, the fist poised like a black mamba in the Sub-Saharan brush.

Eddie McMahon was unable to get Brown a title shot. That fact didn't bother him as much as it did Brown. A Panama Al Brown fight was a good draw for the Commonwealth. The more Brown fought, the better for the promoter. But finding flyweights who were willing to sign on the dotted line had become increasingly difficult.

Don't try to knock anyone out were the instructions relayed to Brown.

When the bells rang, he danced circles around his opponents and flashed a wide smile when they missed. In between he dusted his rivals with glittery combinations that left the crowd in awe and his opponents without bruises. The charade lasted 15 months. During that time Brown ran a streak of 19 consecutive fights without scoring a knockout.

Brown learned the promotion was more important than the fighter. He had no choice but to comply. Promoters had the bank to hold out longer than boxers. Eventually boxers gained an appreciation for the promoters' ideas. With fights going on five or six nights per week, healthy boxers were a premium. Fighting at half steam kept injuries down, fighters busy, and promoters in business.

It was a ho-hum existence Brown quickly tired of. Winning spectacularly didn't bring him any closer to fighting for the championship or the big money anyway. On the contrary, it made it harder to get fights. So he went along with program. He made enough money to pay the bills, his debt, and, for the first time since working in the lawyer's office was able to send money home.

Boxing was his job and after work it was happy hour. He paired up with Siki on many nights and drank until the night was interrupted by the sun. Occasionally, they put down their glasses long enough to squeeze some training in. They even sparred each other. Mostly, they drank.

Going easy on an opponent was common enough to have its own name. Plenty of boxers "carried" their opponents. Jack Johnson allegedly did it. Archie Moore admitted he did too. In fact, Moore said failing to carry an opponent was sometimes considered a violation.

After Lloyd Marshall knocked out Harvey Massey, Moore confronted Lloyd. You had him beat. You didn't have to knock him out was the gist of what he told Lloyd. With no commercial endorsements to beef up their income, fighters relied on steady work. And the "Black Murderers Row" circuit of fighters, and those willing to face them, was about as populated as Detroit's Brush Park neighborhood.

Lloyd brushed Moore off.

Moore never forgot.

Next time the two fought, Moore set out to teach him a lesson. He knocked Lloyd out in a vicious confrontation. Afterwards, Jimmy Bivins confronted Moore. You had him beat. You didn't have to knock him out was the gist of his message. Next time Bivins fought Moore, he knocked Moore out for "doing Marshall that way."

Ironically, boxers benefitted in many ways because of those arrangements. No longer able to rely on their punch, punchers were forced to box and became better-rounded fighters with clever footwork and nifty defense. Their conditioning increased from the additional rounds. When involved in fights where their hands were free of the handcuffs, their repertoires were more complete and they possessed nuances they may not have learned with quick knockouts.

Brown's defense improved along with his ability to clinch. His footwork, dance steps actually, rarely seen in those days and rarely seen in these days, became harder to predict than a reaction ball. He couldn't help but smile and sometimes laugh after making an opponent miss wildly. Fans filled the 3,000-seat arena as much to see him dance circles around his opponents as to see him win.

He boxed like a *Torero,* the bullfighters who face the raging bulls with only a red cape and tire the beasts for the *Banderilleros* who spear them before the *Matadors* do the slaying. But his fights during this period featured no slayings and Brown, like the toreros, did not attain the fame of the matadors.

Moving up to the bantamweight class did nothing to change his fortune. He was no closer to a title shot in that classification than he was at flyweight. His role remained the same. Don't get hurt and don't hurt anyone. Brown learned that the fighter meant little in boxing. The fighter was just the flesh used by the greater interests to peddle.

It had been that way since the sport's infancy when street gangs sent their toughest fighters to settle turf wars and early political rivals settled their scores at the expense of boxers' blood. They call it boxing but exploitation often fits too. The boxer gets the fame, the admiration of the fans, and sometimes hero status. They can make money but only if someone else stands to make more because, in boxing, the real ballers don't get hit.

Only recently have we seen more and more boxers take more control of their careers by co-promoting fights and signing advisors from outside the usual boxing circles. In the era in which Brown boxed, if a fighter refused to take a dive or box with kid gloves, the risk of never fighting again was real.

The opponents no longer mattered to Brown. In some cases, neither did the decisions. On at least one occasion he was seen heading to the showers before a winner was even announced. His career went from a promising venture to something worse than a dead end. It was a continuous loop leading nowhere.

He stopped paying attention to the career of Pancho Villa. Until that thick-aired day in July when news of the Filipino's death brought the rope jumping and bag hitting in the gyms to a stop.

Back from his excursion in the Philippines, Villa had a few fights lined up in California. The morning of July 4th, 1925 he had a tooth pulled.

That night despite a swollen jaw and doctor's wishes to the contrary, he went ahead with a scheduled ten rounder against future champ Jimmy McLarnin. With a heavy dose of painkillers in his system, he toughed out the ten rounds. He lost a decision. Two days later three more teeth were removed. Two more fights were scheduled for that month.

When he developed the often fatal throat infection Ludwig's angina, promoters reluctantly cancelled those fights. Not yet 24 years old, Pancho died on a San Francisco operating table on July 25th. His wife, who gave birth to their son the day before, claimed he was deliberately given an overdose of anesthetic by doctors who were coerced by a crime syndicate that Pancho infuriated.

Pancho's death and the rumors swirling through the gyms over the "real" cause had Brown thinking briefly about returning to Panama. Instead he kept fighting and drinking. In between he sent telegrams back home. He missed the family and informed them of his intentions to return as soon as it was economically feasible.

That summer Stanislaus Loayza of Chile challenged Jimmy Goodrich for the lightweight championship. It was a disaster for Loayza, who had impressed in previous engagements. He was floored multiple times and only lasted a round and a half.

Brown was kept very busy that year. He scored a pair of wins over Breslin and closed out the year with a decision over Tommy Hughes on December 12. The rest of the weekend he spent drinking and dancing. Battling Siki, along with the other French boxers, was with Brown for part of that weekend.

Tuesday morning, while most New Yorkers were eating their breakfast and bracing themselves for the morning cold, detectives from the W 30th Street station were busy putting together the pieces of evidence they needed to find the murderer of Battling Siki.

When Brown found out that Siki was shot in the back and the street lawyers concluded it was the police themselves who pulled the trigger, he went into a funk that lasted for days. He could hear his father's voice inside his head telling him once again the reasons why he left Tennessee. While Brown helped carry the mortal remains of his friend and sat through a ceremony presided over by the Rev. Adam Clayton Powell, Siki's murder was still unsolved. Brown decided it was time to find a way out of New York.

He lost his next bout to Dominick Petrone, a fighter he had beaten earlier. Three months after the death of Siki, undercover cops dressed as gangsters stepped into a dinette for a late breakfast. While eating they overheard a phone conversation by 18-year-old Martin Maroney.

"The bulls are on to us," said the teenaged laborer who lived one block from the murder scene. The "bulls" put down their forks and nabbed him. Maroney denied involvement at first before ultimately confessed to the crime.

When the idea of going to France was first broached inside the bistro on 47th the night of the Goldstein fight, Brown hesitated only slightly before accepting.

Abe Goldstein was once considered by his contemporaries to be the best fighter in Harlem. In his prime he was thought to be as good as anyone not named Jack Dempsey, Gene Tunney, or Harry Greb. The Abe Goldstein who climbed into the ring against Brown at the Pioneer Sporting Club, on E 24th where the Baruch College campus now stands, was past his prime. A winner of only two of his previous nine matches, the Whitey Bimstein-trained former champion didn't have to turn back the clock to beat Brown.

In a fight the NY Times described as "tame" and "unimpressive," fans started walking out the doors during the seventh round. Though Goldstein staggered Brown in the second and fifth rounds, the rest of the fight saw Brown "battered" but "not groggy" according to the Times write up.

Most of the French contingent returned to Europe after Siki's death. The few who remained waited for Brown and Eddie McMahon in the bistro after the loss. You'll be better off in France they suggested. A change of scenery was what Brown needed according to the bistro's owner Mr. J. Villepontoux.

Some twenty years removed from his championship cycling days, Villepontoux needed a break from the long hours of the restaurant business. He also needed a paid ticket to France where he could tend to some personal matters. Still a semi-active motorcycle racer whenever the French cycle team was in town, Villepontoux was willing to leave his business in the hands of an assistant while he returned to France as Brown's European representative.

Eddie was hesitant. Ultimately he agreed, for a slice of the action, if Villepontoux was able to secure a few fights. With Brown's stock at an all-time low following the two losses, the promoter reasoned he had nothing to lose. The very next day Villepontoux sent France's premier promoter, Jeff Dickson, a telegram outlining his plan.

Villepontoux was prepared to deliver two of New York's finest fighters he wrote, in exchange for room, board, and transportation. The fighters were Al Brown, the dynamic punching bantamweight and Jimmy Brown, a middleweight also from Panama. They eagerly awaited Dickson's response.

Villepontoux knew Brown would find better luck in Paris. While New Yorkers bickered for three years over whether or not children should be allowed to play in Central Park, Paris embraced change. Women wore their hair short, like men, and their skirts were high enough that their calves could breathe.

Brown was fighting with the passion of a man stuffing envelopes. He drank in the morning, the afternoon, the evening, and at night. He drank not to have a good time, but to keep from having a bad time. This was ten years before Bill W. started Alcoholics Anonymous. Had those Clinton Street meetings been taking place in 1926 and "Al B" attended, he may have been told he was in the second stage of alcoholism.

Villepontoux and Brown pushed Eddie to pull his brother's strings and get Brown a match on the upcoming Garden card. Eddie figured he had nothing to lose and possibly something to gain. Within a few days his brother Jess managed to squeeze Brown in against Teddy Silva.

Teddy Silva was the type of fighter people are referring to when they talk about a throwback. He was a fight anyone, anytime, and anyplace kind of guy who was coming off a solid win over contender Tommy Milton on the Brown-Goldstein undercard. Before that, Silva picked himself up from two knockdowns and went the distance against Jimmy McLarnin, extended Fidel LaBarba, and boxed draws against former title challengers Clever Sencio and Johnny Buff. His record wasn't a pretty one. Neither were the faces of his opponents after a few rounds with him.

It wasn't the prospect of fighting Silva that rejuvenated Brown. Fighting in Madison Square Garden did. On top of that, it was on a benefit card headlined by French hero Georges Carpentier. Though it was intended to be a Paris audition of sorts, Eddie and Brown knew a good showing on that stage would help his interests locally if Paris didn't call.

Brown's fight was the first of three ten round bouts. The 14,000 in attendance who saw Carpentier salvage a draw with a last-round rally also saw what a motivated Brown could do. It was bombs away from the first round. Without breaking a sweat, Brown did what McLarnin could not - he stopped Silva in three rounds.

It was a night of promise and congratulations. About the only thing missing was a response from Dickson. A month and a pair of wins at the Commonwealth over fighters with losing records followed and still no word. Eddie managed to get him on another Garden card scheduled for July 8th.

Buried on the undercard of the Jimmy Slattery-Bob Sage fight, Brown outclassed the durable Pete Zivic over ten rounds. Called the "Elongated Negro" by the *NY Times's* James P. Dawson, the fight was reported as a dull affair with boos and "outbursts of condemnation throughout" by the crowd of 4,700. The only time the crowd, which was half the size that watched Mickey Walker two weeks earlier, cheered was after the final bell rang. Referee Dick Peters repeatedly asked Zivic to fight but Brown was unhittable that night. The only thing he couldn't do was knock out Zivic. The Zivic brothers weren't easy to stop. Between the five of them, they failed to make it to the final bell only 25 times in over 600 fights.

Along with the boos, Brown heard the usual racial slurs during his walk back to the dressing room. In between he heard a fair share of "ugly comments." Those comments, he said, stung more than the punches.

After a ten-round decision win over the world-rated Harry Forbes in Albany, Eddie got Brown on an all-bantamweight card at the Garden kicking off Labor Day weekend. Rickard showcased what the papers were calling the eight best bantamweights in New York.

With the streaking Chick Suggs going against the popular Bushy Graham in the main event, Brown was again buried on the undercard. His bout, against Brooklyn's Joe Ryder, was the first of the four featured bouts to go on.

Suggs was described by the New York papers as being the "best Negro bantam since George Dixon." Graham was coming off of wins over Frankie Genaro, Davey Abad, and Dominick Petrone. Graham won the fight and the New York papers wrote he was the best bantam at the time. Brown boxed well but repeated low blows by Ryder led to his being disqualified in the fourth round. Though Brown was considered a hard hitting prospect, a title shot remained beyond his long reach. There were no reservations about him leaving when the telegram from Paris arrived.

Uncrowned Champion

"It was my second voyage but this time I had luggage and a passport," Brown said about his first trip to Paris. He, Jimmy Brown, Villepontoux, and another described only as the Eskimo traveled third class at Dickson's expense. Unlike his first trip through the Atlantic, he sat at the communal tables in the wide-open dining halls while he ate potatoes someone else peeled.

When they arrived in Le Havre six days later, the only walking Brown had to do was to the curb where a car waited to take them to Montmartre. Dickson greeted them at the hotel with a hot meal and keys to separate rooms for all. He left them to eat with instructions to get a good night's sleep and a schedule for the following morning - an early press conference, followed by a training session at the gym.

Since the days when welterweight Harry Lewis and lightweight Frank Erne introduced the "American" style of boxing, French enthusiasts flocked to arenas whenever Americans were in action. Parisian fight fans waited for the next American star to fight in their rings with the eagerness of high school seniors scoping out the female freshman on the first day of school. The opportunistic Dickson was always willing to showcase American boxers on his cards. It didn't matter that the two fighters who came with Villepontoux were Panamanian. In France, Al Brown and Jimmy Brown were Americans.

While Harlem was going through a renaissance and the rest of the country was celebrating the Roaring Twenties Paris was in the midst of *"Les Années Folles"* and Surrealism. Gone were the so-called "Apaches," street hooligans that outnumbered the police by far and terrorized citizens with violent muggings. In their place were street fairs on just about every other block and artists, writers, dancers, and musicians plied their craft without the restraints of censorship. Books like *My Life and Loves,* banned in the US and UK, sold for as much as one hundred 1920s dollars in France.

It was a popular destination for black entertainers, who found more opportunity and a less suffocating type of racism in Paris.

After the three course meal, the two Browns went to their rooms, tucked themselves into bed and napped for about two hours. Just after midnight both sneaked out of their rooms and spent the night hopping from one establishment to another taking in the sights and drinking the prohibition-free champagne. Live bands played the familiar jazz heard throughout Harlem and everywhere they went they were well received by groups out for a good time.

Champagne corks popped and the people he met his first night made a toast to celebrate the birthday of French inventor Charles Cros. Brown learned the story of the Frenchman who invented, they told him, the phonograph, colored photography and possibly, the telephone. He was literally a few minutes later than Bell, Edison and, Ducos du Hauron when it came to getting the patents. They drank a toast to Cros and to just about any other thing that came to their minds.

There weren't enough hours in the night to visit all the clubs like the *Bal Negre* and the *Cabane Cubaine*. Plans were made to see them the following night. And the night after that and the night...

When the sun brushed aside the night's darkness the two found their way to the press conference hung over and without having slept.

The press conference was held at Eugene Bullard's Athletic Club at 15 *Rue Mansart* in *Pigalle*. Eugene Bullard, who spoke French with a southern American drawl, was a former boxer and stable mate of the great American boxer Dixie Kid. A war hero with the French Foreign Legion, he also owned *Le Gran Duc* and *L'Escadrille* night clubs where Langston Hughes and Ada "Bricktop" Smith worked.

His gym catered to a broad range of people from professional boxers like Victor "Young" Perez, to celebrities like Hemmingway and Louis Armstrong, and even politicians such as Chinese Ambassador to France, Wellington Koo.

Bullard, who became a good friend of Brown's, had a life worth sidetracking though it would take an entire book to do him justice. In short, he left America after his family split apart following an attempt to lynch his father. His brother Hector wasn't as fortunate, becoming one of the more than 2,500 African Americans who were lynched in Georgia alone.

Bullard left home when he was eight, lived with gypsies, picked cotton, became a jockey, and rode the rails by night until he reached Norfolk, Virginia. Once there, he stowed away on a German ship headed to Scotland and eventually found his way to Liverpool.

He held a variety of jobs including dock worker and whistle man; a lookout role usually on a rooftop or at an intersection where his loud whistles alerted gamblers to approaching police. He was also a "moving target." That job saw youngsters wait against a wall while bouncing a ball. Passing males would taunt them and, for a few shillings, get the chance to try to hit them by throwing the ball at them.

In his spare time, Eugene did odd jobs at Chris Baldwin's gymnasium in Liverpool. He kept one eye on the broom in his hands and the other fixated on the lessons being taught to the boxers working out. It wasn't long before he put down the broom and donned a pair of boxing gloves, eventually fighting on Dixie Kid's undercards.

Bullard was the first black fighter pilot. Before his missions he'd write on the wings of his planes "all blood that runs is red." He was wounded in the battles of Artois and Champagne, befriended the famed Sentinel of Verdun- ace pilot Jean Navarre, played drums for the Zig Zag band, married a countess, and was the inspiration for the character Lloyd in Hemmingway's The Sun Also Rises.

He was also a good friend of promoter Jeff Dickson. Dickson was a war photographer from south of the Mason Dixon line who stayed in France after the war ended. He promoted races, bullfights, figure skating, wrestling and boxing. Dickson became best known as a boxing promoter, most notably perhaps for his work with Primo Carnera. Before he theatrically promoted the "two meters tall" heavyweight, Dickson was selling the public a "six-foot-tall bantamweight."

When Villepontoux wrote to Dickson he mentioned that Brown was 5'9." Someone in Dickson's office took it as 5.9 feet and when they converted his height to the metric system, 5.9 feet equals 180cm, which equals 5'11."

Brown was closer in height to 1990s bantamweight Junior Jones than he was to Roy Jones Jr. The two inches were easy to pull off for the slim Brown. Especially when his opponents were a full head shorter than he was. As far as Jeff Dickson was concerned, 5'11" had a better ring to it than 5'9."

On the topic of acoustics, once again Brown's name was tinkered with. "Panama" was dropped. In France, and throughout Europe, he would become known as the bantamweight from Harlem - Al Brown, Alf Brown, or, as French papers often spelled it, Alf Braun.

On November 11th, 1926 at the Salle Wagram, Europe had its first look at Al Brown in action. His opponent was Antoine Merlo, former challenger for the European championship. A sold-out crowd lined up on *L'Avenue de Wagram* and waited anxiously hours before the doors opened.

When Brown made his way out of the dressing room and down the carpeted aisle of the Troubadour Style arena in a sky blue silk kimono with white polka dots and his beige checkered newsboy cap pulled down to the side, he had no idea he was about to embark upon the most intense love-hate relationship any fighter ever had with his fans.

Merlo was good though no match for Brown. Brown ended the fight in round three when he landed a right hand that dropped Merlo and at the same time made the crowd grimace.

After the fight, Brown hit the streets again with Jimmy, who boxed to a draw with Albert Lepesant on the undercard. Everywhere he went he was congratulated on his win, his shoes, and his checkered cap. At every club they went to he was surrounded by smiles and people asking him to join them.

Brown made more money that night than he ever had for one fight. He also found more places to spend it. In Paris, no matter the color of his skin, he could walk through the front door of any of the pubs in Quartier Pigalle.

BLACK INK

And there were the horse races. Originally he bet for the win. Then he discovered forecasting and trio betting. There were boutiques with fashions he'd never seen before. The champagne cost less in Paris and the dollar stretched longer in those days. His nights were buzzed and his days began with a headache that went away after another drink.

"All I need to live is 2,000 bottles of champagne," he once said.

While Brown lived it up, Dickson secured his next opponent. The never-before-KO'd Roger Fabregues was booked for the first of December. Coming off a ten round loss to the excellent Kid Francis, Fabregues was expected to take Brown into the later rounds. On the undercard, Jimmy, billed as Al Brown's brother, was fighting a rematch with Lepesant.

Jimmy lost his fight. Brown, however, electrified the crowd in mere seconds. A straight right that landed like a bolt of lightning left Fabregues looking like a newbie on ice skates before crashing to the canvas for the count.

In his first two fights in Paris, Brown had outperformed two of the better bantams in Europe. Merlo had gone the full 15 against the undefeated Londoner Teddy Baldock and Fabregues previously went the distance against Kid Francis.

Following the fight, an entourage chose Brown to gather around. They recommended places to party, to eat, to drink and even made the reservations for him always making sure there were enough seats for themselves.

Dickson booked a fight for Brown on December 14th. It was against Belgian Henri Scillie, European bantamweight champion. Scillie, who had lost only once in his previous 40 fights, was more experienced than Brown. The French writers got the call correct when they predicted Brown would not stop him early and would lack the conditioning to hold him off in the later rounds.

Scillie was unbeatable at that time. His recent wins were over Domenico Bernasconi, Kid Francis, Bugler Harry Lake, and André Routis. While Brown was getting a taste of the good life, his opponent was preparing for the fight of his life.

Scillie, the brother of Gustave Roth, came in behind a high guard and used his forearms to block the rapid combinations aimed at his face. Around the fourth round, Brown began to slow down and Scillie opened up with body blows. A tired Brown fought back courageously as Scillie poured it on. The decision of a draw after 12 was met by a scattering of catcalls by the fans that had gotten behind the Belgian.

A bad night Brown would tell everyone. Next time would be different he said between sips of alcohol. Edouard Mascart was picked as the next opponent. The bushy haired featherweight counted fine fighters like Harry Corbett, Bugler Harry Lake, and Charles Ledoux as his victims. In 1925, he and Brown crossed paths back in Harlem while Mascart campaigned for fights against Johnny Dundee and Louis Kaplan. It was at The Pioneer gym about two weeks before Siki was killed.

Mascart's American campaign proved unsuccessful. In Paris his only loss in the three years leading up to the Brown fight was against Routis. A reported record crowd filled every seat at the Cirque de Paris to watch the two exchange punches.

Brown did his training in the French Riviera, spending equal amounts of time at the gym and along the sandy shores. Villepontoux had to return to New York and his portion of Brown's managerial rights went to José Saura, a weightlifting aficionado also involved in the auto racing industry who had no knowledge of the fight game. Allegedly, he had even less knowledge of accounting since he somehow ended up with more money than what his contracted share called for.

Boxers were, and many still are, the last ones to see the money. Promoters made the checks out to their managers who paid any expenses not covered by the promoter including their own cuts and trainer's fees. Then, after everyone else got their slice, the boxer was paid.

The best managers earned their pay by finding the best trainers and sparring partners, handling the publicity, booking flights and car rentals, reserving hotel rooms with few distractions, making sure unbiased officials worked the fights, making sure the ring is the right size and properly padded, and dealing with anything else that might come up.

Saura did none of that. He was a nightmare that got worse after awakening. He signed contracts and simply told Brown what he was earning. Brown trusted his managers to do the right thing. Though he wasn't getting everything he was supposed to, he got enough to send some home, buy the finest clothes, and go out every night of the week. Brown was too busy living it up to realize his hands weren't the only ones in his pockets.

The trip to the Riviera was a productive one. Brown easily stopped the heavier Mascart in round five. After the fight, Brown purchased a Bugatti. Then he gave it away. He bought another one, a convertible Type 43, in March from the money he made knocking out Kid Socks. A few miles after leaving the dealership, driving along the *Bois de Boulogne*, with the odometer reading three kilometers, the car caught fire and blew up. He walked back to the dealership and bought another one on credit.

He made more than enough from his next fight to pay for it. His opponent was Eugene Criqui, former French flyweight champion and featherweight champion of the world. Criqui, whose face told a million stories, was over the hill when he faced Brown. He was coming off a loss in Argentina against a former sparring partner.

In 1924 Carlos Uzabeaga was competing in the Paris Olympic Games when he met and befriended the retired Criqui. Two years later, Uzabeaga looked out for his down on his luck friend in the form of a nice payday in Buenos Aires. The two squared off in an allegedly simulated match staged before a big crowd.

The Brown-Criqui fight was allegedly fixed as well.

The once slick boxer was, since returning from the war, a bruising infighter with unquestionable heart. He was a survivor of the Battle of Verdun where he caught a German bullet with his face that tore half his jaw off. Despite nearly losing the left side of his face, Criqui held on to his rifle and adhered to the universal creed of soldiers to never let go of your weapon. His jaw was reattached using wires, a silver plate, pieces of plastic, and according to some sources, fragments of a goat leg.

A crowd described by the NY Times as "fashionable," and dressed in "evening clothes, with a brilliant display of jewelry, ermine and sables by the women," jammed the Velodrome and witnessed Criqui get cleanly outpointed for the majority of the ten rounds.

The lone exception was the third round. Brown landed a hook and then a right which sent Criqui rolling onto his back for an eight count. Criqui rose and suddenly tore into Brown sending the Panamanian down briefly. It all may have been part of a script.

Arroyo mentions in his book that a secret meeting took place the week before with both fighters present. In a room with no windows and at least one wall that could talk, everything down to the knockdowns was discussed and agreed upon days before the first bell rang. Years later, when Brown boxed and lived in Algeria, *L'Echo sportif de l'Oranie* summarized Brown's career and mentioned the Criqui match. Despite much ink being used to evoke comparisons to the Carpentier-Siki match, the evidence shows the fight was a fair one, the paper wrote.

Criqui was beaten badly by the ruthless Gustave Humery in his next fight. He fought once after that loss before retiring. As for Brown, his honeymoon with Parisian fans was about to end. Fans booed him after the Criqui fight. Beating an old hero is never a popular feat. If anyone thought that was the only reason behind the booing, it was eradicated in subsequent fights. What developed next was a strange yet fascinating, sometimes hostile, and at times violent affair with Parisian fans.

Brown was the biggest attraction in French boxing at the time. In Paris he found many poets and writers from Harlem and through them, came into contact with the writers, poets and artists of the French surrealism movement. His appeal crossed over into the arts.

The previous year, Josephine Baker made French hearts, both male and female, skip a few beats with her performances of *Danse Sauvage* with dance partner and actor, Joe Alexi in *La Revue Nègre* at the *Théâtre des Champs-Élysées*. Around the time of the Criqui fight, at the *Folies Bergère,* she dangled 16 semi ripe bananas from a string around her waist and called it a skirt for her performances in *La Folie du Jour.*

Among those in the audiences were Pablo Picasso and Ernest Hemingway. Brown could be found among them too and at times was invited on stage to dance.

Strolling along the cobblestone *Rue de Martyrs* or *Boulevard de Clichy,* the beating of drums and the mellow tones of a sax seeping through the door cracks were often coming from the hands of Brown. They were hands that seemingly could be taught to do anything. As a fighter, his hands were wrecking balls capable of dropping light heavyweights at Grupp's Gym. One of them was a high-ranking battler. Legend claims it was Battling Siki who was knocked off his feet; others say it was Larry Johnson. Sports columnist Alvin Moses confirmed it happened, getting an admission from the fallen fighter but declined to give a name, saying only that it was "a noted 175-pounder."

Like every major city, Paris had its gay quarters. In the 1920s those areas included parts of Montmartre, Montparnasse, and especially Pigallé - a place U.S. soldiers called Pig Alley. Word got around faster than influenza- Brown was more than a curious observer in these places. In places where women dressed liked men and same-sex couples walked hand in hand, the premier attraction of the most macho sport was a regular.

He was a regular at the popular gay spots like the *Moulin Rouge* and the *Monocle* on Edgar–Quintet Boulevard. Straights often passed by and gawked at the gay couples with the same shocked amazement as a tourist at a safari. Seeing Brown wearing the latest fashions in those places was their lion moment.

By his next fight, the word was out. The "American negro" who was beating the local fighters was queer. A ballerina he was called. When he made his way into the ring against Young Ciclone, he heard just about every homophobic slur that existed.

Ciclone, a featherweight from Barcelona whose real name was Jose Omedes, was treated like the hometown fighter that night. A pro since the age of fifteen, Ciclone was national champion of Spain at seventeen. When offered the fight against Brown by Dickson, Ciclone said Dickson asked him if he thought he could last two rounds with the Panamanian.

"Not only can I last two rounds, I can last the entire fight and even win it."

Dickson, he said, just smiled and said "I'll be satisfied if you can last two rounds."

With the crowd cheering his every move, Ciclone pressed forward swinging but missing the long, elusive target. Brown shot out a right hand that was programmed to knock out the Spaniard. It landed on the top of his head and sent a familiar jolt of pain up Brown's arm. His right hand once again was broken.

Unable to launch his right hand missiles, Brown attempted to win the match with his jab. The increasingly anti-Brown fans jeered him throughout the match. A reporter for the French paper, *Excelsior* wrote, "I have seen few men cheered and applauded for as much as they did the Spaniard. The entire hall was on his side, partly, to spite Brown, and also because of the audacious and gallant way he fought."

Ciclone did his best to beat the one handed fighter. He kept his arms busy but Brown could be as hard to hit as Willie Pep. Brown won the decision and, as his skinny arm was raised, many in the crowd lashed out with insults directed at him while they cheered the Spaniard. Years later when reflecting on his career, Ciclone said the hardest he ever was hit was by Brown. In comparison, the blows of his rival Antonio Ruiz, who scored 34 knockouts in his career, felt like love taps.

It took five months for Brown's hand to heal. Those months he spent traveling throughout Nice, St. Tropez, and Monte Carlo drinking and dancing. By the time he stepped into the ring again, he'd become the boxer the fans loved to hate.

On October 18, he clubbed Alberto Ryall into defeat in two rounds. Henri Scillie was up next in a match scheduled for thirteen rounds. Scillie was favored to win and an audience of anti-Brown fans occupied the seats. Cheers flooded the arena as Scillie bopped up and down in the aisle on his way to the ring. Catcalls, racial slurs, and homophobic insults were directed Brown's way when he climbed into the square circle.

The NY Times reported Brown "out-boxed Scillie by a wide margin for ten rounds, but then tired and permitted the Belgian to get in enough punches to swing the verdict." The crowd, the report stated, "was with Scillie all through, but there was a considerable chorus of catcalls at the end from those who thought the Pana-man should have received a better break."

The French paper, *Le Matin,* described an overconfident, smiling Brown, sure of his "remarkable" skills, nonchalantly sweeping the first six rounds. Scillie, tucked safely behind his turtle-shell guard, never eased up on his aggression. A flurry of hooks in round seven had the crowd cheering and left Brown searching for his confidence. The crowd jeered and voiced their displeasure whenever Brown landed a counter.

A concerned look pushed the smile out of the way as the two battled on even terms until the tenth round. Scillie's hard shots to the chest and sweeping hooks to the side of Brown's face took their toll on Brown. The last three rounds were swept by the Belgian fighter amid applause and emphatic cheers. After thirteen rounds, Scillie was declared the victor.

Brown's first loss in France left fans thirsty for more losses. Dickson knew this and sought a French featherweight who could turn the trick because, as one French paper put it, "for a bantamweight to defeat Al Brown he would have to be a featherweight, and a very good one at that."

Brown expressed a desire to return to New York. To win the title he said publicly. To friends, he confided displeasure with the sour turn of events. Not getting the decision against Scillie along with the selection of opponents being considered for him convinced Brown there was no future in Paris. He still wanted to be a champion and if he remained in France, he felt, he was only going to become an opponent.

After notifying Dickson of his intention to return to New York at the end of the year, the promoter quickly scheduled two fights for Brown. The first, on December 10, would be against André Routis and the second, eight days later, would be another go with Henri Scillie.

Routis was a former French bantamweight champion who was campaigning in both the featherweight and junior lightweight divisions. He had tussles against the whirlwind Jackie Kid Berg and perennial lightweight contender Joe Glick. Routis had been campaigning successfully in the United States when he was contacted by Dickson. His battles with Tony Canzoneri and Eddie Anderson in particular endeared him to the New York fans. *Le Journal* indicated the match could easily have been a match of champions had Routis been more popular with Tex Rickard and, had Brown not been "colored."

The French papers touted Routis as the hero. He played into the hype and according to Arroyo, stated he was out to avenge the losses of the other French boxers. Arroyo wrote that French papers published racist statements attributed to Routis.

Brown's motivation was the paycheck. A crowd of 12,000 chipped in enough for the fighters to make one of the largest paydays of their careers.

It was money Brown needed. His time off saw him spend more than he made. Gambling was the biggest culprit, especially his knack for picking slow horses with heavy jockeys. And an entourage with a bigger thirst than his own contributed to the debt-laden state Brown was in when the bell rang.

The large crowd loudly cheered Routis's every move and booed Brown's. The early rounds featured wicked exchanges. By the third round it became a maul fest with the referee ignoring Brown's clinches and allowing Routis to rough his way out of them. Routis used low blows, elbows, shoulders, and wrapped his right hand under Brown's arm and yoked his shoulder while he slugged away with the left.

With the Scillie fight and the big payday it brought only eight days away, Brown tried in vain to avoid a brawl. Routis took control in the second half. He trapped his skinny foe on the ropes and hit him at will while the crowd screamed themselves hoarse. Routis was the clear winner and exited the ring amid praise and adulation while Brown walked down the steps with a swollen ear, a small mouse under his right eye, and no complaints as he headed towards his dressing room once more bombarded by insults.

Eight days later he swapped blows again with Scillie. It was a closer fight than their previous slugfest but this time Brown did not fade towards the end. The fight was considered a toss-up and when the decision was announced as a draw, the protests were minimal.

Brown had mixed feeling about Paris. There were some aspects he adored. He was a box office magnet, drawing sizeable crowds even when he made an appearance as a celebrity referee or judge. In between keeping his entourage's glasses filled with the sparkly stuff and being flooded with compliments on his clothes and smile just as the tab was tallied, he managed to forge legit friendships. He was a fixture in clubs and had a mob as big as that of the Pied Piper. He made more money in France than some champions did in America.

The fame he found there was bittersweet, however. Many wished him harm. Ultimately, he felt it was better for his career to return to New York. When he boarded the ship for New York harbor Brown did so with no regret and no real intention of returning.

Awaiting him in New York was Eddie. Brown recalled noticing Eddie's appearance had changed drastically in the year and a half he was away. Eddie looked tired and older than his age. Brown told him about his experiences "over there," many of which weren't written or spoken about "over here." Eddie showed partial interest. We can only speculate what he was thinking as Brown spoke. Perhaps it was what many others thought when they first saw Brown after his return from Paris.

Back when championship matches were still scheduled for 15 rounds, just about any gym in New York had an old timer or two eager to retell the stories from the radio days. Their stories ranged everywhere from the bizarre- "Harry Greb had his nuts slashed by a prostitute," to the disheartening, "You can't trust any of the decisions from the forties."

When they spoke of Al Brown, there was consistency in the stories. Eddie wasn't the only one who looked different they said.

Brown had the same wide smile, the inquisitive eyes, and he still had the lisp. But his clothes were more flamboyant and he'd become more particular about his appearance. There was more of a limpness to his wrist and his hips swayed a tad more when he walked they said.

Eddie renewed his contract with Brown and immediately went to work finding him a match. His brother Jess was putting together a show for the Broadway Arena featuring bantamweights. "The top four," according to Jess.

The closer the card got, the more its significance grew. The bantamweight title picture was a muddled one and Jess stood to profit from it by strengthening the claims of his fighters.

The card was shifted to Madison Square Garden with Dominick Petrone headlining against Ignacio Fernandez. The co-feature saw Archie Bell against Kid Francis. Rounding out the card was André Routis against Sammy Dorfman and Brown, unlike his days in Paris, buried on the undercard, against Benny Schwartz. The New York papers published the odds showing Petrone, Bell, and Dorfman as the favorites. No line was given for the Brown fight. His wins in Europe did little to boost his reputation in America and the recent losses had no one calling him a future champ.

Schwartz was a top notch fighter. Still hovering near the top ten, he had a record dotted with a brow-raising number of big names. There were Pancho Villa and Joe Lynch in title fights. There were Charley Phil Rosenberg, Joe Colletti, Frankie Ash, Joe Ryder, Johnny Buff, Tommy Ryan, Pete Zivic, Johnny Erickson, and, after the Brown fight, Petey Sarron, Speedy Dado, and Pete Sanstol.

While the fighters went through their final workouts, did their final equipment checks and, checked their weight, word arrived from the other side of the Atlantic that the British Boxing Board had suspended Al Brown for six months for failing to fight Kid Pattenden in London on New Year's Eve.

BLACK INK

The New York commission, which reviewed suspensions twice a week, contemplated scratching the bout. After a round of last-minute discussions, the commission allowed the Schwartz match to take place since it was arranged before the suspension was announced. Following the bout, Brown's license to box was suspended.

In the main fights Petrone and the Filipino fought to a draw; Francis outpointed Bell; and Routis beat Dorfman on a foul. Brown floored Schwartz for nine counts in the first and third rounds and outpointed his rival who was simply unable to cope with the "cleverness" of Brown.

Two weeks later Corporal Izzy Schwartz successfully defended his title against Chilean battler Routier Parra at the St. Nicholas Arena. Like Firpo, Parra fell short on his quest to become the first world champion from Latin America. The fighters in the best positions to become the first were three fighters from Panama. Along with Brown, featherweight Davey Abad and Santiago Zorilla, who also started out at the Strand Gym in Colon and was described by the press in America as the "bouncing brown featherweight from the jungles of Panama," were ranked in the top five of their divisions.

Before Brown could think about winning a championship, or any fight, he had the matter of the suspension to tend to. Representing him at the hearing was an insurance broker from New Bedford, Massachusetts named Dave Lumiansky. Lumiansky made a name for himself in boxing by steering Chick Suggs and Andy Martin to contention and also had a close working relationship with NBA President Tom Donahue.

Lumiansky used his influence to void the suspension by having Brown draft written testimony of his side of the story. Whatever it was, it worked. Brown was free to fight and the man who helped him would remain in the picture for years to come.

Lumiansky wasn't in the business of helping random fighters out of the goodness of his heart. Within days of the Schwartz fight, unbeknownst to Brown he enticed McMahon with an offer to buy him out. McMahon, who was becoming increasingly ill, accepted and initially transferred a percentage of the managerial rights to Lumiansky.

Before the year was up, Lumiansky had sole possession of the rights to Brown.

The first week of April 1928, when Lumiansky advised him he was fighting in Toledo the following week, Brown found out he had a new manager. He boxed twice in Ohio scoring a win and fighting to a ten round no decision before returning to New York. He was matched against Billy Shaw on the undercard of a huge show the first day of summer featuring Jimmy McLarnin.

McLarnin, the last man to fight Pancho Villa, drew 15,000 fans to Madison Square Garden for a fight that was short but "packed with thrills." It lasted 2 minutes and 45 seconds. Brown flashed his power that night as well, crushing Shaw in 1 minute 43 seconds with a straight right-left hook combo to the jaw that was thrown so quickly the punches seemed to land at the same time.

That summer a boxer from Cuba arrived in New York with a reputation that exceeded reality. 100-0 was his record according to some reports while others had him at 21-0 with 21 knockouts. Called "Yi-Ye" by his closest friends in *Cerro*, "*el bon bon de Havana*" in Cuba, and, Kid Chocolate by the rest of the world, he and Brown soon struck up a friendship that would last the rest of their lives.

Both had similar upbringings. And as adults, both clung to style like a spider to a web. In their heyday, they were trendsetters, fashionably late and fashionably early, and changed their plans so quickly and so often, it gave the impression they couldn't make up their minds.

Chocolate was managed by Luis "Pincho" Gutierrez. A respected and connected newspaper editor from Havana, Gutierrez amassed a stable of fighters that included Black Bill, Gregorio Vidal, Canada Lee, Ignacio Ara, and many others. Brown wanted Gutierrez to be his manager.

Gutierrez was already leery of the New York fight scene. He called all the people involved "fake" and said the policies could be bought off. Some days, he said, he refused to leave his Broadway office in order to avoid the phonies. The idea of managing Brown thrilled him. Lumiansky didn't share the sentiment and demonstrated as much by naming an astronomically high price when Gutierrez came asking.

Gutierrez backed off while Brown pleaded with Lumiansky, explaining that he would not have signed an extension if he knew Eddie was ill. Lumiansky didn't bat an eye. Brown rebelled by going on a work stoppage. It lasted about a month and proved fruitless. If Brown wanted to box, he would have to do so with Lumiansky as his manager.

Lumiansky was the eleventh child of Russian immigrants born in 1887 in Pittsburgh. Not quite six-feet tall, he was a neat, well-groomed man, with round, thin-framed spectacles. A few months before he died in 1962, Lumiansky was accepted into the Free Mason Lodge of Realtors. He was in favor of prohibition, hated nightlife, and preferred reading contracts over the classics. In many ways, he was the exact opposite of Brown.

While Brown sulked during his self-imposed exile, Lumiansky worked any and all angles trying to get Brown a title fight. While he knocked on doors, the heads of the various ruling organizations attempted to clear up the bantamweight championship picture and, in the process, made it worse.

There is no easy way to explain the complications. The trouble was those attempting to clear it up were the same ones responsible for much of the murkiness. Before we get into it, I'll prime any readers new to the backrooms of boxing as best I can.

To understand how boxing was - and still is - imagine the big market baseball teams. Because of the markets they play in, they get the best television deals, commercial endorsements, play in the best stadiums, and can sign the best players. Now give those teams the power to hand-pick the teams they play against along with the power to veto games against the better teams. Additionally, teams willing to play them have to accept endless concessions including the weight of the bats, the size of the balls, the distance down the right field line, and the type of gloves the fielders wear. If that weren't enough, remember too that all the umpires and officials get paid by the big market teams.

If you can imagine that, you understand professional boxing.

Understand too that title fights are box office gold. The designation of a title, almost any title, increases a promoter's earnings like magic. Because of that there's a Black Friday type of madness among promoters lining up to get whatever title is sitting on the shelf. Sitting on the bantamweight shelf in 1928 were several boxes.

Charles "Bud" Taylor could no longer make the 118-pound limit and was forced to relinquish his claim early in the year. In 1927, Teddy Baldock, a British claimant, lost to Willie Smith, who immediately lost to Dominick Petrone. Smith then began campaigning in South Africa and Australia. By 1928, any claims by the British fighters were lightly regarded outside of the UK.

On May 23rd, 1928 Bushy Graham was matched against flyweight champion Corporal Izzy Schwartz. That day the NY Times reported in detail that the NBA, "Following the lead of the NY officials placed its stamp of approval on the match as a title affair," with the condition that the winner box Kid Francis.

No one seemed to pay any mind to the condition. What the leaders of the organizations should have done was use the word "eliminator." Instead, since the stamps of approval from both the NBA and NYSAC were issued, Bushy, his fans, and many more acted and believed he was the champ after he beat Schwartz.

On May 30th, "Executive Secretary Bert Stand contradicted the impression that Bushy Graham, Utica bantamweight, is entitled to recognition as 118-pound champion."

On June 25th, NBA President Donahue ordered Bushy Graham and Kid Francis to meet, with the winner to fight Brown within 60 days. The Graham-Francis match didn't take place. Graham lost to Fidel LaBarba on September 11th in a bout contested above the bantamweight limit. But some newspapers were still reporting months after Bert Stand's announcement that LaBarba defeated the reigning bantamweight champion.

This effort to explain the situation should not be mistaken as an attempt to rectify the title lineage. The line was scribbled over, smudged, and left with a stain that could not be removed. I make that disclaimer now because the situation gets even more confusing.

With Graham somewhat out of the picture and LaBarba hovering somewhere between divisions, Lumiansky stepped in with the suggestion of having Francis and Brown fight for recognition. The NBA concurred. In a fight scheduled for 12 rounds at Madison Square Garden, Al Brown met Kid Francis for the vacant NBA title.

Kid Francis, by virtue of his victory over Archie Bell, was the new sensation in the division. Called a sawed-off Hercules by one writer and a mini Jack Dempsey by another, Francis was tabbed by many as a sure bet to become champion. His style and appearance brought nostalgic tears to the eyes of the cognoscenti, who according to one write-up, likened him to pre WWI champion Kid Williams. Kid Williams' name was a faded one by the late 1920s but to the few who remembered him, he was a better fighter than even George Dixon or Terry McGovern.

Francis didn't hit as hard as Williams some complained. His fans countered that he was quicker and threw many more punches. Bell ranked second behind Charles "Bud" Taylor and graced the cover of Ring Magazine just before losing to Francis. Ed Hughes tabbed Francis as the next champ back in 1927. NBA president Tom Donahue was ready to declare the winner of the Francis-Bell match the NBA champion if Bud Taylor, active against featherweights, officially announced his departure from the bantamweight division.

After Tex Rickard's failed attempt to match Kid Francis against Bud Taylor in an outdoor match during the summer of 1928, Kid Francis was considered the premier bantamweight along with Bushy Graham. A match between the two was discussed but, for various reasons, failed to materialize.

With Graham unavailable, Tom Donahue advised his ratings committee that the winner of the Francis-Brown match would be declared the NBA champion.

That decision was met with resistance. Behind the scenes, high ranking officials in the NBA were against Al Brown fighting for their title. With the match set and Donahue's mind made up, others in the

NBA held their collective breath and hoped for a win by Francis. The *NY Times* called it a match "calculated to eliminate" one of the combatants from the title picture.

It took place on September 13th, 1928 on the Young Corbett III–Sgt. Sammy Baker undercard. In the months preceding the match, the local papers were filled with articles that expressed their frustrations with the confusing bantamweight title picture. The Golden Bantams were leaderless. But the Francis-Brown match received little coverage. James P. Dawson of the Times treated it like any other undercard match, dedicating a few sentences to it before and after and making no mention of Donahue's decision to crown the winner.

Though reporters were in their usual seats in press row typing away with lit cigars in their mouths, all of them ignored, or were told to ignore, Donahue's declaration that the winner would be considered champion by the NBA. Some might have been on board with the notion that a gay champion was a no-no. Others may have been confused by the conflicting statements made by other officers of the NBA, which seemed to indicate an announcement being made but only if Francis won the fight. Lumiansky however, had gotten word directly from Donahue that the winner, no matter who, would be NBA champion.

When the bell for round one rang, the confusion lingered. As for the fight itself, the *Brooklyn Daily Eagle* described the result as being a "surprise." Brown, described as the "towering colored bantam with the extension ladder reach," won the decision in a "sizzling" bout over "the most dangerous challenger for the title."

Brown used his left jab to keep Francis at bay and puffed up and nearly shut the left eye of his opponent. Francis, loser of only three fights out of 73, got in under the jab and launched a vicious body attack during the middle rounds that had Brown doubling over. "The colored boy," as the papers called Brown, changed gears in the seventh and used "nimble footwork" to "baffle" Francis over the last six rounds. Brown was now the class of the division the Brooklyn paper stated.

BLACK INK

He was much more than the "class" of the division. On the night of September 13th, 1928, Alfonso Téofilo Brown, also known as Kid Téofilo, Al Brown, and Panama Al Brown became the first boxer from Latin America to win a world title in boxing.

The congratulations were short lived. The next day, the title was taken away from him. While Brown did the Lindy Hop until the wee hours, Lumiansky met with a press corps who refused to report Brown being a world champion. Initially, papers in France and Spain put out reports declaring Brown champion. On subsequent days, they ran reports stating there was confusion about the status of the championship.

Some reached out to Donahue. *El Mundo Deportivo* reported that he confirmed to them that Panama Al Brown was indeed champion. Promoter Dickson too got word from Donahue that Brown was champ and immediately cabled a few offers to Lumiansky for a series of fights in France.

Over the next few weeks Lumiansky knocked on doors that didn't open and rang bells no one answered. The press ignored Brown, Lumiansky and Donahue and refused to report his championship status. Brown received bittersweet congratulations from other fighters like Norfolk, Gans and Kid Chocolate, who could only shake their heads at the injustice. Brown publicly shrugged it off and popped open a bottle but inside, friends later said, it stung him deeply. He won the championship the way it's supposed to be won - by beating the leading available contender inside the ring. That moment when a fighter's hand is raised high into the air and is supposed to be the pinnacle of his career was denied him. The moment all young fighters dream of and aspire to was taken away from him not by a more skilled opponent, but by officials and without explanation.

The press appeared to be under a gag order. A small piece of evidence has survived into the digital age. On October 14th the NBA sent out a press release over the wires with a list of their boxing champions. The press release was printed in various papers including the *NY Times* the next day under an *AP* banner.

BOXING CHAMPIONS LISTED BY N. B. A.

Genaro, Brown, Routis, Mandell, Dundee, Walker Recognized—Delaney Contingent.

LOUGHRAN IS CONSIDERED

Rated Leading Contender for the Heavyweight Title—Other Class Contenders Named.

TORONTO, Oct. 14 (&P).—The Championship Committee of the National Boxing Association, in session here tonight, recognized champions in the various classes by the adoption of a list submitted by President Donohue of the association.

The champions were recognized as follows:

Flyweight—Frankie Genaro, New York.

Bantamweight—Al Brown, Panama and New York.

Featherweight—André Routis of France.

Lightweight — Sammy Mandell, Rockford, Ill.

Welterweight—Joe Dundee, Baltimore, Md.

Middleweight — Mickey Walker, Rumson, N. J.

Light-heavyweight—Jack Delaney, Bridgeport, Conn., in the event Tommy Loughran's graduation to the heavyweight ranks is permanent.

Heavyweight—The winner of the elimination tournament in which it is suggested that the following men participate: Tommy Loughran, the leading contender; W. L. (Young) Stribling, Johnny Risko, Jack Sharkey, Knute Hansen and the winner of the Paulino-Roberti bout, if it is held.

BLACK INK

In a session of their championship committee the night before in Toronto, the champions were recognized in every class and broadcast via the wire. Whoever it was who handled the wire reports for the *NY Times* that day must not have been privy to the plan to make the smiling, gay boxer disappear because, on page 21, the bantamweight champion listed was Al Brown of Panama and New York.

It must've been quite the scene inside the offices of the NBA the day after the report appeared. That day, the NBA held their elections for a new president and Paul Prehn of Illinois beat Thomas Donahue by a landslide. One of the first orders of business for Prehn was to make the Brown championship issue disappear.

On his first day as president, Prehn sent out an NBA press release for the sole purpose of removing the crown from the head of Al Brown. "In the previous list Al Brown was recognized as the bantamweight champion, but now that championship is declared vacant." No explanation was given.

Brown was neither the first nor the last boxer to be stripped of a title. It has happened a handful of times and when it does, it's accompanied by an explanation no matter how lame. It doesn't seem to be because of his color. Tiger Flowers re-broke the color barrier a few years earlier and welterweight Young Jack Thompson was on the verge of competing for a championship. It doesn't appear to be for failing to defend the title- the reason given when they stripped him again in 1934.

Despite not giving an official reason, the NBA wasted no time.

N. B. A. REVISES LIST OF BOXING CHAMPIONS

Al Brown Not Recognized as King of Bantamweights—Title for Class Left Vacant.

TORONTO, Oct. 15 (Canadian Press).—At today's meeting of the National Boxing Association here the Committee on Titles issued a revised list of champions and contenders differing slightly from that issued last night.

In the previous list Al Brown was recognized as the bantamweight champion, but now that championship is declared vacant, with Brown made a contender along with Bushy Graham and Fidel La Barba.

The new list of champions recognized follows:

Flyweight—Frankie Genaro.
Bantamweight—Open.

Brown was an ex-champion. Prehn said so.

This was the same Prehn, who upon being appointed Illinois State Athletic Commissioner in 1926, proclaimed that his primary focus would be to eliminate corruption. He was the same Prehn who witnessed Commission Chairman O.W. Huncke, the next in charge after himself, resign because of the favorable treatment the Commission, meaning Prehn, extended Tex Rickard during the Tunney-Dempsey promotion in the face of a ticket-selling scandal.

Huncke was said to have refused payment for his services as Chairman and stood up to "lawless elements" in his role even amid threats against his life and home.

Tex Rickard and the NYSAC went along with the new NBA president and ignored Brown too. NYSAC leaders put their heads together in search of another boxer they could recognize as champion.

Lumiansky was unable to find a promoter in the New York area who was willing to put on an Al Brown fight. Whether it was because they felt it was bad for business, or a bad look for an already scandal ridden sport, or because of moral or homophobic reasons, Brown was mostly ignored by the press, promoters and by the commissioners.

Madison Square Garden wanted nothing to do with him. He was never given the opportunity to fulfill his dream of headlining a card at boxing's Mecca. His fight against Kid Francis was the last time he boxed in the famed arena.

In his year-end review feature for the *NY Times*, James P. Dawson reflected on 1928 and considered it a down year. Citing the bantamweights, he mentioned that the championship picture came down to Kid Francis and Bushy Graham despite Brown having beaten Francis and LaBarba, a West Coast fighter, having won over Graham. It would've been logical to have Brown and LaBarba ahead of their victims. But logic was apparently an elusive trait in the boxing world. Recall that this was a period when boxing insiders criticized the superb Gene Tunney for not fitting the tough guy image a heavyweight champion was supposed to have and mocked his affinity for Shakespeare. As for Brown and his sexual preference, the general sentiment seemed to be one of wishing he would go away.

World Champion

A few days after the NBA's first press release, *El Mundo Deportivo* of Spain reported having received news from New York confirming that Brown was "definitely" the champion of the bantamweight class. The report added that the IBU accepted the naming of Al Brown as champion and mandated a rematch between Brown and Kid Francis.

The report went on to say that Brown replied to Dickson's offer to return to Europe for a match against Harry Corbett provided Corbett come in under the 118-pound limit. Coming with Brown was a light heavyweight named Jimmy Mendes fans were sure to love.

Lumiansky had zero offers for Brown in America. Jeff Dickson in Paris on the other hand, couldn't wait to put on an Al Brown fight. As far as the American boxing circles were concerned - Paris could have him.

We can't be sure if Lumiansky knew what to expect when he boarded the ship to France. The money offered was enough to make him close his business and leave his fighters, aside from Mendes who joined them, in the care of an associate. Whereas in New York they wished Brown went away, in Paris he was an attraction. It didn't matter if they came to boo him or to cheer him on, they came in droves.

Waiting outside his hotel room when they arrived were a bunch of the boys from Pigallé. The boys had queer written all over them. Lumiansky knew all about Brown and his ways but now, with adjoining hotel rooms, he had a front row seat. Brown was hardly ever in his room during the nights which infuriated his manager. Of his antics and reckless spending, he said, "Brown is like a kid. If someone compliments him he treats them to a drink."

His first fight back in Paris was to be against a 120-fight veteran who was cooler than snow. Lumiansky worried that Brown, because of his irresponsible behavior, would lose. By then he wasn't fond of Brown personally and if Brown wanted to live the way he did, that was his choosing. What bothered Lumiansky was the fact that his decision to leave behind his life and family and put all of his eggs in the Al Brown basket hinged on a fighter who, Lumiansky felt, couldn't care less about that.

He may have been right. When it came to boxing, Lumiansky had full control. Brown couldn't spar, even against a friend, without his manager's permission. It's a common clause but one few managers strictly enforce. Animosity grew between the two. Brown wasn't welcome in Lumianksy's room unless given prior permission and Lumiansky began insisting Brown refer to him as Mr. Dave even admonishing him publicly when he didn't.

Despite Lumiansky sending Dickson a telegram before setting sail for Paris where he assured him Brown was in great condition, he was nowhere near peak form. His opponent, Johnny Cuthbert, wasn't the type of guy to fight on an empty tank. He was a featherweight and recently fought Routis and Baldock to draws. His career would see him score wins over rock-hard opponents like Harry Corbett, Dom Volante, Edouard Mascart, Gustave Humery, Nipper Pat Daly and a draw against Nel Tarleton. A fighter stepping into the ring out of shape against Cuthbert, even one as gifted as Brown, was asking for trouble.

And trouble he got. The fight was called a draw. Brown was lucky to get that draw. *El Mundo Deportivo* reported a Brown that did not appear to be the same marvelous fighter they remembered. After sending Cuthbert to his knee in the first, Brown tried unsuccessfully to land a big right cross again. His best move of the night was the wide smile he flashed whenever he made Cuthbert miss the paper reported. Cuthbert for his part wasn't able to completely capitalize on the ill-prepared state Brown was in. It was a disappointing fight, they wrote, that was met with a chorus of jeers by the disappointed crowd.

The *NY Times* didn't ignore this fight. "The decision was greeted with protests from the public, who regarded it as an injustice to the British fighter," the Times reported.

L'Écho De Paris which incidentally listed the order of the bouts in a way where it seemed Marcel Thil fought the main event, concurred with the Times report and added that the fans booed vehemently throughout and came to see Brown lose.

Lumiansky was livid. He let Brown know that his performance was unacceptable. "If I can't get you fights when you're the champion, what do you think will be the case when you're not?"

After he reminded Brown that there were no offers in New York, Brown assured his manager and promoter he would be ready next time.

The opponent for "next time" went unknown for a while. Scillie and Corbett were the leading candidates with Corbett being confirmed a few days before the fight. Again, the fight was above the bantamweight limit. With stablemate and fellow Panamanian Jimmy Mendes winning by disqualification in nine rounds on the undercard, Brown closed the show with a dominating performance.

He dropped Corbett with a right in the third round and won at least half of the 12 rounds from the resilient Englishman. Once again, amid the cheers, there were the hateful faces that shouted obscenities when he passed. There was an occasional racial slur but mostly it was a lewd remark about his sex life.

A week later, Brown threw a mega Christmas bash in his apartment in Neuilly-Sur-Seine. Turkey with truffles, sweetmeats, and butter poached lobster. The "dantiest" ice creams, according to *The Afro American*, along with wine and champagne "though Brown himself only drinks water." Among the guests were journalist and war correspondent Joel Augustus Rogers and vaudeville and pantomime star Johnny Hudgins.

He also spent time in Deauville during the holidays where he rushed back and forth from the race track to the baccarat tables, with drink - not water - in hand. Back in Paris, the nocturnal lifestyle continued. The sharply dressed fighter and his pretty boy entourage caused a minor commotion at every club they visited. Even in clubs more crowded than a rush hour train, room was made for the champ and his party because it was common knowledge that wherever Brown went, the money that used his wallet as a pit stop would follow.

BLACK INK

In the afternoons there were shopping sprees at the trendiest boutiques. At night, he and his friends wore the new clothes to the top night spots. In those pre-antiperspirant days, Brown changed out of his sweaty clothes for a fresh set several times a day.

Jazz players invited him onstage with them and asked him to play. He obliged with a competent performance on either the drums or the sax. Artistic friends liked using him as a subject. Stripped down to his shorts, their brushes transferred his likeness onto canvases throughout the gay quarters.

Getting into shape for a fight became an afterthought. Making weight was his biggest concern. Bill Miller was unable to accompany him for all of his European bouts. Georges Mitchel filled in as trainer during this period and later as caretaker of his stable of horses.

Gustave "Tiger" Humery was the next foe lined up for him and he posed a big risk. Coming off a disqualification loss, Humery had recently scored victories over Cuthbert, Scillie, and retired Criqui. Much shorter than Brown at 5'4" but with more density in his bones, Humery would eventually fight at welterweight including tussles with Marcel Cerdan and Ernie Roderick.

Having just turned 20, Humery agreed during the referee's in-the-ring instructions to forego the customary touch of gloves at the start of the round.

The opening bell's echo was still in the air and most fans in the smoke-filled arena were still looking for the comfiest part of their seat when the fight ended. Brown knocked out Humery with the very first punch he threw. It was a right hand launched like a UFC superman punch. There was no feint, no wind up, just a short straight missile thrown from his jaw while his back foot, the right, lifted off the ground. The fight lasted half as long as the ten count.

To the fans who could not hear the ref's instructions, it looked like a cheap shot. They voiced their displeasure with Brown and called him stupid and a cheater and continued booing even after he left the ring. On his way back to the dressing room, items were flung his way and some of those closest to him leaned in with their faces and spat at him.

In Spain he found a place that spoke his native language, ate similar foods, and had many of the same customs. Unlike "The Big Apple," or the "City of Sky Scratchers," as the Spanish press called New York, the media in Spain had frequent features and interviews about the fighter throughout his European excursion. They said he was "all bones" and bumping into him felt like walking into wooden furniture.

The press in Spain admired his fighting ability and appreciated his musical talents. His dancing was top notch, his guitar, piano, sax, and drum playing about average, and his singing bearable at least while he was champion. His mannerisms were described without malice by the Spanish newspaper *ABC* as being "ballerina-like" and his voice as being "extra sweet."

Only part of the entourage came with him from Paris but the remaining spots were readily filled by a contingent from Madrid. They took him to a bullfight in Valencia where he watched from the front row as the *Toreros* in their flamboyant "suit of lights" sidestepped the charging bulls and stabbed them in the shoulder with spears.

"That's how you fight," they told the smiling champ.

When the *Matador de Toros,* or killer of bulls, came in to apply the finishing touch, they again leaned in and told Brown, "You can do that too."

The compliments came too fast and from too many angles for Brown to defend against. Before he could digest the words and shift out the real from the fake, there was another compliment in his ear. Brown was overwhelmed without knowing it. There were people whispering in his ear every second until a smile flashed across his face and when it did, those watching his every step took note of what made him smile and repeated variations of it.

Compliments on his appearance were his Achilles heel. A simple "nice shoes Champ" was enough to get him to smile and buy that person a drink. This aspect of Brown's personality irked Lumiansky. He never understood why Brown was so gullible or why so many people in Europe were drawn to him.

BLACK INK

Spain was Brown's preferred location in Europe. In his later years, sitting unnoticed and barely recognized in the corner of the Salem Crescent Gym, he often said in his then somewhat husky voice that he probably should have stayed there. He visited the country often, sometimes for a weekend getaway, while living in France. But France was where he made his money and once the Spanish Civil War and the German occupations started, neither place was an option. Gay black men didn't fit the description of Hitler's master race.

His first trip to Madrid for the Bernasconi fight left him with a longing to return home to Panama. He seemed to think about that more than the task at hand. "I'm thrilled to be here. It reminds me of Panama," he told a reporter when asked how he was feeling two days before the fight.

Domenico Bernasconi was the same age as Brown and likewise had never been knocked out. It was the fourth appearance in Spain for the globetrotting Italian and this time he came as the European champion.

In a bout billed as being between the world champion and the Euro champion, Brown won after ten rounds. Lumiansky, upon his return to New York, told reporters Brown held the IBU title and, along with the NBA title that was rightfully his, Brown should be deemed if not champion then the premier fighter in his division.

As for the IBU mandate for a rematch with Kid Francis, it was scratched when Lumiansky asked for 10 grand. Dickson replied, "If you think your man is such a drawing card ... I'll loan you the Velodrome d'Hiver free…and you organize and run the show," adding all he needed in return was 10% of the receipts. Lumiansky had no response.

He did have a response to Dickson's other offers. It was no thanks to fights in Denmark and the United Kingdom. Lumiansky was determined to return to the United States and win big there. He offered a certified check of $2,500 to be deposited by the NYSAC as a forfeit in exchange for them sanctioning a title fight against an opponent of their choosing. He was prepared to beat the establishment with Brown's own two hands.

After a quick win in Paris over lightweight Joe Cadman on a benefit card for the war widows and orphans, a cause Brown donated his purse to - minus Lumiansky's cut - they returned to New York.

The boxing honchos in America were still playing blackball with Lumiansky. In their haste to crown a bantamweight champion, anyone other than Brown, the NYSAC put pressure on two featherweights - Kid Chocolate and Fidel LaBarba - to do whatever was necessary to get down to 118 pounds. LaBarba previously said no to a Brown fight because, his trainer, George Blake explained, he was no longer campaigning as a bantamweight. Despite that, members of the commission urged both fighters to shed the extra pounds throughout their training camps right up until the weigh-in which was done a few hours before the fight.

They tried but neither fighter came close to making the bantamweight limit. Chocolate weighed in at 121 and LaBarba a fraction less. The fighters, drained from trying to make the bantam limit, put on a stale performance. Ed Hughes, *Brooklyn Daily Eagle* writer, called it a "moderately interesting fray" that lacked sensation and disappointed. The NYSAC's thirst to declare someone other than Brown as champion was strong enough that they placed the health of two fine fighters at risk.

It's easy to shake our heads at their actions from the vantage point of our 21st Century perch. It was a different world then and their actions were probably considered to be in line with the norm. Whatever supporters Brown may have had remained silent. The commission's campaign to blackball the boxer was succeeding.

Kid Chocolate got the decision over Fidel LaBarba in a bout ringsiders were split on who won. Lumiansky made an offer for what would have been a historic showdown - Kid Chocolate vs. Panama Al Brown.

The truth is neither was anxious to box against the other. Lumiansky couldn't care less about the feelings of his fighter. He wanted to be the manager of a champion and the fighter, as far as he was concerned, had little say in the matter.

BLACK INK

Luis Gutierrez brushed off Lumiansky's pesky offers. They don't want to fight each other he tried to explain and when that fell on deaf ears, he did what Lumiansky did to him when he offered to buy Browns contract - he made a ridiculous counter offer. Luis Gutierrez "demanded something like $50,000" Lumiansky told reporters. Gutierrez's "offer" forever ended any Chocolate versus Brown ideas.

With no fights on the horizon and the commission yet to reply to his offer, Lumiansky accepted a June 21st, 1929 match in Copenhagen against featherweight Knud Larsen. Brown was set to sail on May 28th for Denmark while Lumiansky planned on remaining in New York where he would continue his efforts in persuading the NYSAC to recognize a title fight involving Brown.

On May 24^{th,} Lumiansky met with the commission at their downtown offices and once again stated his case. *The NY Times* that day reported that Lumiansky "undoubtedly will have the support of boxing followers who are eager to see a champion." The article added that the manager should have "whatever moral support there is in the fact that Brown now is recognized by the National Boxing Association as the world's bantamweight champion."

Whatever transpired in that meeting was enough for Lumiansky to abort the Larsen fight. While that was going on, another bantamweight from Harlem created a bit of a stir - a mini sensation actually - when he held the unbeaten Kid Chocolate to a draw. Joey Scalfaro floored the Cuban with the first punch of the fight and boxed gallantly the rest of the way against the stylish fighter. Punching to pay his way through pharmacy school, Scalfaro almost repeated the feat in his next fight, decking highly rated contender Archie Bell in the first round before fading down the stretch.

Scalfaro emerged as a stern test for anyone. Only the very best were beating him and only after escaping a close call or two. On May 17th at Madison Square Garden, an aggressive Spaniard out of Philadelphia ignored the bombs Scalfaro was bouncing off his face and crushed the "Fighting Chemist" in just two rounds. Gregorio Vidal's impressive performance had many in the offices of the NYSAC believing they had found the next bantamweight champion.

A match was arranged between Kid Chocolate and Gregorio Vidal for June 5th in Philadelphia's Shibe Park. A win would, in the eyes of the commission, make Vidal the leading contender in the bantamweight division. And anyone who could beat Kid Chocolate, they thought, would beat Al Brown.

Kid Chocolate was given the decision but Vidal won the fight. Having injured both thumbs early in the fight, Chocolate was unable to properly fend off the swarming Vidal. Fight reports nearly unanimously sided with Vidal as the winner, crediting his wicked body attack as the deciding tactic. "Verdict Is Unpopular" read the *NY Times* the following day. "When the announcement was made by Joe Griffo that the judges favored the Cuban the crowd of 20,000 set loose a roar of disapproval," the paper added. When Chocolate headed back to the dressing room via the first base dugout, fans hooted at him and threw programs and newspapers at him and his handlers.

"Even Kid Chocolate Was Surprised When He Got The Decision" was the headline the *Brooklyn Daily Eagle* ran the day after. Chocolate was clearly outfought according to the reporter, who scored the fight seven rounds to two in favor of the "The new Spanish sensation." Chocolate's mouth was agape and pain written across his face at the end of the "cyclonic" affair according to the report.

The officers of the NYSAC concurred. Brown and Chocolate were considered to be more or less on the same level. If Vidal, the reasoning went, could snuff the fire out of The Kid, he surely could do the same to Brown.

The NYSAC was willing to take Lumiansky's $2,500 and designate the winner of a Brown-Vidal fight as the champion of the bantamweight division. That winner, they believed, would be Gregorio Vidal. Most in the local press agreed.

The money was backing Brown 6-5 but writers like Ed Hughes advised readers to pay no mind to the gambling trends. "After witnessing Gregorio in action against Kid Chocolate in Philadelphia, I cannot subscribe to this sentiment." He felt Vidal would "upset the dope and win."

BLACK INK

Writing about Brown's victory over Kid Francis, a fighter he wrote "had been trumpeted along the rialto as a sure thing for the title," Hughes stated it had made life harder for the Panamanian. The "dangerous colored boy" he continued "found it so difficult to obtain work after disposing of Francis…so much so that he departed for Europe." Brown returned to New York, he wrote, for "a 'break' that was as sudden as it was fortunate. I use the latter advisedly. The little Senegambian may have reason to view the matter in murkier tones after his setto with the Spanish boy tonight."

The fight took place at the Queensboro Stadium in the Long Island City section of Queens under the auspices of the National Sports Alliance Relief Fund for Destitute Fighters. "It's a good cause," wrote Hughes, "providing destitute fighters get the relief, of course."

The straight-shooting Hughes was wrong about two things. Brown was no *Mandinko* and, Vidal did not win the fight. It wasn't even close. The last time Brown fought with anywhere near the motivation he had for the Vidal fight was when he stepped into the ring as a homeless dishwasher to spar with Ansel Brown.

The press and fans in Spain initially didn't know who Gregorio Vidal was. As recently as the Brown-Cuthbert fight, he was fighting in Spain under the name Young Marti. His fists carried him to victories in Spain, France, Argentina, England, and Belgium. He was the first to beat Gustave Humery and Nicholas Petit-Biquet before settling in Pennsylvania where the 5'6 bantam became a local attraction after wins over Matty White and Johnny Erickson.

Exhibiting the resiliency of his father, Brown repeatedly fired a wicked jab that tenderized Vidal's cheeks. Vidal managed an occasional body shot that didn't appear to affect Brown. It wasn't until the ninth round that Vidal began to have some success.

The left jab alone was enough for Brown to build a comfortable points lead. With each jab that smashed the features on Vidal's face, the commissioners in attendance began dreading their decision to sanction the fight. One round at a time, the "ballerina" was getting closer to history and there was nothing the officials could do about it.

He sidestepped his opponent's rushes and spun him around to face him so that he could pop off the jabs again. But in the ninth Brown lingered too long in a clinch and Vidal was able to land enough punches to win the round. Vidal continued his resurgence in the tenth and the commissioners breathed more easily, the smirks returning to their faces.

The smirks were wiped off in the thirteenth round when Brown sent Vidal to the canvas three times. The game Vidal did not quit. He rose each time and each time went back at the superior boxer before him and tried with all his ability and might to win. It was not to be. Brown was the clear winner that night.

Brown boxed for justice that night. And he boxed for the pride of his people.

It was something the American boxing press chose not to write about or, perhaps knew nothing about in the 1920s. Black Bill, the Cuban flyweight, was described by one writer as a tar faced boy who looked like he just dropped out of a coconut tree. Columnist Joe Williams, when writing of his death, said Black Bill looked like a minstrel performer and, when he smiled, like a gashed watermelon. That narrative wasn't limited to boxing writers.

In 1932, when women in Puerto Rico were given the right to vote, writers in the fifty states questioned what the ramifications would be. One writer stated, as fact, that the role of motherhood was the role nature intended for Puerto Rican women and juggling that with their new role as citizens would be a challenge.

It wasn't until recently that boxing writers grasped what *"orgullo"* was and how that pride – and not machismo – fueled the championship runs of Latin American boxers.

"America is the epitome but I know in time, Latin Americans can compete," Brown said in 1930. Not only did Brown know that Kid Gavilan, Sixto Escobar, Pascual Perez, Carlos Monzon, Antonio Cervantes, Alexis Arguello, Roberto Duran, and Julio Cesar Chavez were coming; he held open the door for them.

Having had one title taken away from him, Brown was determined once again to become the first fighter from Latin America to win a world championship. His countryman and former gym mate in Colón, Santiago Zorilla, came close only months earlier. The previous December, Zorilla challenged Tod Morgan for the junior lightweight championship.

Despite suffering a flash knockdown in the final round, some felt Zorilla won the match. The *AP* reported it being a close fight with Zorilla having thrown more punches and closing the champion's left eye and Morgan having landed the harder shots. The fight was a draw. Going into the Vidal match, Brown was determined to leave no doubt who the winner was.

In their haste to find an opponent Brown would lose to, the commissioners in New York did not stop to consider that the alternative could happen. Stories leaked to the Spanish press about the strongarm tactics the NYSAC used to get Gregorio Vidal to fight Brown that night. A few days before the fight, his manager, Pierre Bertys, petitioned the commission for a postponement. Vidal suffered a broken nose in a sparring session against Milton Cohen in Pomptom Lakes.

Absolutely not he said they were told. According to the Vidal camp, Gregorio fought while struggling to breathe. "It would not be a good career move," he was warned by the New York honchos when they requested pulling out.

Reporter D. Walters chronicled the events leading up to the fight in *El Mundo Deportivo*. Walters wrote that Vidal's manager, who he referred to as "Perry Betty," pulled him to the side after the weigh-in and whispered to him that Gregorio's nose was broken in three places.

"They wouldn't let us cancel."

He went on to say that for days the Commissioner William Muldoon repeatedly "vomited" expletives about the Panamanian while singing the praises of Vidal. In Walter's estimation, Vidal had no chance against Brown even with a good nose. Brown possessed every punch in the book and, he concluded, it was a lack of experience that did Vidal in.

But universal recognition as champion still eluded Brown.

The NBA sent out a press release the night of Brown's victory and announced they "no longer recognize" anyone as champion of the bantamweights. Brown, they said, "holds no title as far as the NBA is concerned."

The commission in Pennsylvania decided to go against the NYSAC, which bestowed on Brown the awkward designation of "defending champion." Pennsylvania did not recognize anyone as bantamweight champion until two months later when it declared Bushy Graham the champion following Bushy's decision win over Vidal on August 26th in Philadelphia.

Throughout his stay in New York and France, Brown and his family wrote to each other constantly. Brown smiled when he told friends and writers in Europe that his sisters and mother hated boxing and implored him to stop. The money was great but not necessary, or even worth it, they explained in vain.

It wasn't just the money that drove Brown. The feeling that consumed him when the bell rang had no price tags. When the bell rang, he was chief, king, the boss and everyone watching knew it. For someone who was often told he should be ashamed of who he was, that feeling of superiority was addictive. The respect and awe his ring dominance earned him spilled out into the cabarets and streets where Brown was often the richest, most famous, and toughest man in the room. As a result, he was the best dancer, best singer, and best looking man in the room too. When he couldn't box, he was a poor, skinny, gay drunk. Walking away from boxing meant walking away from being special.

But in 1929 New York, even with partial acceptance as champion, Brown could not get a big fight. He scored a win in Newark and another in Portland, Maine. Then on July 10, the NBA suspended manager Lumiansky for spreading "rumors" that Brown was NBA champion.

Brown thought it was a good time to return to Panama. Lumiansky, undeterred by frivolous suspensions, disagreed. He thought it was time to cash in. Unable to secure a challenger in the bantamweight division, Lumiansky booked Brown for three fights in the featherweight division during the month of July. The last of those fights was in Hartford against the superb Battling Battalino.

Fights and suspensions kept the duo busy that summer.

On July 17th, it was reported that the NBA would permit Brown to go ahead with a July 25th bout in Hartford despite having been "recently" suspended by them.

On July 25th the Pennsylvania Athletic Commission announced Lumiansky was suspended indefinitely for Brown's failure to appear at a fight against Matty White in Philadelphia.

On July 26th, Brown was in Hartford climbing into the ring to meet a fighter much more dangerous than White.

Christopher "Battling" Battalino was as famous for knocking people out as he was for saving a drowning child in Park River. For that act of heroism Hartford Mayor Walter Batterson paid a visit to Battalino at his wedding and presented him with a gold medal.

The match against Brown was described as a fast-paced one that resulted in a ten-round decision win for Battalino. A few days later Brown wrote the commission in Connecticut to tell them that he was forced to enter the ring against Battalino ill-prepared and in less than optimum condition. In his next fight a few weeks later, Battalino became NBA featherweight champion with a victory over Andre Routis. Brown, the bantamweight champion, was reduced to fighting bigger men in their hometowns.

On August 1st the NYSAC followed Pennsylvania's lead and suspended Brown and Lumiansky. They were reinstated three weeks later. Around this time Brown was suspended by the Illinois commission for failing to fight Knud Larsen in Denmark. It's interesting to note that Larsen was white and Illinois at the time prohibited mixed race matches in the state because of a riot that followed the Jackie Fields- Young Jack Thompson match the previous March.

Herman Landfield, a 38-year-old milliner, was pushed off the balcony overlooking ringside to his death. Thirty-seven more were taken to nearby St. Luke's hospital with serious injuries including broken limbs and a fractured skull.

Also worth noting is the request made by Illinois Governor Louis Emmerson on August 1st asking the members of the state athletic commission - Paul Prehn, Sam Luzzo, and Al Mann - to resign effective August 10th for what would "undoubtedly be for the best interests of boxing." On his second-to-last day, Prehn, who kept his post as president of the NBA, went public with the news that two years earlier, though he said nothing about it then, he received an offer of $10,000 from a "gambler" to appoint a certain individual as referee of the Tunney-Dempsey fight.

While the various state commissions in America found reasons to suspend Brown and/or his manager, the two of them boarded a ship for Europe to face Knud Larsen. The match took place on August 28th, 1929 but not after some posturing from the IBU.

The organization threatened to strip Brown of his title if he went ahead and boxed Larsen. The reasons for that action were never explained but a reporter in Spain was compelled to write that it was "a shame Al Brown isn't Al White."

Another speculated that the organization and promoters feared Brown would spend the majority of his time boxing in the United States, which would have limited the opportunities of European boxers, where the IBU was based. But someone in the Danish commission either pulled the right strings or greased the correct pockets and the match was finalized.

Larsen was the European featherweight champion and was coming off a win over Scillie. At 5'7" with a 70" reach, Knud, a Fritzie Zivic look-alike, and his potent uppercuts posed a legit threat to Brown. A wild, enthusiastic mob of 20,000 greeted Brown's arrival in Copenhagen according to the NY Times. Brown's training sessions were packed by curious fans anxious to a get a glimpse of the stylish boxer.

A sellout crowd flocked to the outdoor arena and the thousands more who were turned away at the door remained in front of the arena where they were notified of who was winning by low-flying planes that circled above after each round with lights on the wings signifying the leader. A red light meant Brown was in the lead. Six times the planes flew overhead and six times they saw red.

The fans inside watched as Brown fought like the Scarlet Pimpernel: he was here, there, seemingly at the same time, and his calling card - a stiff combination instead of a red flower. The crowd, who cheered each time Larsen threw a punch, was mostly silent. In the seventh the tide changed. Larsen threw a wicked low blow and Brown dropped in agony. Slowed down by the blow, the next few rounds were closely contested. In the tenth, Brown resumed control. It was a clear-cut win for him after 12 rounds.

Brown returned from Denmark via Norway on the Berengaria and was set to commence training for an October 2nd match against Teddy Baldock at the New York Coliseum in the Bronx. Baldock left a lasting impression on the local scene during his 1926 tour of the states. Too young back then to fight in bouts scheduled for more than six rounds, Baldock was considered a serious threat to Brown's reign.

A week before the match was set to take place, papers published reports that Baldock was on his way back to England taking with him the $1,600 in training expenses promoter Jess McMahon gave him, citing difficulty making the weight limit. Others indicated that a disagreement over the purse was the reason for Baldock's sudden departure.

A scramble ensued for a replacement but no suitable opponent was found. However, an October 1st match against Blas Rodriguez in Mexico City before President Gil was proposed. Brown went into training alongside Spanish heavyweight Paulino Uzcudon at Madame Bey's gym outside of Summit, New Jersey. But the match never materialized.

His spirits rose slightly on October 7th, when new NBA President Stanley Isaac held a teleconference with his championship committee and advised them they had no choice but to recognize Al Brown as champion. That day Chairman Edward C. Foster announced publicly that Brown would be recognized as champion by the NBA.

The announcement did little to help secure a fight. When the stock market crashed on October 29th and the promoters paused for a while to contemplate their next move, Brown seized the opportunity and returned to Panama.

Before doing so he and Lumiansky were once again at odds over their contract. Brown asked once more to have the contract rescinded so that he could join the camp of Gutierrez. At that time Brown was leasing an apartment in a five-storey building at 156 West 141st Street for $65 per month. Living with him was Kid Chocolate and two other males. During those few moments when the two fighters slowed down from their bustling lives to catch their breaths, slumped on the couch with legs sore not from morning roadwork, but from the miles they put in the night before at the dance clubs, the topic of being managed by Pincho often came up.

Brown wasn't shy when complaining about the things his manager said and did. Chocolate pleaded with Pincho to do something. The two fighters, among the greatest ever, hadn't yet learned that the power of contracts was stronger than steel. That quick little glance and scribble he did when Eddie McMahon told him to "sign this" forfeited any say he had in his career.

Brown released a statement to the press that accused Lumiansky of not "holding up" his side of the contract. Without elaborating, he closed his statement by announcing he was off to Panama where, "A certain young lady anxiously awaits my arrival."

A marching band, school children, and a slew of mounted police led the way through the streets of Colón. Hundreds of friends and neighbors surrounded the champion as he made his way around town with his mother following behind in a convertible. People lined the streets and jammed into the second-floor porches waving hats and handkerchiefs when he passed.

The next day he boarded a train to Panama City where six rooms were reserved for him and his guests at the *Hotel Central*. More marching bands and a Boy Scout troop were among the parade of well-wishers that greeted him. He visited schools and hospitals and was ushered to the governor's building where he was given the honor of pardoning four, any four, criminals.

Standing close enough to pick his pockets, onlookers filled his ears with the names of friends and friends of friends. To be fair, he decided on two males and two females. The males were acquaintances from his youth. As they were freed before the throng, Brown, embarrassed by their countless thanks and hugs, gave them each fifty dollars and told them not to mention it.

At a concert that night in his honor at the main plaza, Mayor Abel DeLa Lastra presented Brown with a championship belt and a gold medal on behalf of President Arosemena, who told the *Diario de Panama* that he was, "Very sorry not to be able to present the belt personally."

Funds for the belt were raised from collections in the street, workplaces, and even the elementary schools where donations of "not more than one cent" were accepted. This was the championship belt Brown was proudest of.

At party after party Brown delighted in showing the dance moves he picked up in Harlem and Montmartre. He flashed the moves he learned dancing to Chick Webb at the Savoy Ballroom.

"Yeah I know Louis Armstrong," he told his friends, "And Smack Henderson too." He was asked about the jazz clubs, the speakeasies, and if there really was gold in the streets. "No of course not," he replied. "But some streets have clocks embedded in them."

The question he was asked the most was, "when are you fighting here?"

The idea of a championship match in Panama created a buzz among the locals but his homecoming was about to go from hero worship to embarrassment.

It was bittersweet to begin with, as Brown had felt compelled to announce that a certain young lady was anxiously awaiting his arrival. Just who he was talking about and what happened to necessitate that statement we can only imagine. An even bigger issue was a report in the paper about his citizenship. Brown applied for U.S. citizenship they wrote. Rumors spread throughout Panama that said he was born in the United States. Those accusations cut right to the heart of the Panamanians. Their champion, the pride of Panama, didn't want to be – or wasn't – Panamanian.

Where the rumors originated was not reported. A National Guard Enlistment Card exists for an Alphonso Brown dated September 4, 1923. The age is listed as 21 years 1 month old and the place of birth Cristobal, Panama. Cristobal is a part of Colón much like Coney Island is a part of Brooklyn. The complexion is listed as "C" for colored and Alphonso Brown was dropped for desertion in January 1925. Alphonso is a common spelling, and misspelling, of Alfonso. Of course this could be a different person. But a few things stand out on the application. Besides the name and age, the height was similar and the address given was the staff entrance of the Commonwealth.

It's strictly conjecture but maybe Brown sought Naturalization through military service before having a Riddick Bowe-type change of heart. Maybe he was simply complying with the Selective Service laws just to get his boxing license and deliberately misspelled his name.

Those who questioned his birth pointed to his American father and flawless English as evidence. The rumors were significant enough that Brown addressed them publicly.

Through the newspapers he assured everyone that he was and always would be Panamanian. As an added bonus, he announced that he had agreed to box in Panama against Mexican Blas Rodriguez. The announcement was met was enthusiasm and the wheels were set into motion. The proceeds of the fight were to be donated to athletes preparing for the upcoming Central American Games in Cuba.

Rodriguez, a former leading flyweight contender who two years prior was one of four chosen to participate in an elimination series for the vacant flyweight championship, had sparred many rounds with Brown.

Brown sent a telegram to Lumiansky, who stayed in the states because the trip, he thought, was "frivolous." The Panamanian government agreed to sponsor the match and in case Rodriguez couldn't make it, former foe and current Panamanian featherweight champion Pedro Troncoso was on standby he informed his manager.

Lumianksy's response was short and to the point. "No. Since when are you the manager?" Return to New York immediately he told Brown.

Lumiansky's permission was needed and an invitation from the local government was extended to him. Once again his response was to the point. He wasn't interested, he reiterated, and instructed Brown to return because *he* had fights lined up for him.

With the drama playing out publicly, friends and public began whispering louder and louder about the champion. He wasn't his own man they said. While Brown ran back and forth with telegrams, the public lost interest. The best Brown could do was engage in a pair of exhibitions that were staged before a small crowd.

The parties continued and so did the disappointment of not being allowed to stage a fight before his hometown. He spent the last day at home and his embrace around his mother's shoulders had to be pried apart by his brothers so he wouldn't miss his boat.

It was the last time he would see his mother.

Exile

On his way back to New York, he made a pit stop in Cuba for a ten round bout against Pinky Silverberg at the end of January. Brown's punches lacked their usual snap and quickness and his legs, heavier than normal, moved as though they were stuck in sand. Pinky never threatened to win however, and when the ten rounds were over, Brown had his arm raised for win number 60.

On February 8th, 1930, he was set to make the first defense of his titles at the old Commonwealth location on 135th and Madison. Then called the Olympia Boxing Club, the Harlem crowd that filled the arena witnessed a disgraceful display.

The challenger, Johnny Erickson, was well known throughout the city as a rugged customer. His biggest win was a decision over future featherweight champion Petey Sarron. Going into the Brown match, he rode a streak of eight consecutive losses, all against top notch rivals. There was Kid Chocolate, Matty White, Archie Bell, Gregorio Vidal, and Pete Sanstol. A borderline contender, it was the best opponent they could get and for Erickson, it was a once-in-a-lifetime opportunity - his *Rocky* moment.

Shortly after the bell rang, it became clear that Erickson was not as good as Rocky and Brown was better than Apollo. With the Lindy Hop crowd in the seats, Brown fought like he had the jitter bugs. Nimble and light on his feet, Brown darted left or right with the same grace as a Jamal Crawford crossover.

By the second round, Erickson shifted his focus below the belt. He attacked Brown's nuts with blow after blow. At the end of the round, after the bell, he sneaked in a right that brushed the champion's chin. Brown did his best to keep his opponent at the end of his punches. Occasionally Erickson got in close enough to unleash a volley of groin shots. In the clinches where Brown managed to tie his arms up, Erickson used his head to butt the champion. The referee, Jack Dorman, finally began to warn him for the low blows-repeatedly.

After Brown was forced to take a knee following a low blow, the referee moved to disqualify Erickson. But Brown waved the referee off. Let me handle this he said. He advanced towards Erickson with knockout intentions. Erickson ducked low and once again let out with a combination below the belt leaving the disgusted referee no choice but to disqualify Erickson.

After that fiasco was a series of fights officiated by lenient officials. Punches strayed low, clinches with forearms pushed against his jaw were common, and the bells ending the rounds were a signal for his opponents to throw an extra punch. His fights were way off Broadway. The only way he made it into Madison Square Garden was to watch the Kid Chocolate-Midget Wolgast bout.

He beat future featherweight champion Tommy Paul in Buffalo. There was a first round stoppage over the never-before-stopped Milton Cohen in Waterbury. One opponent, KO Morgan, well known for his moves on the dance floor and called the Charleston Kid after performing the Charleston in the ring during and after his fights, was disqualified for being "outclassed."

Morgan, born Andrea Ettore Esposito and called Andrew by friends, ended up in Toledo, Ohio as a teen because that's where the boxcar he jumped onto in Connecticut took him. The southpaw trained at the Toledo Athletic Club on Superior Street and reportedly went unbeaten as an amateur. As a pro, he defeated Jackie Callura and Sixto Escobar and was rumored to have more than three hundred wins including his stint in the Scottish boxing booths.

But against Brown at the Convention Hall in Toledo, he had no chance. Floored twice in the early rounds, Morgan quit trying to win after the third round. He clutched, grabbed, and held whenever the champion got close. By the fourth round, Brown stopped trying to hit his rival. He motioned to the ref to stop the fight but referee Ollie Pecord, a former pro baseball player and bareknuckle boxer, ordered them to fight.

Brown, who was not recognized as champion by the Ohio authorities, held back and Morgan tried but had no defense for the occasional flurries the champion threw. Pecord, who refereed the Dempsey-Willard fight disqualified Morgan and considered doing the same to Brown for "not trying."

Six days after the Morgan fight Lumiansky thought it a good idea to stage a homecoming. Not Brown's homecoming, but his own. He arranged a match between Brown and Al Gillette in his hometown of New Bedford, Massachusetts. The manager's friends, family, and business associates all got to watch Brown train and fight.

While Brown was in the ring doing the fighting, stopping Gillette in nine rounds, it was Lumiansky who was the featured attraction. Sitting in the front row with his friends, family, and local politicians, Lumiansky was the star that night.

They remained in New Bedford while Lumiansky secured fights in the New England area. During this period Brown was billed as being from New Bedford for his fights in Connecticut and West Springfield, Massachusetts.

As soon as they returned to New York, the topic of being managed by Luis Gutierrez was broached again. There was no convincing Lumiansky. He would remain Brown's manager.

Brown and Kid Chocolate continued their late night romps through the dance clubs and setting fashion trends. A May 3rd 1930 headline in the *Afro American* declared the two "Set Harlem Styles for Men." The article described their attire as "feminine," and stated their "Flowing coats, high belts and tams tickle observers on Seventh avenue."

The two fighters, neither of whom the paper said could be called "handsome lads," were considered the best dressed men in Harlem. The windows of various establishments, they wrote, were adorned with pictures of the two fighters decked out in the latest fashions.

"Gown like overcoats with wide belts and hats with tams were a grotesque fashion for men spurred on," according to a tailor in the article, by men who were "jealous because women were wearing long skirts."

South of 110th Street, the flamboyant Brown was still ignored. Ed Hughes wrote the game was in a sorry state, calling heavyweight Max Schmeling a "synthetic champion." Mickey Walker was a good slugger he said, but overrated and the beneficiary of careful managing. "Except the night Jack Kearns permitted him in the ring with Harry Greb." Al Brown, though possessing "talent," was no match for the champions of the past like Pete Herman, Joe Lynch, Kid Williams, and Johnny Coulon he wrote.

Those weren't fireworks people in Baltimore heard on the 4th of July. The crackling sounds coming from the Maryland Ball Park were from the mighty fists of Al Brown as he hammered away at Calvin Reed. Brown, described by *The Afro American* as a defensive master with dynamite in both hands, "toyed" with Reed in the first two rounds. In the second, a right hook dropped Reed to his knees. The 130-pound Reed rose at the count of one with both hands blazing. Brown slipped the majority of punches with the few that landed being duds.

Brown, who trained at Joe Dundee's gym for the fight, worked his arms like "pistons" in round three. Reed winced from the blows and was "almost reeling" when he came out for the fourth. The champion wasted no time unleashing a barrage punctuated by a left uppercut that landed on the point of the chin and knocked Reed cold before he crashed face first into the mat.

Still out when the referee counted ten, Brown walked over to Reed and lifted the fallen fighter off the floor and carried him to his corner. He remained in the corner with Reed until the Philly fighter came to. Only then did he raise his hand and leave the ring to applause. Any plans Brown had for after the fight were delayed. At his door was a mob seeking autographs and photos of the champion.

His next match was a rematch against Bernasconi in a ten round bout at Ebbet's Field. Squaring off in the same area where Babe Herman chased down fly balls, Brown defeated the Italian slugger in a fight the *NY Times* described as "uninteresting, with no sparkling moments." Unlike their first match in Spain, there was no wrestling to the mat or roughhouse tactics. It was target practice for the champ and miss after miss for Bernasconi.

Five thousand fans filled the stands that night. In contrast, Kid Chocolate, who Ed Hughes described as the "Cuban Sheik, idol of Harlem's blackamoor set," pulled in over 15,000 the year before against Ignacio Fernandez in the same arena. Later that year, at the Polo Grounds, 40,000 watched him trade hooks with Jackie "Kid" Berg.

In a time when Tony Canzoneri and Jack Sharkey pulled in crowds of over 25,000 for their matches at Ebbet's Field, the five thousand Brown drew was disappointing. Two weeks later Jeff Dickson showed up in New York with two goals. The first goal - signing Jackie Berg to face Al Foreman in London- he was unable to realize. The second - signing Al Brown to defend against Eugene Huat in Paris - was easily accomplished. Brown had no other offers. Once again he was forced to pack his bags and sail the Atlantic.

"And we all played on." Ada "Bricktop" Smith

The Great Depression hadn't yet affected Paris. At a packed club at 66 Rue Pigalle called "Chez Bricktop," Ada Bricktop proclaimed the music never stopped. That suited Brown fine. Around this time Brown began indicating his displeasure with the sport. Training was becoming an interruption to his partying. The cabarets were where he preferred spending most of his time.

While staying at the Hotel Scribe in Paris, he was interviewed by Luis Melendez, a Spanish reporter. Luis Melendez waited in the lobby until Brown showed up, on time, with a friend, Paulino, from New York.

They sat on the red velvet stools of *Le Bar Américain*. Brown handed him a photo of himself in pose and remarked how much he enjoyed Spain. He ordered a drink. It was a concoction neither the bartender nor the reporter had heard of. Brown walked the barkeep through it step by step while bopping in his seat to the Jazz music playing in the background. His Spanish was proper, though cadenced and highlighted by a lisp, "dragging the 'S,'" he wrote.

"So you're from Panama?"

"Yes from the capital," Brown answered.

His father was North American and his mother Spanish.

"You can see it in my name -Alfonso Téofilo Brown."

"Then why, 'Al Brown'?" Melendez asked.

"Because," Brown explained, "In America it sounds better, more American, and as a result better suited for the masses."

"Did you start boxing in New York or Panama?"

"I started in Panama but perfected my craft in New York. Because of boxing I had to leave Panama for New York in the hopes of making more money."

He stopped dancing in his seat for a moment.

"You see, after my father died we lived a life of deprivation. We were deprived and in the poorest of poverty. We lived off the good graces of a few benevolent souls who helped out my mother. If not for the graces of a few generous and kind hearted neighbors..." The last words were drowned by a gulp of the drink the bartender made for him.

"Seeking a better life," he continued, "led me to jumping aboard ship as a stowaway to New York at the age of 17."

"Are you satisfied today?"

Dancing again, "I think I am. I think so because I could never hope to be more than what I am. I am world champion, have made good money, can afford a comfortable life and, have provided supported for my mother and sisters."

"How much money have you made?"

"Not sure exactly but it's around $300,000. I don't ever have to worry about my finances since the government of Panama pays the salary of a trusted person to take care of my finances. That was one of the gifts they gave me last time I was in Panama. That and this belt I'm wearing in the photo I gave you." Pointing at the photo, he added, "The belt was paid for by a collection of the people."

He reminisced about the car he left in New York. A 1929 Packard Model 645 Sport with six wire wheels - a car, Paulino added, that caused great jealousy among the other boxers in New York. "It cost $5,400. It's a magnificent car that I might bring here if I decide to stay for long."

"Are you staying in Europe for long?"

"Depends on how many fights are lined up for me. Right now I only have the Huat fight. But it depends on what promoter Dickson can line up. In New York he told me he was working on arranging fights in London, Paris, and Barcelona. I'd really like to fight in Spain. When I fought Bernasconi in Madrid, the desire to return once again for a fight and to witness again a running of the bulls remained. I think Dickson can find me worthy rivals in Spain. I believe he is close to finalizing matches against Carlos Flix and Jose Girones."

"How much will you make?"

"I don't know. My manager handles those affairs but, as a gauge I can tell you I'm getting $7,000 for the Huat fight." A fighter who Brown said had "made good progress but I don't consider him a threat."

A different song played in the background and Brown's legs were unrestrainable. "I think you should dance," the reporter told him.

"May I?"

"Yes, before you explode."

Brown went on to do a perfect rendition of the Charleston while Paulino cheered him on.

Eugene Huat fought with the typical French style wrote Ed Hughes. Like the other French fighters who boxed in New York, Huat took his "boxing lightly," and his "hitting and slugging heavy." The year before the Brown match, Hughes called him a "small Carpentier," and a thunderbolt, one he thought might become flyweight champion.

That was before the copper haired fighter lost to Black Bill. Before the Bill fight, Huat defeated Corporal Izzy in New York and his early European record reads like one a UFC fighter would possess.

Nearly half his opponents "tapped out," deciding to remain on their stools when the next round began. After being outclassed by Black Bill, the Cuban sensation who often crashed at Brown's apartment, Huat moved up in weight to the bantamweight division.

He lost his first two starts in the heavier division but Huat was rolling again coming into the Brown fight.

Huat didn't like Brown. He called him a "disgusting n*****." Every time he saw Brown, Huat shouted out a profanity about his race or sexual preference. As a result, Huat became the only opponent Brown ever disliked.

"He's not in my class - inside the ring or out," Brown said.

Huat, nicknamed "The Wildcat," had the crowd behind him that night. The insults continued in the ring. But the elusive champion brought his A-game with him and Huat, determined and battered, resorted to fouling. Huat landed his best punches after the ref called break. Brown flashed a wicked smile over the last two rounds as he punished his opponent at will. After 15 rounds, Brown's arm was raised and Huat's mouth, swollen, alternated between asking for a rematch and insulting the slim champion.

On October 6th, 1930, British paper *The Daily Mail* published a cartoon of the Brown-Huat fight. Titled "The Shadow Man," it depicted a stick figure with a normal sized head and extra-large lips under a caption that read, "Napoleon stirred uneasily in his tomb last night when Eugene Huat, a fighter of France, was beaten BY A COON."

The last three words appeared capitalized. It was a bad fight, the paper wrote, because Brown was "too thin to look at."

Before going to Spain for an October 22nd match against Jose Girones, Brown sat down for an interview with a Spanish reporter. He spoke of his mother, three brothers, and two sisters back in Panama.

"I am happy to report they are doing well. I did not purchase any extravagant items for myself until they were looked after."

Brown was in a "radiant mood," and eagerly awaiting the arrival of the belt he was given in Panama.

"They collected a penny per person to pay for the belt. Even the elementary schools donated."

As for the fight with Girones, Brown said he was informed by reliable sources that his foe was a serious puncher and not one to take lightly but he was expecting to win nonetheless. The day of the interview, October 16th, he weighed 56 kilos, (about 123 ½ pounds) and expected to weigh 57 kilos, (125 pounds) the day of the fight.

When asked if getting back down to the bantamweight limit would be a problem after the fight, he stated, "not at all. Simply, and without denying myself in the slightest, I am accustomed to losing a pound per day like I did after the Knud Larsen fight. Naturally, one day-perhaps soon- I will encounter difficulty making the bantamweight limit. When that day comes, I have little to no doubt what to do. I will compete in the featherweight class."

Satisfied with the session, the reporter closed his notebook and extended his hand to Brown and wished him luck.

"Wait, one more thing I'd like to say," Brown said with urgency and pointing to the notebook. "Regarding my age - it's wrong. They say I'm 27 but I'm only 24. It all started when I arrived in New York from Panama. I said I was 19 but I was really only 16."

The fight was held in Barcelona. Brown and his entourage from France stayed at the *Hotel Oriente*. Described as eccentric by the press in Spain, a man who owned 50 suits, 20 pairs of shoes, and purchased a new hat each day, Brown drew as many as three thousand viewers to his public workouts.

A reporter with *ABC* asked what he trusted most, his arms or his legs.

With a description that could be used for Michael Jackson, the writer illustrated how Brown lifted a finger and, gently pointed to his forehead.

"My head, Sir."

His nose was flat, the writer said. Two jagged scars marred his upper lip, which was permanently deformed years before. When asked if he was confident of victory, he replied, "Without underestimating my opponent, I'd be lying if I said I wasn't."

BLACK INK

He moved about the hotel with a "childish vanity" according to the reporter. At the hotel's entrance during Brown's stay a large crowd awaited his arrival. They were there to catch a glimpse of the smiling, waving, and somewhat embarrassed-looking champion as he sauntered in and out of the hotel.

A tale of the tape was published the morning of the fight. Supporting 21" thighs were 13" calves. A 26" waist held up a 36" chest and sprouting out from that chest were arms that, when outstretched, measured 72" from fingertip to fingertip. His biceps were 11" and his neck 14.5" around his Adam's apple. His height was listed as 5'8.5" tall.

The weigh-in took place at the offices of the *Nuevo Mundo* magazine a few hours before the fight. Brown tipped in at 56 kilos 100 grams, a shade less than 124 pounds.

In the dressing room before the fight, an inspector noticed something unusual with the champion's hand wraps. A closer look revealed a layer of duct tape between the wraps. Duct tape was commonly used in workouts by fighters with brittle hands. But it was forbidden in competition, possibly because of its greater resistance to water. Water, or ice, hardened the hand wraps and with duct tape, it was harder to detect if a fighter wrapped his hands in moist wraps or, dunked his wrapped fist in a bucket of ice before the fight.

"It's a mistake," explained Brown's corner.

After having his hands re-wrapped, Brown made his way down the same path the matadors did, past the wooden holding pens where the bulls awaited their demise, and into the pit of the circular arena where the echoes of the estimated 25,000 screaming fans made it next to impossible to hear his trainer's instructions.

The crowd was completely behind the local fighter. Girones was a better than good fighter. He awaited the opening bell with a record of only six losses and two draws in 75 fights. The European featherweight belt was wrapped firmly around his waist and his experienced fists were too much for the likes of Mascart, Larsen, Ciclone, Luigi Quadrini, and future featherweight title holder Maurice Holtzer.

Introductions were skipped - the speakers didn't work. And when the bell rang, Girones wasted no time implementing his battle plan. He applied pressure and threw quick hooks to the body. Brown stayed away and squashed the efforts of Girones with jabs and uppercuts.

After a few rounds, the Spaniard tried turning the match into a brawl. He held, he pushed, and never stopped applying pressure. Brown caught Girones coming in with his rapid one-twos before niftily-side stepping the wide-swinging featherweight. The crowd jeered Brown as he evaded exchanges and thwarted any attempts by Girones to turn it into a slugfest.

The decision after ten rounds was a draw.

ABC gave the edge to Brown in their blow-by-blow write-up. Brown landed more punches they felt, and his superiority was evident. Girones, however, never quit and was very much in the fight the whole way. The draw didn't bother Brown he told a reporter. It did him no harm, he said, while at the same time did wonders for Girones who, he thought, was a notch below the top Americans and whose punching power he did not feel.

Back in Paris he had a chance encounter with famed runner Jules Ladoumégue. A silver medalist at the previous Olympics and then the Men's 1500-meter world record holder, he questioned Brown about his training practices and preparation.

"What's your weight and height?"

"One meter and 75 centimeters and I weigh 56 kilos. What about you?"

"A meter 72 and 57 kilos," the runner replied.

You're a featherweight Brown replied. Curious about how Brown made the bantamweight limit, Jules continued.

"What are your meals like?"

"I eat light. I shouldn't gain weight. Extra weight is an enemy. I believe, in all sports, speed is the best asset. And speed can only be maintained by keeping off the extra weight. You have to be quick and accurate…" he demonstrated with a one-two.

"Did you ever try running?"

"Yes," Brown said with a smile. "Back in Panama when I was young but I quit. Now I regret having stopped," he mumbled without a smile.

Jules patted his shoulder and told him, "You did well. Boxing pays in cash. Running just gets you medals and suspensions."

They spoke for awhile with Brown telling him his life was mostly a normal one, without excesses. "I start serious training 12 days before a fight. The rest of the time I stay fit and watch my weight."

"How do you make bantamweight?" he asked Brown.

"I have a process. I lose 400 grams per day for ten days. That way, four days before the fight, I'm a kilogram under the limit. The last few days I gain 100 grams at a time. That way, I don't feel weak."

As time went on Brown would deviate greatly from his disciplined regimen. He was at his peak when he met Jules and the late-night partying and all-day gambling excursions to Deauville hadn't affected him yet.

After an uneventful ten-round decision over Nic Bensa in Paris on November 8th, 1930, Lumiansky and Dickson had a falling out. While his manager worked out details for a run through Great Britain, a fledgling promoter approached Brown with an enticing offer.

An American living in Paris, Charles E. Sriber dabbled in the preliminary levels of the boxing and entertainment fields. Through an acquaintance in the entertainment business, he approached Brown with an offer. When Brown agreed, Sriber felt he had reached the big time.

Sriber encountered difficulties from the start. Unable to find either a venue or an opponent, the plans for an Al Brown fight were put off until after the holidays.

Brown, who still considered New York his base, boarded the *Ile de France,* told the crew he was 25, and sailed home to watch Kid Chocolate challenge Battling Battalino for the featherweight title.

Battalino was still considered something of a mystery to the New York press. After beating Brown and Routis, he lost to Young Zazzarino, twice to Cecil Payne, Louis "Kid" Kaplan, Bud Taylor, and Roger Bernard and was dropped by Taylor, Ignacio Fernandez, and Bushy Graham. But Chocolate was considered on the downswing after losses to LaBarba and Jackie "Kid" Berg. With a chance to join Brown as champion of the world, a rejuvenated Kid Chocolate entered the ring that night.

Battalino found himself on the deck again in the opening round.

The *NY Times* had Chocolate winning nine of the fifteen rounds. The decision, however, went to Battalino and had Brown pondering getting out of the fight game.

That sentiment was still in the back of his mind when he returned to Paris. Sriber booked the *Salle Pleyel*, a venue better known for musical performances. Eugene Criqui was the sole official and the only opponent Sriber could find with the little money he had left was Nic Bensa.

With the fight teetering on cancellation, Brown's training was lax. The decision against Chocolate still lingered in his mind. Lumiansky, who was not ready to see his meal ticket drift into the tropical sun, sought to distract Brown with a bevy of fights. He booked a series of fights for Brown in England following the Bensa rematch.

Sriber no longer looked to break even. His goal was to minimize his certain losses. His hopes hinged on a sizeable number of people willing to pay again to see a rematch of a fight that was not competitive to begin with.

Brown spent the last few days leading up to the fight in taverns expecting it to be canceled. It wasn't. He headed for the arena half drunk.

The ring stood where a concert piano usually did and most of the red velvet seats that faced it were empty. Bensa smiled sheepishly and immediately began bouncing on his toes away from Brown. Brown did little more than stalk the first three rounds. In round four he started fighting and by round five, the fight was essentially over.

Criqui scored the fight for Brown stating that Brown was in a class all by himself.

Sriber was ruined financially. *Paris-Soir* reported he was some 100,000 Francs in debt as well as being mired in personal problems.

BLACK INK

Five days after the fight, Sriber was found lying in a pool of blood on his bed with a gunshot wound, thought to be self-inflicted, in his head. He was rushed to *Beaujon* hospital where they found the bullet lodged between his eyes only two millimeters from his brain. Doctors felt surgery was too big a risk. Sriber died shortly after.

Lumiansky booked five fights over the next eight weeks. The British debut was set for ten rounds in Manchester against the unranked Billy Farrell. The money was good and Lumiansky was glad to keep Brown away from the toxic distractions of Paris. Bad influences he said of the tail-like entourage that followed Brown everywhere. He was also tired of the gay friends who, it seemed to him, were only interested in having a good time and reading *La débauche*. To his delight, the entourage remained in Paris.

Brown knew the birthplace of modern boxing was England. It was created by a Welshman, Dai Dollings often reminded him. John Graham Chambers of Llanelli drafted the set of rules which were adopted in 1867 by John Douglas, then Marquis of Queensberry. The Queensberry Rules supplanted the London Prize Ring Rules and instituted Three-minute rounds and disallowed boots with spikes on them, among other things.

The fighters occupying British rings when Brown arrived were more than capable of keeping alive Britain's boxing tradition. The famed boxing "booths" that dotted the landscape were so crowded many quipped there was a fighter in every family. Leading the way was Len Harvey, a fighter good enough to have beaten Marcel Thil and Dave Shade and who was busy at that time fighting on more or less even terms against Vince Dundee and Ben Jeby in New York. Among the lighter weights was the fascinating prodigy called the "Boy Wonder," Nipper Pat Daly, who turned pro at about the age most kids are learning cursive.

Just like in America, their good ole days were stained with racism. For a reminder of that, Brown needed only to turn to his left in the gym where Len Johnson was working the bags. A top-ranked welterweight and middleweight in the mid-1920s, Johnson held area titles and even the Commonwealth title, but was barred from British honors because of his race. When he and Brown shook hands for the first time, Johnson was the reigning Northern Area light heavyweight champ.

The "colour" ban had been in place since WWI. Formed in 1911 by the National Sporting Club because of Jack Johnson, it would stay in place until 1948. It was an odd and stubborn stance when taken into account that after the 1930s a dark-skinned fighter could be champion of the world except for that part under the Royal Coat of Arms.

Curiously, according to one of the founders of the National Sporting Club, the color ban was initiated in part to spite Jack Johnson for skipping out on a debt. Arthur "Peggy" Bettinson partially funded Johnson's trip to Australia when he challenged Tommy Burns. In exchange, Bettinson claimed Johnson agreed to return to England to face Sam Langford in a title fight provided he beat Burns.

Johnson won easily and Bettinson sent for Langford. Johnson however had a change of heart. The original offer of 1,000 pounds, already paid, plus a third of the proceeds from the bioscope earnings were no longer enough. He asked for an additional 6,000 pounds.

The fight was never made. Langford fought Iron Hague, a white fighter, instead and Bettinson was out the cost of the fare to Australia, the potential earnings of the title fight, and the thousand-pound advance which, he said, was long ago spent on "chicken and champagne." The furious Bettinson commenced a campaign against Johnson that ultimately led to, or at least contributed, to the color ban.

"A Black Cloud Looms over England" read one headline when Brown arrived. Just as he had done in France and Spain, Brown polarized the masses. Some people were taken in by his unmistakable ability. Others appreciated his acts of generosity and were thrilled to have a world champion perform on their soil. But some felt he had an unfair height and reach advantage and couldn't help but think of him as a sort of bully beating up on smaller fighters. More than a few couldn't get past his color or sexuality; sometimes both.

Brown bounced down the narrow aisles of the King's Hall amid some cheers and plenty of jeers. Billy Farrell proved to be no match.

BLACK INK

He was dropped five times in three rounds. No one expected him to rise from the fourth knockdown. He did, but barely, and when the referee waved Brown in to resume the assault Brown looked at him with a "you gotta be kidding" expression on his face. Box on, the referee instructed and Brown extended his right and pushed Farrell down for the final time. The ref called halt to the contest without a count.

On his way back to the dressing room, fans booed his every step until he was no longer in view. Once there, Lumiansky reprimanded him for coming in overweight at 123 pounds. He took his percentage from the pre-penalty amount. He was not going to pay for his mistakes, he told Brown, who seemed more concerned with matching his shoes to his belt.

A knock on the door interrupted them.

His friends were waiting for him someone advised. Not expecting anyone, they all turned towards the door to see who was on the other side.

The door was opened wide enough to see a group of well-groomed and sharply-dressed young men. The locals stared admiringly at the champ and smiled bashfully, their hopeful eyes waiting for a reaction. Brown smiled back, tied his shoes and to Lumiansky's chagrin, joined his "friends."

The referee Joe Bowker, a former British bantam and featherweight champ who swapped punches with the likes of Owen Moran, Pedlar Palmer, and Jim Driscoll in his day stated that Brown was every bit as brilliant as his contemporary, George Dixon. He questioned whether the slim champ could stand up to heavy pressure but from what he saw, Brown was fully deserving of the title of champion.

Two weeks later he turned back the challenge of 100-fight veteran Douglas Parker. Four times he floored the 130-pounder. The last knockdown prompted one of Parker's handlers to toss in the sponge.

1928 Olympian Jack Garland was next. Once again boxing at the King's Hall in Manchester, the fight went the entire 15 rounds with Brown the winner.

Two days after the rough fight with the Olympian, Brown was back in Paris and back in the ring against Roger Simende. The match against the muscular Simende was part of a benefit to raise money for an artifact-collecting expedition across Central Africa. Brown donated his entire purse to the Trocadero Museum in Paris.

The anthropological expedition spanned from Dakar to Djibouti and was financed almost entirely by Brown. The director of the museum, cited as Eduoard Riviere in a 1931 article but likely was Georges Riviere, introduced Brown to the world of anthropology. He met Brown while studying the differences between "American Negroes, West Indian, Sudanese, and Senegalese Negroes from among the living specimens along the black colony of Paris."

Riviere was considered a good man to go to for advice on everything from getting a permit to play in a jazz band - to phoning the proper authorities and straightening out a situation that would have "kept a negro hot and bothered for months." Through mutual friends in the black colony, Riviere came into contact with Brown and took him around the museum's African exhibits and demonstrated to the fighter how they related to him. When Riviere showed him "racial resemblances between himself and certain natives still living in a state of savagery; showed him how his own ancestors probably lived, what weapons they made and used, how they hunted, what huts they built, what their tribal gods and customs were, he got under the black boy's skin."

That was from a write-up that appeared in the *Brooklyn Daily Eagle* under a heading that said Brown was Tunney's intellectual rival. The exhibition was well publicized and filmmaker Luis Bunuel was invited to film the mission. Brown kicked off the festivities by boxing an exhibition with one of the anthropologists before stopping Simende in three rounds later that day.

Others mocked the intentions of the exhibition. In the same article where he criticized Kid Chocolate's pink-and-purple-striped shirts, John Lardner claimed the proceeds went towards buying a livery cab for Brown's personal chauffer.

The match against Teddy Baldock was finally realized on May 21st.

Brown trained at the National Sporting Club for Baldock, who had seen his best days. Whatever was left of Teddy's skills was sent off by Brown to that unknown place where lost hair and wrinkle-free skin resided. In a fight that would have been stopped about five times had it taken place after the 1990s, Brown battered Baldock to the canvas four times, the final one seeing Baldock collapsing on his forehead for a stoppage in twelve rounds.

Even with his best days in the rear view mirror, Baldock was a tough-out. Brown used all his might to keep his rival down. Afterwards he complained of an unusual pain in his right hand when he reached his dressing room. When his glove was removed he couldn't move his fingers and a large lump sat between his wrist and knuckles. A specialist was called in. Four bones were wedged out of place from the force of his blows, *The Brooklyn Daily Eagle* reported. The health of Brown's right hand joined Teddy's skill in that far-off place.

Still, Lumiansky wanted Brown to go ahead with a Paris match against Andre Regis two weeks later. "Use your left," he told the fighter. Lumiansky refused to cancel the fight and when Brown balked, threatened to sue his fighter for breach of contract. He told Brown any financial losses incurred by the promoter were his responsibility. In addition, Brown would be suspended by the commissions for an indefinite amount of time. If he didn't fight then, there was no telling when he would.

Brown's lifestyle did not permit a lapse in activity. During his time in England he discovered Saville Row and spent many an afternoon seated on the quilted leather sofas sipping tea while a tailor custom altered a couple of suits to his dimensions.

He also had purchased a stable of thoroughbreds that he kept in *Maisons-Laffitte*. Horses and big cats were his favorite animals though - unlike his late friend Battling Siki - he chose not to take in the latter.

Two days before the Paris fight, Brown woke up with a lesion on his face. Brown was not allowed to fight with the open sore visible. Regis boxed Dominique Di Cea instead and the fight with Brown was pushed back until June 13. The fight didn't come off on that date either and newspaper reports cited the still-unhealed hand as the reason.

Lumiansky's hunch that Brown's uninhibited lifestyle would affect him was being realized. The lesion was syphilitic. As soon as it began fading, Lumiansky booked a fight for Brown in England for June 15th.

Johnny Cuthbert was approaching 150 fights that included five 15-rounders in one month. Among them was a victory over then-unbeaten Jackie "Kid" Berg. Cuthbert entered the rematch with two good hands and the home court edge. He was coming off of two wins and the previous December he boxed a 15-round draw against knockout artist Al Foreman for the British Empire Lightweight title. At the time, Foreman trailed only Young Stribling among active boxers in career knockouts and ranked about sixth all time behind Sam Langford, Stribling, Wilde, George KO Chaney, and Joe Gans (and possibly Peter Maher) in career knockouts.

Like Brown, Cuthbert had a wiry build with large knuckles and a crooked nose. He was trained by Bobby Diamond, known in his mother's homeland of France as Robert Diamant. Bobby Diamond knew Brown from their days in New York where they often crossed paths at Villepontoux's café.

After the echo from the final bell of his ring career faded, Diamond traded in his gloves for a knife and fork and ate himself out of his flyweight body and into one that resembled a snowman. His round face, framed by prescription lenses, was unrecognizable from his fighting days. Those who knew him when he was trading leather with the likes of Andre Routis did a double-take when they saw his stubby fingers wrapping the hands or rubbing the backs of the fighters under his charge. He would go on to be one of the prominent handlers in Europe and Northern Africa. Glimpses of his guile were evident during the Brown-Cuthbert match.

Brown floored Cuthbert in the third and fifth rounds and was winning easily with his one good hand. Then, in the eighth, he threw a hook to the stomach that dropped Cuthbert to his knees. Tom Gamble, the over-seventy referee, disqualified Brown for a low blow.

Brown was previously warned in round three for a stray shot. Diamond told Cuthbert to go down and stay down if Brown hit him low again.

But ringside reports stated the punch that led to Brown's disqualification was a fair one. *The Daily Mirror* reported the crowd booed lustily and the official decision could not be heard. The booing was directed at Brown who was showered with jeers and insults along with accusations of being a dirty fighter as he left the arena.

Gamble meanwhile became the focus of great controversy in the days after the fight. How old was too old was the question the public began asking about a referee's age. A slew of fighters came to his defense. Gamble was deemed young enough and went on to referee fights for another five years.

Brown left for Paris the following day craving an extended rest. His hand was not fully healed and the complications from syphilis were beginning to take their toll. Lumiansky, however, was eager to campaign on American soil. He returned to the U.S. and began negotiating.

Before departing for America, Brown received a correspondence from the *London Mail*.

"How do you keep such a wonderful figure?" asked a female reporter.

Three reasons replied Brown. He never drank alcohol, ate plenty of raw fruits, and never went a day without riding his horse.

He overpaid for his stable, the people snickered. He entered them in races though they rarely placed. Despite that, he betted heavily on them because he didn't want their feelings to be hurt. He purchased the horses, a friend said, not because they promised victories but because no one else wanted them.

Having given his age as 24, Brown arrived in New York from Cherbourg aboard the Bremen on June 28th. Two weeks later he rushed over to Philadelphia to watch Kid Chocolate become the second boxer from Latin America to become a world champion.

Brown's hand was still not completely healed when the time came for his next fight. Lumiansky, unwilling to jeopardize another payday, lobbied for heavily padded gloves. His request was met with resistance. After some back-and-forth, both camps agreed and Brown readied himself for what turned out to be one of his toughest foes.

More than 12,000 jammed the Forum in Montreal. The crowd was decidedly behind his opponent, Pete Sanstol. A Norwegian with a long track record of fights in New York and Montreal, Sanstol had lost only two of 84 going in. He was also considered world champion by the Canadian commissions. But he was coming off a fight against Eugene Huat in which he was knocked down and many felt he lost.

Brown jumped out to an early lead. He landed combinations at will and danced off to the side whenever Sanstol countered. The battle was thrill-packed. Brown's looping right hands were quick and lashed out like cobras wrote the *Ottawa Citizen*. Sanstol bled from the left eye early and by the second half of the fight, he was a one-eyed fighter. Brown targeted the purple lump that covered Sanstol's eye repeatedly with straight rights. But Sanstol weathered the storm and when the bell rang for round ten, he made his stand.

Jolting Brown with vicious uppercuts on the inside, Sanstol walked down the fading champion and had the crowd on its feet in the fourteenth. The fifteenth and final round saw possibly the two biggest hearts in boxing that year stand their ground and battle it out toe-to-toe until the final bell.

The decision was split in Brown's favor. The majority of fans gave both fighters a big hand but some "local die-hards" loudly booed the verdict. In his dressing room Brown stated he hurt his left hand in the later rounds. He also said "Sanstol is the toughest man I ever fought."

Despite two bad hands, deteriorating health and a wicked bout against Sanstol, Lumiansky booked a fight for Brown three weeks later in Wales. One month after that, it was back to Montreal for a title match against Eugene Huat.

Brown was approaching burnout. He received word from Panama that his mother was not in the best health. He wanted to visit her. But he didn't want her to see the condition he was in. His skin was covered in a rash and his elbows and knees began to ache so much that he was taking painkillers daily. With Panama on his mind, he sailed for Wales.

Because of Dollings, Brown was excited to be in Wales. The Ginger Jones fight was a routine victory for Brown. More important were the exhibitions and donations he made to various youth and hospital charities while there.

Before he could do more good, he was off to Montreal for the rematch with Huat. Years later Brown would say Huat was the only opponent he didn't like personally. In his mind, he expected more respect from a fellow boxer. Regarding what the public and the writers felt and said, he had no expectations. But a fellow boxer was his equal he said, and had no business thinking he was a better person.

"Milo Pladner, him I liked. Hurting him hurt me as much as it did him. But Huat - him I don't like. He says horrible things and calls me a disgusting n*****. Against Milo I wanted to get the fight over with as soon as possible. Not with Huat. Him I wanted to hurt and drag it out as long as possible. I wanted him to remember this disgusting n*****."

Brown took his time when the bell rang. Boxing just far enough away to hit without being hit, he worked his jab repeatedly through the high guard of the crouching wildcat. Occasionally he dropped a long right but by this point in his career, when his right hand was beginning to look like a hawk's talon, the left was the punch he began relying on more.

Brown kept his distance, poised like a harpy eagle waiting to make a kill. Except there would be no "kill." This was a torture session. "Stop the fight," shouted some spectators. Brown's uppercuts lifted Huat's chin into the air repeatedly. Each time the referee thought about stopping the fight, Brown shifted into neutral.

Huat began aiming for the body starting in round four with very limited success. Brown stepped it up in the eighth round, bouncing thudding combinations off the chin of the Frenchman. Huat never quit advancing. In the clinches, he resorted to roughhousing and trying to hit on the break. At one point, he nearly shoved Brown through the ropes.

By the eleventh, Brown was once again in complete control. A left hook to the gall bladder froze Huat in his tracks. The champ landed a right-left to the head that had Huat wobbling on his heels. Brown stalked icily. He threw one hard punch at a time and stared into Huat's eyes. The final two rounds he let Huat swing away while staring at him with a look that seemed to say "You ain't shit."

Lumiansky kept booking fights. They headed west to Los Angeles for two fights.

On December 15th, 1931, he lost a ten-round decision to Newsboy Brown. The *Associated Negro Press* reported that Brown "did not extend himself" and was "content" to let Newsboy "hammer his body." The result was called a surprise by the *United Press* who credited the "New York Brown" with winning four rounds while the Newsboy won five.

Exhausted and sick, Brown asked out of the January 4th fight. Lumianksy brought him to a doctor the week of the 20th to examine the "injuries sustained in the fight." The doctor pronounced him "nearly physically fit." The day after Christmas Brown was back in the gym.

They rang in the new year in Los Angeles - Lumiansky counting receipts and Brown drinking away. Brown was mired in a perpetual cycle of receiving cash advances from his manager. And many of the gambling spots in France allowed him to wager on credit. The money was going out as fast as it was coming in.

1932 got off to a bad start. On January 4th, he lost on points to Speedy Dado. He was reportedly drunk when he climbed through the ropes. Things went downhill after that.

Dado would later in his career lay claim to the bantamweight title. The following year, Dado's promoter made an offer of $10,000 to Brown to put his title on the line. Lumiansky countered with $20,000. Champions were reluctant to defend their titles in California, the *Afro American* reported. There were several reasons but the report cited the main one as being a series of peculiar wins by west coast fighters over east coast fighters. The rematch with Dado was never made.

Despite a successful career Dado spent his retirement selling pencils that too few people bought out of a tin cup in the lobby of the Olympic Auditorium. A handwritten sign that said something along the lines of "Please help, I am blind," hung from a shoelace around his neck.

1932 was also the year Brown's mother died.

Some say it was the year Al Brown died too.

Following the Dado fight, a January 11th match against Mose Butch in Pittsburgh was cancelled at the last minute. Brown was quickly admitted into a New York hospital. The published reports said he was recovering from an illness brought about by an alleged low blow he received in the Newsboy Brown fight. Three other scheduled bouts were canceled as well.

Brown hadn't contracted an illness from a low blow.

The syphilis was progressing. Where and when he caught it is not certain. It might have been aboard a ship crossing the Atlantic in a cabin too dark to notice the chancre sores. Perhaps it was concealed in a flirtatious smile inside a dimly lit cabaret in Montmartre. However it happened, it was about ten years too early. Though penicillin was invented in a London basement around the time Brown was pardoning prisoners in Panama, it was not used as a cure for syphilis until the 1940s. Instead, Brown rubbed mercury ointment all over his body and sweated it out.

Just like his buddies.

Black Bill was almost completely blind by the time Brown lay in the hospital. He told anyone who would listen that it was from a fight he had in Cuba where his opponent rubbed his gloves in rosin dust before the first round. Despite his claim, it was commonly accepted that his sight was fading before that night and that it was from syphilis. Black Bill turned to liquor to soothe the misery. It didn't work.

Black Bill died the following year. While most New Yorkers filed their taxes and others celebrated the legalization of liquor sales, Black

Bill felt his way down the corridor of his apartment into his bedroom. Once there, he grabbed a pistol and pumped a slug into his abdomen. When the police arrived he was still alive. "Don't save me," he told them as they took him to a Harlem hospital.

Kid Chocolate might have been infected around the same time as Brown. It was common knowledge throughout boxing circles that the Kid fought not just his opponents but also the "Great Imitator." Bacteria *Treponema pallidum* is the official name and the list of famous people who were infected with it includes writers, athletes, actors, mob bosses and, heads of state.

Lumiansky simmered while Brown was being tended to in the hospital. "Don't touch me," was his directive when the fighter got out. A fight was scheduled for March 14th in Lumiansky's hometown of New Bedford. His opponent was a local welterweight named Osford Golf Ball Bernard. Originally from Panama and known as Ossie, he was thought to have over 100 fights. Brown won a decision in a fight where neither tried too hard to hurt the other.

Nearly one in four Americans were unemployed during 1932. Interest in boxing was dropping. Heavyweight champion Max Schmeling was known as the "low blow champion." Writers criticized the splintered championships with multiple state commissions declaring their own champions. "The situation would be worse if anyone cared," wrote *The Brooklyn Daily Eagle*.

Brown didn't seem to care about boxing either. His health was in poor condition and he developed an addiction to painkillers. He couldn't sleep without first taking a few shots because, he said, the "nightmares only happen when I'm sober."

When he found out his mother was gravely ill, he wrestled with the urge to return to Panama. He decided he would, but not until he was better.

What would she think when she saw the sores?

He wondered, would she have the same thoughts some of the gym goers did? Would she feel like they felt about sharing the same shower and insist, like some did, that the walls and floors be scrubbed down afterwards so that they wouldn't catch what he had?

He would visit his mother as soon as his sores vanished.

When the chancres healed, Brown decided he would make a pair of quick paydays before visiting his mother. He and Lumiansky sailed back to Europe. When they arrived in France, it quickly became clear that they did not have the same plans.

While his manager hammered out deals for much more than a fight or two, Brown headed for the casinos on France's north shore. Between the two of them, they were juggling six of the seven deadly sins.

The Hotel Normandy in Deauville was a favorite spot of Brown's. Seated at the baccarat table, the dealer almost always passed the face-down card from the shoe to Brown, since he often was the biggest bettor. His bets were usually on "ties" and after the hands were revealed, Brown didn't bother keeping track of score on the cards the house handed out. He often lost track, if he even kept track, of the money he lost, remembering only to place increasingly higher stacks of chips each hand.

While Brown played on credit at the tables, Dickson and Lumiansky reconciled long enough to shake hands on a deal that included three fights in a span of thirteen days. When Brown was informed he told them, "Afterwards I'll visit my mom."

Just before the May 18th match in Paris he was told by Dickson, "Don't knock everyone out. It's difficult finding you opponents." Brown obeyed, letting his opponent last the ten-round distance. Just over a week later he was in Cardiff, scoring a between-rounds stoppage of Luigi Quadrini in a match where Brown donated his entire purse to The Royal Infirmary in Cardiff.

Three days after that fight, he outpointed Francois Machtens over ten rounds. Brown once again could not use his right hand during the fight. Poet and fight writer Guy Levis Mano covered the fight and compared Brown's precise ring movement to that of an expensive watch. Brown played with Machtens he said, and it was understandable that the crowd voiced its displeasure with his antics.

Antics that included smiling at his opponent when he missed and spinning him completely around and had him punching south when

Brown was standing north. At times, Brown dropped his hands to his sides and exposed his chest. He invited his opponent to hit his chest and when Brown had enough, he simply danced away. But the general public was missing out on a gifted performer, according to the poet. Brown had shown the French what a ring artist was and the public couldn't appreciate it.

Perhaps Brown dropped his guard because he wanted to be punished by Machtens. It was around that time he received word that Esther had drawn her last breath.

A ton of guilt pushed down on his chest. The stream of a thousand tears could not wash away the sadness that covered his still-boyish features. He was tormented when he found out that she spent her final days scrubbing clean the dirty clothes of rich families while fending off the critiques that her rich son sailed the world. For a while, nothing eased the pain that burned inside. He soon found something that did.

Inside the bars of Paris was a thriving narcotics business. And Brown, a defensive master inside the ring able to anticipate danger and evade it, walked right smack into trouble. Under the bar, on the shelf next to the brand liquor, was where they kept the dark little opium pills.

You sure you want it?

Yeah. I need it. Nothing else is working.

"To it I owe my perfect hours" poet Jean Cocteau once said of the powerful effects of opium. Brown found his way to the back rooms and basements of the clubs where patrons lit up and passed the pipe. Lying on his left side, like all righties, on a soft mattress covered with layers of quilts, Brown placed a pill inside the pipe's chute and inhaled.

The smoke, described by some as sweet smelling and by others as smelling like bbq chicken, filled the room and Brown felt no pain. You'll sleep better, the pushers told him. You won't hurt anymore and your orgasms will last longer, was a common pitch. As long, they continued, as you're high.

Eventually he discovered the dedicated opium dens. Unlike 1980s New York City crack houses with their missing steps, burned out light bulbs and armed lookouts, the opium dens had friendly hosts and comfortable couches covered in red and gold velvet. The pills and pipes were brought to the user nestled inside decorative wooden boxes adorned with Chinese drawings. Entire families could be found at the dens, especially on graduation nights when parents brought their teens to marinate in the smoke. Artists in search of inspiration and university students needing a lift were a common sight. Brown too became a fixture.

When the final bells rang and the fans went home and the bars closed and the entourage remembered where they lived, Brown often found himself alone. In public he wore his happy face. In his room, alone with his inner demons, he was much like a veteran who saw his leg blown away forever in a jungle with a name he couldn't pronounce. The ones who are paraded around as inspirations and tell every reporter who asks that they wouldn't change a thing. When the director yells "cut" and the grip packs the last of the equipment, they find themselves forced to cope by smoking joints alone in their kitchens with a half-empty bottle of Percocet nearby.

Brown was no war hero. But the public façade he put on to conceal his private emptiness was nonetheless similarly debilitating.

The opium felt like hope. Among the most addictive of all drugs, opium cured him of his ills. But it was only temporary. The drug is a con artist. The first few times you sample it, it lets you walk away feeling like you're in control. Without warning, your body is sick without it and the only cure is more. Brown became trapped in the grip of his vices. And in the grip of his manager's too.

On June 13th, 1932 he traveled to Liverpool for a match against local legend Nel Tarleton. If Tarleton ever tired in a fight, he was excused. He boxed his entire career with only one lung. Despite having lost the function of one lung to tuberculosis while still a child, Tarleton had developed into one of the smartest defensive fighters of his day.

The featherweight decided to make Brown come to him. Fighting in reverse the entire night, he attempted to pot-shot Brown whenever he got too close. Brown, who didn't have his usual inches-long height and reach advantages, jabbed from the outside and avoided being ambushed by his cautious rival. Between rounds he drank liquor from a water bottle wrapped in a white towel. The decision was a draw. Tarleton threw a tantrum. Brown just wanted his paycheck. Money was his other addiction.

Five days later he faced Eugene Huat for the third and final time. He floored Huat in the second round and battered his nemesis with his left. A week later, Brown was in Italy to face Olympic Gold Medal winner Vittorio Tamagnini. When he met with the press before the fight, he was more concerned with his age than with his opponent.

"I'm not as old as you guys say I am," was the message he wanted to drive home.

As for the fight, the Italian proved too fast for the fatigued champion. Brown reinjured his right hand and could not keep the younger man at bay. He fought most of the fight with his back to the ropes covered up in a high guard. Brown advised the media afterwards that his hand was injured early in the fight and that it was too great a handicap against the caliber of opponent Tamagnini was.

"He beat me. I accept that. With two hands he would be difficult to beat. With one hand, I just couldn't do it."

He needed both hands and both legs for his next fight. Kid Francis was still hanging around the top ten. Time was running out however for the once "sure thing." Since their Madison Square Garden match, Francis had a winning streak that included wins over Bernasconi, LaBarba, and highly rated Eddie Shea. LaBarba beat him in a rematch and contenders Earl Mastro and Lew Feldman, a featherweight, got the best of him too.

Born in Naples, Francesco Buonaugurio and his brother Guy became boxers. Adopting the name Kid Francis early on, the naturalized Frenchman lived in Algeria and Argentina before settling in Marseilles. He grew up in the era of Mussolini and his family was part of the so-called population surplus of Italians who branched out into other countries.

His second cousin was Francois Spirito who, among other business undertakings, functioned as his defacto manager. An offer by a Mr. Sol, who had a ton of underworld muscle backing him, was extended to Lumiansky. Against Dickson's vehement protests, Al Brown was set to defend his bantamweight title against Francis in Marseilles.

"It's stupid!" exclaimed Dickson. "Stupid! Stupid! Stupid!"

As soon as Brown arrived, the promoters in Marseilles did everything they could to make the champion feel comfortable. They provided unlimited liquor, the best foods, and VIP access to all the best clubs. Prostitutes of all shapes and colors were made available. All Brown or anyone in his entourage had to do was ask.

Spirito had plenty of experience with prostitutes. He ran prostitution rings in Egypt, France, Spain and Northern Africa. It was in Egypt that he met Paul Carbone. They partnered in a variety of endeavors including a cheese smuggling ring, drug and arms trafficking and gold bullion. Carbone became the godfather of the Marseilles underworld with Spirito a trusted capo. Aside from his responsibilities as mediator of the French underworld, where he settled disputes between rival gangsters at his bar named "Friendly," Spirito allegedly fixed fights for his cousins.

One of Kid Francis' fights was billed, announced, and reported as a match against American Georgie Mack. It would have been a good win for the fighter had it happened. Months later it was revealed that it was a not Mack, not even a boxer, in the ring that day but a local dock worker.

Brown was approached by people who, after looking around to make sure they were alone, made him offers to lose the fight. Brown politely turned them all down. Around the same time, at least one of the ring officials was approached as well.

The night of the fight, Spirito sat directly behind one of the judges. With one official already understanding his role, a second official needed to be convinced. Unbuttoning his suit jacket and holding it back far enough to let his piece show, he spent the night loudly giving his version of the blow-by-blow.

"Another round for Francis!' he bellowed at the end of each round. "No way Francis loses this fight! No way!"

When Brown landed a combination, Spirito quickly chimed in, "Missed!"

"Brown is hurt!" was another one of his favorite lines that night.

The crowd wasn't much different. Each time Francis threw a volley, they roared as one. When Brown did, there was silence. The crowd was silent most of the fight.

"One more round and we have a champion!" shouted Spirito throughout the final round. "Just one more round," he said while rising to his feet. He was joined by dozens as the entire arena chanted for the hometown fighter.

But the official, Dr. James Sparks, Commanding Officer of the American Legion in France, was not the type who fazed easily. Not even when guns, at least four, were brandished as he tabulated his score after the fourteenth round.

A man described by newspapers as a hoodlum saw that Sparks had Brown winning the fight by a large margin. He thrust his revolver below Sparks' bottom rib and demanded he hand him the card. Sparks did and when the bell rang for the final round, he climbed onto the ring apron and advised the referee of what happened.

The referee had his own problems by then. At the end of each round gangster types reminded him that Francis was to win the fight. He ushered Sparks off the apron and back to his seat, which was no longer there. In its place were about half a dozen men who pinned him against the ring in a way Francis wished he'd been able to pin Brown along the ropes.

Spirito and his crew blew their tops. More guns were drawn and shots were fired into the air. Shouts of "Change it!" were overheard while a few of them grabbed Sparks and tried to make him change his card. Sparks refused and the gangsters ripped the scorecard into tiny pieces. One of them shoved the pieces into Sparks' mouth and made him eat them.

BLACK INK

Someone threatened to kill him while one bashed his head from behind and sent a stream of blood down his back. The Italian referee, wanting to make it back to Milan in one piece, held aloft his own card in the middle of the ring and, before disappearing for almost an hour, shouted "Look - I voted for Francis!"

Now was when Brown needed his legs most. He, his handlers, and the third official took off for the dressing rooms while a growing mob chased after them. Fists started to rain down on Sparks' face while others decided to take their anger out on the seats. Someone tried to set fire to the ring but the canvas didn't ignite. Women fainted, bottles were thrown and random faces were punched. Hundreds of police and soldiers wearing steel helmets were needed to restore order. Helping to calm the riot was the announcement that Kid Francis was the winner.

Back in his hotel room, Brown was livid at having lost the title. At least he was safe. Word got out about where Sparks was staying and soon another violent mob pushed their way into his room and continued the beating.

Before Brown arrived in Paris, the local commission and the IBU announced an investigation into the result. The next day they officially announced Brown as winner of the fight.

He and Francis would fight once more. In Paris two years later, Brown outscored him again. Carbone and Spirito would later join forces with Mussolini and his fascist regime. After the French Liberation, Carbone was killed when a train he was aboard was derailed by the resistance. Spirito made it out of France alive and settled in South America. He expanded his heroin trade and become one of the orchestrators of the drug smuggling operation known as the French Connection.

Lumiansky was especially eager to return to the United States after that close call. American promoters still weren't champing at the bit to promote an Al Brown fight. The manager signed for a pair of matches in Canada. Originally Brown was scheduled to defend his title against Emile Pladner. Pladner himself was originally set to face Newsboy Brown. When promoter Armand Vincent did not hear back from the Newsboy camp, he went ahead and scheduled Pladner to fight for the title. With the champion already in training at Madame Bey's, Newsboy Brown showed up in Chicago on his way to Montreal with every intention of honoring his commitment to fight Pladner. Rather than pay Brown's training expenses for nothing, Vincent put Brown on the undercard in a featherweight match.

Brown was matched against the unranked Roland LeCuyer of Massachusetts. Just in case there was any lost enthusiasm among the public, the local press advised their readers that Brown abandoned his cautious fighting style when the title wasn't on the line. The *Montreal Gazette* called him a "tearing, heavy-slugging battler" in non-title fights.

The fight was a mismatch. The *Montreal Gazette* wrote the next day that the fight was "no contest from start to finish. The lean negro, master of the left flick and a vicious right hand, stabbed LeCuyer unmercifully." The crowd booed the mismatch throughout the fourth and fifth rounds. LeCuyer, badly cut, stood on his stool when the bell rang for the sixth round.

In the main event, Emile Pladner earned a shot at Brown with a decision victory over Newsboy Graham. Pladner was a fast punching, fast moving fighter with enough wallop to have stopped Frankie Genaro with one of those shots to the liver that freezes a man. Pladner won the flyweight title that night and had plenty of other good nights in his career. There were wins over Corporal Izzy, Victor Young Perez, Frankie Ash, and draws with Sanstol and Huat. There were bad nights as well. Like the first fight against Huat, where he was floored repeatedly and ended up in a coma.

His fight against Brown in Toronto five weeks later was another bad night. At least it was short. Two rapid left hooks to the jaw followed by a straight right to the heart ended the fight in round one.

With Madison Square Garden still not returning his calls, Lumiansky headed back to his second hometown, Pittsburgh. Mose Butch was outpointed over ten rounds in a subpar performance by a half-drunk Brown.

Brown was still very sick at that point. His right hand was swollen, his left hand was tender, and the skin rashes were back. He doubled up on the little blue mercuric chloride pills and chased them down with painkillers.

His jaw hurt but not from punches. His gums bled often and the first of his teeth began to loosen. His knees burned and Brown wrapped them in bandages to ease the discomfort. Arthritis, a consequence of the syphilis, turned his occasional roadwork runs into power walks.

Drunk, gay, and riddled with infectious disease, the American press and boxing promoters preferred to deal with gangsters rather than deal with Brown. The only place Brown could live like a champion was Europe where the promoters didn't mind making bank off of a public anxious to see Brown beaten.

The francs kept pouring in and Brown was getting his share. Joining him in Paris were his brothers. They too were enamored with the sights, the food, and the cabarets of the city. They raced his horses, went on shopping sprees, and were treated to fine clothes with price tags that evoked minor guilt. What bothered them most during their trip was the condition their younger brother was in. He was battered and weary and his preferred healing process was to disappear for the night on a drug binge.

"Quit," they told him about boxing, which they felt was the root of his troubles.

"I can't," was his usual reply.

They accompanied him on his trip to Belgium where he fought twice in five days. Both hands were hurting and he complained of light-headedness. Still, he went through with the fights and like always, blessed himself with the sign of the cross before the first bell. He won both matches but not without being forced to dig down deep. They weren't close fights but Brown had reached that point in the career of a fighter where each fight visibly took something out of him. From here until the day he retired, the man who climbed up the ring steps to do battle was visibly younger and fresher than the one who climbed down less than an hour later.

Another fight against Emile Pladner was set for November 14th, 1932. From about the eighth of November, Brown could not get out of bed. His vision was clouded, his head spun, and his stomach had trouble holding anything down. The day of the fight, he awoke with shivers and cold sweats. His temperature reached 100 degrees Fahrenheit. A doctor was called to his room.

"Don't fight," was the doctor's advice.

"The Palais is sold out," someone reminded.

Perhaps the promoters thought fighters were too tough to let a little cough keep them from fighting. Perhaps they didn't care. The threat of a fighter being sued for a promoter's losses was often floated about. More real was a boxer falling out of the good graces of the game's organizers. Whatever the case, the fight went on.

The nearly 20,000 who crammed into the *Palais De Sports* were treated to a heavyweight match first. Federico Malibran, recently arrived from San Sebastian, Cuba made his Paris debut against Giuseppe Sanga. Sanga won by fourth-round stoppage over the out-of-shape Malibran.

Middleweight Pierre Gandon outscored American Harry Smith in a bout scheduled for under ten rounds. Ben Said got a disputed win over a Spaniard billed only as Hernandez. Hernandez complained vociferously about the decision, one that could have been a draw according to *El Mundo Deportivo*.

LaRoche scored a third round stoppage over Malasagne and Kid Zenti stopped African Hie Hine in five. The first ten rounder saw Jimmy Tarante dominate the determined Bert Melzow. Melzow fought back courageously throughout but was forced to remain on his stool when the bell rang for the ninth round.

While Melzow struggled out of the ring, a Dr. Taubmann prepared a syringe in Brown's dressing room. "This will last ten minutes at the most," he said of the rush Brown would feel from the mixture of amphetamines. "Starting now," he said before sticking the weakened champion in his arm.

At exactly ten that night both fighters entered the ring. The crowd backed Pladner and bought into his story of being the victim of a lucky punch the last time they shared a ring. While both fighters disrobed, the crowd was introduced to two champions seated in the crowd. Marcel Thil and Valentine Angelman entered the ring waiving to the crowd and wished both boxers luck. Pladner was applauded while he was introduced at 5.8 kilos. Brown had a mixed reception of mostly applause when he was announced at 5.5 kilos.

About four of the ten minutes remained from the feel-good shot when the bell rang. It was clear to ringside reporters that something was very wrong with Brown the minute the fight started. His steps, usually a bounce, were slow and deliberate. His guard was high and his elbows were tucked in close to his body. Only occasionally did he attempt a combination. At the end of the round he lashed out with a stinging combination that visibly stunned Pladner.

"You don't have much time," his corner, which included Lumiansky, told the slumped fighter between rounds. Just before the bell rang his manager held a small handful of smelling salts under Brown's nose. "Take him out now," were his final instructions.

In the other corner, concerned their man might get caught while waiting for Brown to tire, Pladner was told Brown had thrown his best shots and had nothing left. Attack now was the directive.

Brown's legs quivered unsteadily when he rose from his stool. At the center of the ring an eager Pladner awaited, his left hand locked and loaded. When Brown reached him, Pladner threw a left with fight-ending intentions towards Brown's diaphragm.

A well-placed hook to the pit of the stomach might have been too much for the weakened Brown to handle. The left hook traveled in a slight arc, gained maximum leverage, then, suddenly, was pulled down to the canvas by the rest of his body.

A split second after Pladner planted his left foot for torque, Brown unleashed a right hand. Both punches were airborne at the same time. Brown's punch was straight. Pladner's took the scenic route. The straight punch landed first.

It detonated on Pladner's jaw.

Pladner rose unsteadily. When the fighting resumed, it was Brown who looked in worse shape. Still, Pladner remained cautious while he gathered the rest of his senses. He kept his guard up and waited while Brown slowly pawed with both hands. After a few seconds, and figuring lightning couldn't strike twice, Pladner took his chance and opened up.

But Brown didn't throw lightning. When he saw Pladner plant his feet, he knew what punch was coming next. Rather than evade the incoming missile, he let out an atomic right hand that carried every last bit of energy he had left. It landed on the temple.

Pladner was out before he hit the canvas. Before the referee reached the count of six, Brown started fainting. Light headed and unaware of where he was he walked over to Pladner's corner where Pladner's trainer placed the stool in the ring and sat Brown down.

After a second or two Brown realized his error and started over towards his corner, just as the ref counted ten, and after taking only a few steps- collapsed into the arms of his trainer who rushed over just in the nick of time to catch him.

The crowd, recognizing Brown's unheard-of effort, gave him a standing ovation as he was escorted back to his dressing room held up by his handlers. Once in the dressing room Brown fainted again.

The next day Pladner told reporters he tried his best knowing full well that an opportunity like the one the night before won't ever come around again.

For his part, Brown was admitted into the hospital *Americano de Neuilly* where the doctors ordered a minimum stay of 48 hours. The press informed he had a fever of over 102 and it was revealed that he had been sick for over four days leading up to the fight.

Those few days in the hospital were among the few he spent resting. He was exhausted, dehydrated, and sick with an incurable illness. What wasn't made public was that Brown was riddled with syphilis. Instead, the papers reported he had an infection in the knee with swelling of the lymph glands in the groin and inflammation- the result of a fall from a horse.

Some 48 hours later Brown woke from his rest to find a telegram from Lumiansky by his side with instructions to check himself out and head over immediately to Sheffield for a December 1st match followed by one in Brussels on December 3rd and then another December 8th in Paris.

Physicians instructed him to refrain from physical activity for three weeks and, after that, to ease back into a training regimen. Brown told Lumiansky he would not be ready for those fights.

Lumiansky told him it was too late; the fights have been announced.

Brown insisted he couldn't - he was medically unfit

Lumiansky insisted the hospital wouldn't have released him if he were unfit. When Brown continued to protest, he told Brown he had no say and his only responsibility was to be in shape when he told him to be.

"It's in the contract."

That winter Alan Gould, Sports Editor of the *AP*, stated the public had little interest in champions and championship fights and again called the game a "legal racket." After the Primo Carnera-George Godfrey performance, he again attacked the game and its managers and promoters. Two sets of contracts, he said, were drawn up for many matches. The first, to satisfy and comply with rules, was filed with the commissions. Then another set, the "working set" was drawn up with very different stipulations.

Brown's own contract was about to become a popular news topic. Some of the clauses became public knowledge including one that stated, should the manager die, a percentage of Brown's earnings would have gone to the manager's then nine-year-old son.

Two weeks after he checked out of the hospital Brown found himself in the ring against Dick Burke. Burke turned pro in 1929 two days after Brown defeated Gregorio Vidal. By the end of 1929, Burke was fighting 15-rounders. Burke, who claimed he was the only one to both box and play a match at Liverpool's FC Stadium, was a hard hitting featherweight with wins over Johnny Peters and Len Wickwar.

The Merseyside slugger was a difficult opponent for Brown. In a match officiated by flyweight legend Jimmy Wilde, Brown mustered up enough strength to win by decision.

Lucky for Brown, his next opponent was only a shell of his former self. Henri Scillie was at the end of his long career. The day after the Burke match, he was on his way to Brussels to get reacquainted with old foe Scillie.

His brothers worried the Pladner incident would repeat itself in Brussels. But Brown, not wanting to bear the brunt of any financial losses from a cancellation, went ahead and fought.

Scillie, fighting his 99th fight, was either unable or unwilling to hurt the exhausted Panamanian. Despite constant icing, the swelling along his knuckles and the puffiness around his left eye from his fight just two days before were still visible when his hands were wrapped.

Brown struggled to make it through the fight. He spent the last round clinging to his opponent, who clung back. The decision was a draw and in the dressing room, Brown passed out.

When he came to an injured right hand awaited him and back in Paris, at the track, a horse with slow legs. Paid only 1500 francs for the fight, at his wits' end, dazed, sick, and ready to quit boxing, Brown headed to the track and placed the entire 1500 on a horse that finished somewhere in the middle of the pack.

Then he disappeared without a trace.

Lumiansky could not find him and no one in boxing seemed to know his whereabouts. If anyone did, they kept it to themselves. Lumiansky turned to the press for help finding Brown. With the fight against Machtens only days away and rumors surfacing that Brown had retired, Lumiansky went on a desperate search for his meal ticket. It was a search that took him to places he otherwise never would have gone and possibly never would have heard of.

That night Lumiansky visited the cabarets, taverns and jazz clubs where he thought he might be able to find Brown. The skinny boxer was nowhere to be found. With each place Lumiansky visited, with each failed sighting, the manager grew more and more frustrated and desperate. Desperate enough that his search saw him take matters into his own hands and head to the places Hungarian photojournalist Brassai dubbed "The Secret Paris."

BLACK INK

Lumiansky found himself in places where lawyers and government officials mingled with artists, plumbers, university students and criminals and engaged in activities everyone understood were not to be mentioned the day after. Each place he went disgusted and appalled him more than the previous ones.

There were the fetish rooms where young men dressed as sailors and pleasured distinguished gentleman who Lumiansky himself might have kept company with and considered respectable businessmen under different circumstances. He walked into places where women dressed as men and men dressed as something in between. He spent the entire night searching for Brown.

Lumiansky visited clubs where men sat close to each other and, sometimes, on each other. When Lumiansky asked the bartenders and patrons if Brown was seen, "no" was the answer he received, sometimes from men with lipstick-smeared lips.

The next day Lumiansky put out word that Brown may have been kidnapped. He enlisted the help of promoter/trainer Bobby Diamond and together they visited the office of French boxing federation president Rousseau.

Brown was reneging on his contract, they told him. Rousseau sent out a message warning Brown that if he failed to honor the contracted match, he would face suspension and possibly revocation of his license along with having to repay any financial losses incurred by all parties.

Word reached Gene Bullard, who Brown was staying with. Too much was at stake. Brown had to box.

On December 8th he battered François Machtens over ten rounds before a crowd that booed almost the entire night. Brown was accused of carrying his opponent and some fans requested refunds. Brown, still fatigued, asked incredulously, "I hit him hard for ten rounds. How considerate is that?"

Brown once again stated he was leaving Lumiansky. He stayed in Maisons-Laffitte and tended to his horses. His brothers, not wanting to witness what would happen first - Brown self-destructing by his own vices or, the destruction of Brown by a manager who wanted to wring out every penny possible - returned to Panama.

Brown cabled the NBA to ask when his contract with Lumiansky ended. The *Brooklyn Daily Eagle* reported "a matter may have come up between the two and Brown wants his freedom." Brown was under the impression their contract ended February 15th, 1933 according to the article. While awaiting word from the NBA, he stayed near his horses, horses he purchased at "prohibitive prices." The article mentioned that despite Brown's assertion that the contract was about to end, Lumiansky went ahead and booked 20 fights in 20 weeks in the United States.

Brown had little interest in returning to the United States and even less interest in dealing with Lumiansky. Before Lumiansky headed to America for the holidays, he set up a fight for February 9th in Paris to be promoted by Bobby Diamond.

Brown stated publicly that he had no intention of showing up for that match. Reporters in France telegrammed Lumiansky in New Bedford to tell him all about what Brown was saying. His response was published in the magazine *Boxeo*. He thanked them for their concern and for advising him of the statements made but he assured everyone that Brown will fight that night and that someone, and he had an idea who it was, must've been whispering half-truths in Brown's ear.

When Lumiansky returned, he once again threatened Brown with a lawsuit if he did not go ahead with the match. Brown stated he was ill, tired, and depressed over his mother's passing. His reply, according to Brown, was a question.

"You're still not over that?"

Brown insisted he was hurt and cited a fall from a horse that resulted in a bruised collar bone. Lumiansky called his bluff. "Report your imaginary illness to the commission," he was told. When Brown reported it, the manager relented.

"You win," he told the boxer. He offered Brown a compromise. Take the 9th off, but, fight for free the next time he stepped into a ring to recoup his and the promoter's losses.

Brown laughed off the suggestion and asked since when do champions fight for free. Lumiansky was ready with an answer. "You have, many times," he reminded him. And if he didn't fight that night, he would be doing so once again.

"Nonsense!" was Brown's reply.

"Then I expect you to be ready on the 9th."

Brown insisted he was injured. Lumiansky sent a doctor from the commission to examine him.

"You're fine," the doctor said after a quick check-up. He deemed him fit for battle. Then Lumiansky asked Criqui to make a plea on his behalf and convince Brown that it was in his best interest to go ahead with the match. Bobby Diamond visited Brown and, in tears, begged him to go through with the fight because, if he didn't, he would be ruined.

The fight was on.

On his way to the ring, Brown passed the doctor who examined him and told him, "You're no gentleman."

Brown defeated Henri Poutrain by decision. Exactly one week later, an article in *El Mundo Deportivo* stated "bad winds blowing throughout the house of Brown." Brown was in a state of depression severe enough that he might quit the game. The cause for the depression was the death of his mother and his inability to visit her.

It was a suicidal state according to those around him. It appeared to some that Brown believed death was close. The syphilis wasn't going away and he wished to be high when it killed him. His health didn't matter anymore.

His chemical regimen continued. Painkillers, mercury, drugs and liquor were consumed almost daily. His clothes were still sharp but his appearance was being neglected, at least by his standards. The weekly haircuts stopped and he wore his hair in a short, nappy 'fro most of the time. He smelled like the dense smoke of the opium pellets - something he always had one or two of in his pockets next to a smoking tube.

When the high wore off and the kinetic movements kicked in, Brown would find a private spot somewhere, anywhere, and take a pellet out and burn it with whatever he had available - a pipe, a candle – anything.

While he waited for the NBA to respond to his request regarding his contract, Brown was matched against London featherweight Johnny Peters. It was a rough fight with lots of clinching, holding and hitting. Brown proved superior that night, winning a decision after 15 rounds.

Around that time Brown received a letter from the California State Athletic Commission notifying him that he was no longer recognized as champion by them. Brown folded the letter and lit another pipe.

They tried stripping him again two weeks later. It happened during the fourth round of his title defense against Domenico Bernasconi in Milan. Brown had the advantage the first three rounds. But each time Bernasconi closed the distance on the dancing master, it became uncomfortable for the champion. Midway through the fourth, when Brown tried to sidestep his way around, Bernasconi grabbed him and held him still. Brown retaliated by wrestling and swinging Bernasconi to the side. The move drew the ire of the referee who admonished the champ and ordered both fighters to a neutral corner.

Nearly two minutes of confusion followed. The referee had disqualified Brown. The ringside officials thought it too drastic a call and consulted with each other. Even Primo Carnera, taking up two spots in the second row, thought it was a bad call.

When word reached one of Mussolini's officers on the other side of the ring, he sent an order to the referee. The fight resumed. Years later, that officer said his directive to the referee was a simple one : the government under Mussolini was not interested in winning in that fashion.

By the end of the fourth round, the fight turned into a slugfest. Round five saw a continuation of the brawl, with Bernasconi getting the edge despite suffering a cut on his brow. He came out aggressively for round six and landed a straight right to the jaw. For two seconds, the champion was the only one in the *Palazzo Dello Sport* who wasn't on his feet.

BLACK INK

The simultaneous cheers of everyone in attendance filled the arena for the remainder of the round, a rumbling roar that drowned out the sound of the bell that ended it.

Brown's title was in danger of being legitimately taken from him. In between rounds his handler refused to give him a swig of whiskey. He emptied the contents from the bottle onto the floor and made Brown drink water. You can't lose today, he was told. Like he had done many times in his career, the skinny *Campeon del Mundo* dug down deep and pulled out another victory.

Bernasconi could match Brown when it came to partying but was no match for a motivated champion in the ring. For the next five rounds, Brown turned Bernasconi's face into a swollen, bloodied pulp. Alternating heavy one-twos with an occasional dragging of the laces across the Italian's reddened mug, Brown built up a big lead heading into the final round.

When the bell rang for the final round, Brown decided to stand in front of the tired challenger and traded toe-to-toe to the crowd's delight until the final bell rang. The decision for Brown was met with respectful applause and a standing ovation.

Lumiansky had grown accustomed to being the manager of a boxing champion and the life it afforded. Brown's run would end soon he estimated. He scheduled a series of fights in England with which the fighter once again reluctantly went along. When Lumiansky found out that Brown cabled the New York Athletic Commission asking for the expiration date of his contract with his manager, he hatched a plan.

Brown didn't know exactly when Eddie McMahon and Lumiansky made their transaction. He guessed it was sometime during the spring of 1928. Never certain of the expiration date and not wanting to risk breaching the contract when the end was so close, he prepared for what he felt would be the final run under the management of a man he'd grown to despise.

Lumiansky tried scheduling a fight per week throughout the United Kingdom against fighters of any weight. He briefly pushed once again for a match against Jackie Berg but found no takers.

"Let him get by Dom Volante first," British promoter Ted Broadribb commented.

After three fights in three weeks Brown fell ill again. They returned to France to recover. He spent those days and nights trembling with fever under a light blanket or soaking in an Epsom salt bath. As soon as his temperature dropped to normal Lumiansky had him return to England for more action.

Brown still hadn't heard from New York. Depressed, he allegedly showed up for the fight drunk. He managed to ward off a spirited challenge by Dave Crowley, who would shortly afterwards win British titles in the featherweight and lightweight divisions and would eventually challenge Mike Belloise for the NYSAC featherweight title.

Lumiansky immediately set up a defense of the bantamweight crown against Johnny King. It was set for July 3rd at the Kings Hall in the Belle Vue Zoological Gardens in Manchester.

King, a native of Manchester, held a variety of British and Commonwealth titles. A member of the famed Collyhurst three, a stable which included champions Jackie Brown and Jock McAvoy, King was a dangerous striker. When he stepped through the ropes to challenge Al Brown, King was among the top 10 all-time knockout leaders.

Brown wasn't feeling much better as the fight drew near. He dealt with frequent headaches, blurred vision, and pain in his joints. He thought of canceling the fight.

A few days before the fight, Lumiansky found out the referee assigned was Frenchman Rene Schemann. Believing him to be anti-Brown, Lumiansky petitioned the commission to have the ref changed. Schemann was replaced by veteran referee Jack Dare, a move that satisfied Brown. Lumiansky further assuaged his fighter's anxiety in the dressing room just before the fight. He wanted to make sure Brown fought that night.

In the dressing room the day of the fight, Lumiansky cleared the room of everyone except himself and Brown, who was laid out on the massage table facing the cracked ceiling.

"I spoke with King's handlers," he told Brown. "King is throwing the fight."

The rematch, however, would be a legit contest Brown was told. But on the night of July 3rd, 1933, Brown had nothing to worry about.

"You can drop your guard and entertain the fans. Relax."

When the bell rang for the first round, Brown, loose and relaxed, danced towards his opponent with both hands low. King, whose knockout tally reached 74 when he hung up his gloves, launched a right hand aimed at Brown's jaw.

Ten years younger than Brown at 21, Johnny King was a pro before he needed to shave. As a 14-year-old, he graduated from the booths and began mixing it up with other teens and grown men. Decked out in an F.A. Downes robe, he wore his hair, full and dark, parted not quite in the middle and not quite on the side. His nose, bashed flat since before puberty and pointing down and slightly to the right, smelled a victory.

The right landed flush and Brown wobbled back and almost down. Held up by the ropes, the champion seemed confused about where he was. King rushed in a bit too eagerly and missed with his follow-up. The fighters tangled themselves into a clinch and when they were separated, Brown's head was clear. And he was livid.

At one point in the round he peered over the top rope and scolded Lumiansky.

Brown somehow made it through the round. He was forced to tap into that same reservoir he reached into when he fought Pladner and when he was homeless on the streets of Harlem.

In his corner was Bobby Diamond. He doused Brown's face with a sponge then stuck a water bottle under his nose and told him to take a sip.

"You drink it first," Brown replied.

Bobby didn't.

Neither did Brown.

Across the ring, King couldn't wait to come out for the second round. He rushed across the ring and threw punches without aiming.

Brown unleashed a right hand that turned King sideways and made him pirouette to the canvas for an eight count.

It was the champion's go-to punch. He often told people he fought strictly for the money. His left he called his cash flow, his fragile right, which he saved for desperate times, he called his gold reserve and his guarantee.

Again in the same round, his guarantee made King tumble hard into the ropes where he bounced off and dropped to the canvas.

Each time King went down, he would rise, shake the cobwebs that formed between his ears, and resume his attacks. Brown's sudden and nimble movement had King tripping over his own feet and missing badly. As wild as his swings looked, they were all close calls and Brown considered himself fortunate to have evaded them all.

"Just one more and I might not have survived to talk about it," he said afterwards.

When the final bell rang Brown congratulated King on a good fight and walked with him to King's corner. From there he headed over to a neutral corner while the decision was announced. He refused to return to his own corner after the fight ended and none of his handlers rushed into the ring to celebrate the victory with him.

Brown wasn't in the mood to deal with any of his handlers when they reached the dressing room. Speaking out loud, he spoke of retiring and fired everyone in his camp. His trainer, Bobby Diamond, professed his innocence. Through it all Lumiansky sat unperturbed and without saying a word.

Brown showered quickly, haphazardly threw his belongings into his bag and left with the gang of groupies that waited for him. As he did, his manager reportedly mumbled aloud, "Can't anyone beat this sissy?"[1]

---

[1] This alleged comment was made sometime after the King fight., not necessarily at that precise moment.

Betrayal

Lumiansky had been sure that King would be the one to end Brown's reign. He believed it so much he took over as King's manager just before the fight. Brown was past his prime and Lumiansky had no desire to give up the lifestyle managing a champion afforded.

By the time they returned to France the rejected referee, Rene Schemann, had sent an angry letter to IBU president Paul Rousseau complaining of his mistreatment in Manchester by the Brown camp. He reiterated to Rousseau that it was he himself who recommended Schemann as referee.

Feeling his authority may have been undermined, Rousseau suspended Brown until the following July, one year in total, and Lumiansky until March, a six-month suspension. That ruling was criticized and deemed "curious" by many in the press and Brown commented on the unfairness of the decision.

"They never asked me for my side of the story," he told the media.

Schemann told members of the press that when he confronted Brown, the champion told him that he could not accept him as referee due to Schemann's close relationship with Dickson. It would cause suspicions and the appearance of favoritism. This left Schemann confused because, as he stated in his letter, it wasn't the case. He left Manchester "vexed" and surprised by the actions of the British Board of Control and their enabling of Brown's behavior. Behavior, he reminded, that Brown had exhibited before.

Lumiansky, in an effort to both regain Brown's favor and justify his rejection of Schemann as referee, released a statement formally accusing Schemann of being a professional masquerading as an amateur and claimed that he received money for officiating. The French Federation erred in sending a professional to officiate the Brown-King match, Lumiansky claimed, and as a result, they should nullify any and all suspensions.

Officials were classified as professionals or amateurs. Amateurs, the only ones allowed to officiate professional title bouts, were not supposed to accept more money than what they would reasonably expect to spend on travel and board. Lumiansky submitted to the commission a report supporting his claims that Schemann profited above the levels an amateur would have.

Schemann rebutted Lumiansky's claims and added that he received a letter from Brown himself, addressed from North Africa, in which Brown stated that he regretted what occurred and considered Schemann to be a perfectly honest official.

According to some, Brown felt Schemann had something against him. Even if he didn't, there was enough controversy in his handling of fights to justify Brown's camp rejecting him as an official - which, incidentally, was their right.

The referee's career spanned over twenty years and included a fair share of questionable calls. When Frankie Genaro defended his NBA and IBU titles against Victor Ferrand of Spain at the *Plaza de Toros* in Barcelona, he declared the fight a draw despite his card having Ferrand winning. The reason, he cited, was the rule stating a title challenger could only become champion by decision if he won by five or more points.

When Hogan Kid Bassey was floored by Serraphin Ferrer in the first round of their Paris match, the Ferrer camp argued that Bassey benefitted from a slow count by Schemann. Bassey, who was down longer than ten seconds according to the protests, went on to win the fight.

The suspension stood.

When Brown boarded a ferry for Algiers in Marseilles, he was under the impression his contract with Lumiansky had already expired. While he thought he was finally free from the control of a suffocating manager, he still was banned from boxing throughout Europe because of the suspension.

In Algiers he found peace of mind. The climate and the way of life suited him. Boarding with other fighters including Roger Simende, Rene DeVos, Maurice Holtzer and Jimmy Tarante, he rested, eased off the opium, and trained himself back into formidable condition. Brown was under the temporary guidance of Lew Burston. Low on cash but feeling healthier, he was anxious to resume fighting. Much of what he had was spent along the clothing shops of the Casbah and the narrow, stucco-wrapped streets that led to the Citadel. No matter how much he bought, there was always something else he wanted.

Burston had his contacts in the media put a negative spin on the suspension. With every story published, the suspension looked more and more like a personal vendetta against Brown. Images of Schemann as a sharply-dressed high roller who professionally laundered his clothes twice per week and dined at the finest establishments in Europe hinted at a lifestyle too rich for an amateur referee who worked in the shoe business during the day.

Burston also threatened to form his own organization to compete with the IBU. Only when they found out that backing Burston was some serious Algerian money with political connections throughout North Africa and the Mediterranean did the IBU relent. The IBU did not have the resources or the desire to find out if Burston and his deep-pocketed backers were bluffing. Brown's suspension was rescinded to 60 days, which was time served by then.

Burston did all of that despite thinking Brown was still under contract to Lumiansky. When Lumiansky heard Brown was headed to Africa, he contacted Burston and informed him he had an extension signed by Brown that gave him full managerial rights for the rest of his career. In spite of that, Lumiansky was willing to lease Brown to Burston while he took a brief sabbatical in America. Brown did not appear to be aware of this arrangement.

Burston, a former theatrical agent and promoter for Ringling Bros. and Barnum & Bailey Circus, was a highly regarded boxing agent and manager who promoted boxing shows across Morocco and Algeria. He scheduled a trio of fights for Brown to round out the year.

Brown, refreshed from the break, was eager for a new start and to repay a debt to Dickson. Slowly, he became aware that Lumiansky had been pocketing more than double the amount he was supposed to. Almost 75 percent and Lumiansky billed all expenses - including stationery costs and all phone calls - out of Brown's share. For the past few years, Brown had been borrowing from someone who was loaning him what was his own money.

Furthermore, not a single cent was ever sent to any financial advisor in Panama who was supposed to be handling his affairs. While Brown partied in a perpetual drunken and drugged stupor, unknown amounts of his money were being deposited into bank accounts other than his own.

Burston took only a third and paid expenses out of his share. In just three fights in North Africa, Brown was able to pay off his debt to Dickson. Brown was content during those days. The climate agreed with his knees and his favorite champagne, *Mumm Cordon*, cost less than it did in Paris and the open air souks reminded him of the market in Panama.

A few days before the Georges Leperson fight in Algiers he woke up with a stabbing pain in his head and his jaw didn't close properly. A dental implant was infected. His teeth, which had recently begun to drop like flies in the Panamanian heat, were replaced by false teeth. Some were gold, and the one he had done in Algeria while under suspension cut into his gums, turned them from pink to purple, and filled his mouth with blood.

Brown was in no condition to box. He wasn't in a position to turn down a payday either. He was willing to fight despite his mouth being a tender, infected mess. It was probably for the better that he was willing since not once did anyone consider canceling the fight.

Georges Leperson was nowhere in the same category as Brown skill-wise. On September 30th, 1933, a sold-out crowd at the *Stade Communal de Saint Eugéne* witnessed a psychological beat down as Brown, in near agony, followed the instructions of handler Gilbert Benaim to "look mad." He posed menacingly in front of Leperson, a scowl masking his pain, and scared the crap out of his outclassed rival. Shuffling forward, right hand locked and loaded behind a feint-ing left, Brown postured and bluffed his way through ten rounds against a rival who was too afraid to take chances.

That Brown didn't throw many punches suited Leperson just fine as he moved around the ring, hands held high, and was elated just to hear the bell ring ten times. Brown too was glad to hear the final bell clang, being in no condition to get into a real fight. For the crowd and the referee, who repeatedly admonished both fighters to fight, they too were glad the final bell sounded because, by all accounts, there was no fight.

As soon as Brown collected his pay but before he could put it in his pocket, the entourage from Paris, along with one from Algiers, showed up and helped the champ spend it. They spent the night rocking the Casbah while Brown drank nonstop despite heavy doses of painkiller already in his system.

Fighting his own suspension was manager Dave Lumiansky. Since Brown had his suspension lifted, so should his he reasoned. The commission in the UK agreed though he remained suspended in France and by the IBU. While Brown was staying in Africa, the old manager was cutting deals in England. British newspapers reported Brown a no-show for a match against Tom Watson.

On December 22nd, *El Mundo Deportivo* reported that while Lumiansky was booking fights on Brown's behalf, the champ was campaigning in Algeria and no longer had any ties to his former manager. His advisor, Benaim, told the press Brown didn't show up because he, Benaim, was busy booking fights for him in Algeria. Benaim and Lumiansky traded dicey barbs through the press and had reporters wondering if the two would come to blows if ever in the same room. A few days later, the same was wondered about Brown and Lumiansky.

For the next few weeks, the hottest match in France appeared to be one between Al Brown and Dave Lumiansky. Lumiansky insisted he was Brown's manager and Brown would do as he said. Brown declared the only way Lumiansky would be a part of any of his fights was if Lumiansky himself were standing in the opposite corner. Brown publicly challenged his former manager to a boxing match and agreed to have his share go to charity because, he said, putting a hurting on "that man" he'd do for free.

Jeff Dickson, with a smile, expressed a willingness to stage the fight. The question Lumiansky was most asked during this period was when *he* and Brown were settling their dispute *mano a mano*. The manager waved off the talk as drivel and reminded the media that he was a man of business and not a boxer. To that, a new challenge - albeit one with a shorter shelf life - presented itself.

"Then box me," offered Benaim through the newspapers. "If not, then shut up and disappear forever."

On January 25th, 1934, two French papers reported that all was done and the saga called, "L'affaire" between Lumiansky and Brown had come to an end.

"From now on I will be handling my own affairs," Brown announced. "Lumiansky is no longer my manager for two reasons: he is disqualified as a manager by the French Federation and, because our contract expired on October 3rd, 1933. It was a five-year contract and damn any intentions I may have of renewing it."

"Any contracts for fights must be signed by me. However, my friend Gilbert Benaim will handle my affairs. He will work out any details with promoters and when a deal is hammered out, I will give my stamp of approval."

The announcement was premature. Brown didn't know it at the time but Lumiansky was in possession of an "extension" that Brown signed. With his own suspension about to end, Lumiansky was ready to resume his place as Brown's manager. He assured Dickson that everything was in order and that his legal teams in both America and Europe were reviewing documents which confirmed his managerial rights were extended.

With that assurance, he signed a contract with Dickson for a rematch against Gustave Humery. Lumiansky contacted Brown via telegram and advised him he was to report to Paris for the Humery fight followed by a return to the United States for a series of matches he had planned.

Brown laughed it off believing the contract between them was history. When Lumiansky insisted, Brown explained Burston was promoting him and, even if he wanted to, he didn't have the money to get to Paris.

Lumiansky hurried down the *Champs D'Élysées* to a bank, a lot more vibe in his steps than normal, and wired to Algeria enough money for Brown to get a few meals and pay for the ferry that crossed the Mediterranean Sea and the train that would have brought him to Paris.

Brown took the money and made it as far as the nearest pub.

"A round of drinks for everyone," he ordered the barkeep. "On Dave," he and his hangers-on laughed.

Back in Paris, Lumiansky fumed. The Brown-Humery fight was scrapped and a Humery-Johnny Cuthbert match, which didn't sell anywhere near as many seats, topped the bill instead. Feeling humiliated, Lumiansky headed to Algeria, vengeful thoughts sparring in his mind.

Not at all interested in the goods sold in the winding street markets or any of the local attractions, Lumiansky made a bee line straight to Brown's hotel as soon as the ferry docked.

Brown was surprised to see him. "You can't hide from me," he told Brown. "And you can't fight without me." In the hotel lobby Lumiansky explained to the fighter that he was not his former manager but his current manager and that he would remain so for the five years that followed.

"You signed," he said, showing Brown an unfamiliar document bearing his signature. Return to Paris or never box again were the options he gave Brown.

When Brown hinted that not fighting wasn't such a bad idea, Lumiansky reminded him of the riches the sport afforded, riches Brown needed to keep his horses fed and running, and the opium and champagne flowing through his veins. The fighter didn't budge. I've had enough of that for a lifetime, was his reply.

Lumiansky asked Brown what he needed.

They negotiated a deal where Brown would receive an undisclosed, but significant, amount up front. Without hesitating, Lumiansky made out a check payable to Alfonso Brown in an amount that wasn't a loan and was considerable enough to make Brown pack his bags for France that instant.

Not much was said to each other during the trip back to Paris. Brown clutched his check and Lumiansky checked his smile.

A title defense against Victor "Young" Perez was quickly arranged for February 19th, 1934. As that date closed in, the match was in jeopardy. While Perez trained diligently at Eugene Bullard's gym amid the flags of 21 nations, Brown was again missing. He resurfaced one day in the office of Dickson with the news that he wanted to go ahead with the fight but not with Lumiansky. He told Dickson the check he received from Lumiansky bounced and that there was an extension with his signature though he did not recall signing it.

Things were about to come crashing down quickly on David Lumiansky. The French federation called a meeting and after hearing both sides, determined that the extension Brown signed was not valid since it was signed while both parties were under suspension. Since Lumiansky was not operating under a valid managerial license he had no business signing contracts and therefore the extension was nullified.

Lumiansky clawed away relentlessly and stated that Brown's suspension was reduced and so should his have been. But the federation stood by their decision even amid the threats of legal action.

Recognizing imminent defeat, Lumiansky requested he be able to name a replacement manager, since his contract was transferable but only by himself. He named Louis Lerna as the replacement.

The French federation repeated their stance. The extension was signed while Lumiansky was suspended and in no position to act as manager in any capacity. He was not authorized to enter into contract with anyone during that time.

As for the rubber check, the bank reported it to the proper authorities. Lumiansky was sentenced to 60 days by the *Tribunal d'instance de Paris 12eme*.

BLACK INK

Brown's good fortune continued at the racetrack. One of his horses - Stanley Falls - won a race and earned for Brown a considerable amount at the betting parlor. Brown estimated that two or three wins per year could bring in over a million francs. With his winnings, he purchased a few more thoroughbreds.

Brown's morning runs had turned into speed walks because of the arthritis. In his gym bag was an assortment of elastic bandages he used to brace his joints. With a training camp that consisted mostly of shadowboxing and painkillers, he stepped into the ring to face Victor "Young" Perez.

Some sources say his last name was Younki. He grew up in the La Hara section of Tunis. Inspired by Battling Siki, he started boxing at the Maccabi Sports club at 14 with his older brother, Benjamin Kid Perez. Two years later he was off to Paris where he found work as a shoe salesman and hooked up with manager Leon Belliers at the Alhambra gym.

A flyweight world champion after knocking out Frankie Genaro in just two rounds, he returned to Tunis where a crowd of 10,000 greeted him at the pier and along the Avenue Jules Ferry, tens of thousands more waited to salute him. He was awarded the Order of Glory by the Bey of Tunis, Ahmad ll ibn Ali.

Perez married model-turned-actress Mireille Balin and paid for the installation of showers in his old school. After moving up to bantamweight, he lost to Baltasar Sangchili, split a pair with Vittorio Tamagnini, and turned back the challenges of Emile Pladner, Eugene Huat, and Kid Francis.

Eight inches shorter and with a comparable disadvantage in reach Perez had a hard time getting to Brown during their match. Brown used his unique footwork to keep Perez guessing and swinging at a target that used to be there. Brown tired in the second half of the fight but Perez could not overcome the differences in size and speed of foot.

The decision went to Brown after 15 rounds. The crowd voiced their displeasure to the point where some feared a riot was about to break out. Among those who didn't boo the decision was Lumiansky. Immediately after the fight he contacted reporters and told them that he watched the result with great pleasure and interest because he will soon be a part of the Al Brown camp.

"Very soon I will be the manager of the bantamweight champion of the world," he proclaimed. "The contract is in the hands of my attorneys and they are guaranteeing me victory because the contract is extended throughout all jurisdictions and the judges will have no choice but to rule in my favor."

Speaking once more as manager of Brown, Lumiansky advised the press that Brown would soon be campaigning strictly against featherweights and that he intended to secure a challenge for the featherweight championship against American Freddie Miller. An occasional report with similar claims surfaced every few weeks. And in America, Lumiansky continued to accept matches for Brown. But the reports were wrong. Lumiansky was no longer a part of Brown's team.

On March 27th, 1934 the NYSAC suspended Brown because a few days earlier the Mexican Commission had suspended him for not fighting Rodolpho Casanova in Mexico City. Almost immediately, the NBA stripped him of his title. The news meant little to Brown. He was still considered by logical minds to be the real king of the bantams. That was a distinction no organization could strip him of.

Eight days after an April 7th victory over Maurice Dubois in Switzerland, Brown defended his throne against Kid Francis. Jeff Dickson was the promoter and on the undercard, forty-year-old light heavyweight champion Georges Carpentier boxed an exhibition. Looking "paler than before," according to ringside reporter M. Vilaregut, Carpentier started out by shadowboxing for one round then boxed the two-round exhibition against middleweight champion of Oran, Maurice Fumo. The performance left Vilaregut with the impression that Carpentier, even at that age, could come back and give even Marcel Thil a hard night's work.

In the main event, Brown used his clever footwork to evade the motivated rushes of Francis. Keeping the jab in his face and an uppercut on his chin whenever Francis got under the jab, Brown controlled the early rounds.

BLACK INK

The second half of the fight saw Brown's output slowed enough for Francis's occasional volleys to the body to make some of the middle rounds close. It was a fast-paced match that ended with appreciative applause from the crowd followed by another round of clapping when Brown was announced the winner.

Years later, on January 23rd, 1943, a retired Francis was having brunch in a café a block away from the sea. German police descended on the area and took into custody Jews, gypsies, and Nazi dissenters. Francis, as he had done in the ring, did not run and was captured in the sweep. He was taken to Sachenhausen on April 28th, 1943, tattooed and registered under number 64769, and spent the rest of his life fighting twice per week against other prisoners in concentration camp bouts arranged by the guards.

On February 4th, 1945, he was transferred to Buchenwald then, two weeks later, to a camp in Langenstein. On April 16th, 1945, following, or somewhere along, a death march to Trossin, Kid Francis was killed by Nazi soldiers.

Following the fight with Francis, Brown saw a proposed May 16th, 1934 championship defense against Seaman Tom Watson scrapped by the BBC, who recognized and upheld the NBA suspension.

He then accepted an over-the-weight match against old nemesis Gustave Humery slated for May 17th, 1934. By then a full-fledged lightweight with a heavyweight face, Humery had become obsessed with vengeance. He wanted to do to Brown what Brown had done to him.

From the very first round, Humery imposed his 10-pound weight advantage and pushed the bantamweight into the ropes. Brown struggled to keep Humery at a distance. By the second round, reporters wrote, it was clear that Brown could not hold off the charging tiger. Clinch after clinch followed, each warning by the referee a bit sterner than the previous one.

Humery did plenty of damage in those clinches. They traded head butts, elbows, and both punched below the belt. Humery, called "El Poullain de Carpentier," continued the roughhousing in the third, a round reporters stated looked like Brown was seeking a disqualification loss. Despite repeated warnings from the ref, Brown continued to hold whenever the inside action got rough. Spanish papers reported seeing spectators leaving their seats and approaching the ring.

"He's drunk!" They called out.

Spanish reporters wrote that Brown did indeed look drunk. Between rounds he sipped from a champagne bottle wrapped in a white towel and seemed to stare at nothing in particular. No instructions were given to the fighter, just a pat with the towel on his hunched shoulders.

By round four many in the crowd had converged near Brown's corner and hovered ominously. As the seconds ticked, insults turned into threats. Humery landed a few body blows in the fifth round that appeared to shake up the battered champ. There was little doubt Humery was going to win. The crowd craved a knockout. They wanted to see Brown hurt badly. Brown was operating on instinct by that point, no longer trying to win. Instead he walked towards Humery, covering his face like a man at a windy beach, and held every chance he got.

A pissed-off Humery tried in vain to wrestle out of Brown's exaggerated clinch. Part of the crowd went from hostile to riotous. Fed up with the antics of the drunken champ and looking to quell the heated attitude of the crowd, the referee disqualified Brown for "stalling."

"Kill him!" shouted someone in the crowd.

When Brown and his corner climbed down the ring steps, an angry mob blocked the path to his dressing room. Brown and his corner men did an about-face. Before they could circle the ring and take the long way back to safety, about two dozen nasty-faced men formed another an angry roadblock.

One of his handlers shouted to clear the path. The mob shouted back. They tried to squeeze their way through the barrage of insults and spitting. The angry faces got closer. The few guards present were overwhelmed. Hands began pulling at a quickly sobering Brown's robe. Insults turned into shoves.

A brawl ensued.

BLACK INK

A French reporter wrote that Brown was the cause. That the mob, though boisterous and obscene, did not make contact with the champ until Brown lashed out with a punch at one of them for, he wrote, "repeatedly but lightly tapping a rolled-up program on the top of Brown's head."

Fans started to shout that Brown had attacked them. From the rear, bottles were hurled at the champion. Seats were ripped from the ground and thrown towards the soon-to-be-destroyed ring. Completely surrounded by dozens of attackers, Brown and his handlers were trapped. Within seconds, fists bounced off Brown's head and shoes thudded against his legs and groin. His robe was torn completely off and one fan used a cane to strike Brown over the head. Semi-conscious, blood gushed from his nose and mouth and turned his black chest red.

Random unnamed fists, shoes, and spit continued to rain down upon his face and head until reinforcements arrived twenty minutes later in time to prevent a possible murder.

The following day, newspapers reported he was recovering from cuts, bruises, a dislocated clavicle, and a concussion. Max Schmeling's manager, Joe Jacobs, swallowed his cigar and burned his throat during the melee. About the only other time anyone saw Jacobs without a cigar dangling from his mouth was in 1935 when Schmeling fought Steve Hamas. After the win, the crowd of 25,000 stood in unison and gave the Nazi salute. Those in the ring returned the salute, including Jacobs, a Jew. Not wanting to be the only one in the arena not saluting, he raised his hand aloft, lit cigar to the sky. Jacobs was criticized by both the Nazis and the Jews afterwards.

After the dust settled, the French federation suspended Brown until September 1st because of his disqualification. But, since it was finalized prior to the suspension, Brown took his damaged body to Switzerland for a June 30th match against Johnny Edwards.

Suffering from headaches and an occasional flashback of the violent night, Brown walked down the aisle nervously. It wasn't his opponent he was worried about. Johnny Edwards of France, an opponent with 13 wins in 25 bouts, was considered a safe match for the still-healing Brown. On the way to the ring, his eyes scanned the crowd for unruly fans.

For the first few rounds, Brown stayed away and built an early lead. The middle rounds each felt like a marathon to the champ. By the seventh round he had nothing left.

Edwards took the eight round. Brown didn't have the strength to clinch. Instead, he took a pounding in the ninth round. Edwards dropped Brown towards the end of the ninth. The shocked crowd rose to their feet. Brown, never before stopped inside the distance, pushed himself off the ground and withstood the follow-up barrage. Edwards swept the last three rounds to win a close but clear-cut decision.

I know why you lost his trainer told him in the dressing room after the fight.

"Because you didn't bless yourself."

"Yes, it is true, I didn't bless myself, but do you think I needed God's help to beat him?"

While Brown healed during his suspension, the world got worse. The Japanese enslaved and tested chemical weapons on the Chinese in occupied Manchuria, and after the death of German President Hindenburg, Hitler was Fuehrer of Germany.

Though the world was changing, Brown wasn't. He was welded to his vices.

The boxing world was changing too. The NBA moved forward with their plans to crown Baby Casanova bantamweight champion. A teenage knockout artist born in Guanajuato and raised in the *La Lagunilla* section of Mexico City, "Chango" was dubbed the "Uncrowned Champion" by fans and media. Sixto Escobar had different ideas.

Sixto hailed from Puerto Rico, the city of *Barceloneta* - little Barcelona - specifically, also known as the city of pineapples and located just to the left of Manati on a map. At age three, Sixto and his family left for the *Tras Talleres* sector of Santurce. Getting his start in boxing while it was still illegal, Sixto trained as a child in a secret gym in the backyard of Angel Soto, a former boxer from New York. Called

"The Bantam" or *"El Gallo,"* he was one of the few fighters in his division.

When Sixto turned eight, Governor Horace Mann Tower legalized boxing in the sovereignty. Sixto, whose idea of arithmetic was throwing six-punch combinations, left school during eighth grade and trained at the Victory Gardens Gym on *Avenida Ponce De Leon* under Ignacio Penagaricano. He turned pro around the same time Brown was tenderizing the face of Gregorio Vidal, and stepped up his game the following year when Filipino contender, Lope Tenorio made his way to Puerto Rico.

Headlining against local attractions like Pete Martin, Attilio Sabatino, and Cuban star Relampago Saguero, Tenorio took Sixto under his wing and sparred countless numbers of rounds with the future champion.

Competition and popularity being scarce in Puerto Rico, Sixto headed for Venezuela with other boxers including lightweight Pedro Montanez. Squaring off against featherweights and lightweights, Sixto had mixed results. But what didn't show up in his record was the improvement he made despite several losses. Sixto was not just good, he was damn good. New York good. Brought to the Mecca of Boxing by Tony Rojas, Sixto fell under the guidance of Lou Brix and was trained by Whitey Bimstein.

Promoter/matchmaker Armand Vincent contracted Rodolfo Casanova, who was coming off a loss to Freddie Miller, to meet Sixto for the NBA championship on June 26, 1934. But Vincent was a Montreal-based promoter and the NBA wanted the match held south of the Great Lakes. When they didn't get their wish, the NBA refused to recognize the fight leaving only the Montreal Athletic Commission to designate it a world championship fight.

Casanova was the favorite. With a melodic name that evoked memories of Rudolph Valentino and Casanova, coupled with a hard-hitting style, writers could not resist using the name in their articles. They tracked his morning runs through *La Fontaine* park and gathered at his workout sessions at the gym on *Mont-Royal*.

Sixto, pronounced *seeks-toe*, was often called "Skeeto" and his last name meant broom. Almost no reporters came to his workouts. While Casanova dropped sparring partner after sparring partner, Sixto worked on defense and counterpunching.

Close to eight thousand paid to see the match dubbed the "Battle of the Little Brown Guys," by writer Al Parsley. They saw Sixto nearly sweep the canvas with Casanova.

Flashing Joe Louis-type power in his right hand, Sixto cut, confused, and floored Casanova and by the fourth round had his rival attempt fighting out of the southpaw stance. A right-left-right combination put Casanova out for the count in the ninth round.

Sixto Escobar followed up that win with a 15-round decision over Eugene Huat also in Montreal.

On the other side of the Atlantic, while he nursed the wounds from his mob beating - a beating which today would be considered by many a hate crime - Brown received an offer to fight Sixto in Montreal.

Armand Vincent cabled Brown an offer of $7,500 plus 35 percent of the gate. Vincent advised the press Brown unequivocally turned it down.

"I'll never fight in Montreal again," was Brown's retort. Unfair treatment during his fight with Sanstol was the reason cited by the champ.

Vincent then made an offer to Young Perez, who was in Oslo for a match with Pete Sanstol. Perez turned down Vincent's offer, preferring to take his chances in a rematch against the aged Brown, who he felt was ready to be toppled.

Sixto was then struck by an automobile and needed several weeks for his knee and ankle to heal. He returned to Puerto Rico to recuperate and was greeted by hundreds in the streets. The Mayor closed the schools, organized a parade, and singers and poets wrote about the champion - the first ever from Puerto Rico.

Brown and Perez fought their rematch on the first of November in Tunis. Perez had given no indication of being able to defeat Brown during their first go. The rematch was no different. In an outdoor location with no seats, the fans - on their feet throughout - applauded as Perez bobbed and weaved while Brown danced, side-stepped and circled behind a steady jab.

Perez, no quit in him, moved forward ready to capitalize on any mistakes or openings. In the tenth round a left hook to the liver, some say low, landed and Perez, unable to continue, was counted out.

Perez complained vehemently that the blow was low.

When Brown went over to check on Perez after the fight, Perez struck him. "Hey, the fight is over," he told Perez.

Hundreds waited for Brown outside the Hotel Majestic. Wherever he appeared, pedestrian and vehicular traffic jams followed. He received dozens of invitations to appear at cabarets and dance clubs after the fight. He did his best to honor each request and spent the night dancing rhumba and banging out rhythms.

Victor Young Perez lost more than he won for the rest of his career including another loss to Brown in 1937. In 1938 he boxed in Berlin and proudly wore the Star of David on his trunks despite threats and boos. In 1943 he was detained by the French Militia and interned at the Drancy camp before being sent to Auschwitz sometime that fall. He worked the kitchen of the Buna factory and was forced by the camp guards to engage in battles where the winner got a meal and the loser was killed.

While captive, Perez often smuggled soup or bread from the kitchen to feed his fellow prisoners risking severe punishment. Early in 1945, one of only a few survivors left, he was killed. Some believe he was shot after he returned with food for his fellow detainees. French flyweight and Holocaust survivor Gabriel Burah wrote in his memoirs that Perez was emaciated, his back branded by the guards, when he attempted to escape. Too weak to resist, he laid on the snow-covered ground as the guards hovered over him. It was the last time anyone saw him.

Dickson wanted badly to stage a return-to-Paris match for Brown. Worried about his safety, he turned down several offers before accepting a Christmas Eve match against featherweight champion Freddie Miller.

Brown was once again behind on bills. Georges Mitchel no longer cared for Brown's horses reputedly over lack of payment. Mitchel, who also assisted during many of the gym sessions and some of the fights, was no longer seen in any of Brown's training camps. Bobby Diamond, still pleading his innocence every chance he got, became Brown's chief corner man.

On the undercard was Sixto's friend from Puerto Rico, Pedro Montanez. Managed by Burston, Pedro had left a trail of victims on both sides of the Atlantic and throughout the Caribbean.

Brown took him under his wing when he arrived in Paris, shared some pointers and showed him around a bit. Montanez was a much more serious fellow than Brown. Not averse to partying when the time was right, he nevertheless lived a life more appropriate for a boxer. He was as good as any champion of his day not named Henry Armstrong and fought liked a tucked-in Rocky Graziano.

Riding a streak of eight straight knockouts since touching down in Barcelona, Montanez sought another early night. Maurice Arnault had different plans in mind. Each time Pedro attacked, he covered up and then lashed out with sharp counters. Montanez kept up the pressure and dominated the fight but had to settle for his first win by decision since arriving in Europe.

In an upset Joseph Decico, also managed by Burston, scored an eight round decision over former champion Victor Young Perez. Some considered his performance the highlight of the night.

For Brown, the return to Paris was a disappointment. In a bout between two reigning champions where neither was risking his title, both agreed to come in over the featherweight limit.

Depending on which newspaper one read or which insider one listened to, Brown weighed 124.9, 127, or 129.5 pounds. One report described a scene where both fighters weighed in at literally the same time. The combined weight of the two bodies was then divided in half, both boxers being announced at the same exact weight.

BLACK INK

Another version had Brown in his street clothes, winter overcoat included. Inside each of the large angled pockets that adorned the front of the coat, a cement paving stone banged against his hips as he stepped onto the scale. That report had Brown at 124.9 with Miller, who weighed in butt naked according to that report, at 127.1 pounds.

When Brown slipped into his hot-cocoa-colored robe and jogged slowly down the aisle to the ring, he did so under a large chorus of catcalls and jeers. Despite the events that followed the Humery fight, extra security was scarce. Brown considered not coming out. A group of his friends that included one-time champion Maurice Holtzer and undercard fighters Montanez and Decico made a last-minute decision to accompany Brown during the ring walk.

The first round was a cautious one where each landed only a punch or two. The action picked up slightly in the next round as did the clinching. Miller blocked most of Brown's punches with his high guard while Brown used his still-nimble legs to dodge Miller's shots.

Brown landed the jab more in the third while Miller countered to the body. The clinching, where the opportunistic Miller scored with hooks to Brown's flanks and thighs, increased in the third round.

Unable to land cleanly, Miller focused his attacks on Brown's hips and kidney whenever they fell into a clinch. Brown retaliated with shots behind Miller's head.

The crowd grew restless as the rabbit punching increased from both parties. Garbage rained down on the ringsiders as fans protested the lack of action.

Sportswriter John Kiernan wrote that by round 8, the fans in the cheap seats went from hostile to vocal and looked ready to "descend on the arena for the purpose of burning down the joint." Instead, he wrote, they thought of a better idea on the way down and simply left much to the relief of the ringsiders.

Miller, the winner, received lukewarm applause. Brown was derided on his way back to the dressing room though, by then he was reportedly too drunk for it to have bothered him.

The February 9th,1935 *Afro American* ran a piece with the headline "Al Brown Capitalizes on Unpopularity in France." Al Brown was "not at all popular with the boxing crowds. But he makes money by that very fact. The crowds keep coming out in the hope of seeing someone beat him."

Brown's knuckles and knees hurt more that winter than any of the previous ones. His left knee buckled when he moved in the ring. Tightly-wound bandaging that extended from his calf up to his thigh supported his body during the few training sessions he had before his fights. About a week's training, which consisted of mostly shadow-boxing and sparring, became his routine.

Whenever a crowd gathered to watch him train, Brown was still capable of whipping the jump rope through the air. It was mostly all show by then.

After a two-month break, Brown climbed back into the ring for bouts against Henri Barras on March 2nd in Paris and again on March 9th with Gustavo Ansini. He out-boxed Barras over ten but could only muster a draw over the same distance against Ansini. By all accounts, Brown was simply collecting pay checks at that point in his career. While drinking and smoking away most of those earnings, he voiced his displeasure with the business of boxing. But, like the opium that flooded his limbic system with dopamine induced pleasures, the ring was an addiction he could not shake.

On March 18th he faced a fighter who possessed the same hunger that Brown did when he stowed away on that Peruvian liner a dozen years earlier. While Brown showed up for the money, Baltasar Sangchili fought for his future. After ten mostly one-sided rounds in Valencia, Brown watched as the other man's hand was raised in victory.

Two things made the loss bearable – liquor and his ability to convince himself that he lost only because he wasn't motivated. When properly prepared, he still believed, he was unbeatable at his weight. Before the sun rose the next morning, Brown had already shrugged off the loss. And spent most of the money. He remained in Spain and within a few weeks, a rematch with Sangchili was set. This time with the championship on the line.

BLACK INK

When the grainy black-and-white film of the Dempsey-Carpentier fight flickered in the theaters of Valencia, seated among the mostly male audience was nine-year-old Baltasar Belenguer Hervas. Despite knowing the outcome, when the lights dimmed and the film whirled through the projector and filled the crowded theater with the sounds of a typewriter, everyone sat on the edges of their seats.

It was Baltasar's first glimpse of a gloved fight. After the movie ended, a short documentary of the Dempsey fight followed. Baltasar fixed his big black eyes on the beating Dempsey administered to the Frenchman. He returned several times that summer to watch it all again. Each time he bobbed and weaved his way home, his little fists clenched tightly, and threw lefts and rights at an imaginary opponent.

Against his father's wishes, Baltasar and his friend, Zhang Chi Li took up boxing. They graduated from punching bags in Li's house to working out at one of the many gyms that opened everywhere from Bilbao where former champion Dixie Kid operated his - to Valencia. When they came to that breaking point that separates those who boxed a little from those who competed, Baltasar left behind his friend but took his name, his full name, as his own last name. Baltasar Belenguer Hervas became Baltasar Sangchili.

Fighting out of a crouch reminiscent of Jack Dempsey's, he was called *El Alano Espanol* - the Spanish Bulldog. It's a rare dog today, perhaps no longer completely pure, similar to the Presa Canario, a dog some call a pit bull on steroids. And Baltasar, at 5'1 and 118 pounds, was not much larger and could inflict almost as much damage as those bulldogs that guarded the villas throughout the Spanish countryside.

Soon all the locals became familiar with this new bulldog with the Chinese surname. Though they didn't all flock to his fights, Baltasar never became discouraged because he knew from the documentary that all champions, like Dempsey and Carpentier, passed through periods that made ordinary men cave in.

Baltasar never considered himself ordinary.

Not even when he started out his career with just six wins in his first 18 matches did he consider himself ordinary. A little to the left or a little to the right and those fights he might have won, he reasoned. Once his engine was fine-tuned, he slugged his way to victories over Carlos Flix, Young Perez and Brown. Spain, he promised, was about to have its first world boxing champion.

Once he arrived in Valencia for the rematch, Brown announced he was out for revenge. It wouldn't be easy, he said, and he knew Spaniards were anxious for their first world champion but, he "regrettably had to deny them."

The Spanish press initially disagreed. They backed Sangchili and not just for patriotic reasons. The first fight was not a fluke, they wrote. The only question they had going into the rematch was whether or not Baltasar would be the first to stop the Panamanian.

It wasn't just writers who were backing the Spaniard. Former contender Serafin Martinez Fort called Brown a top performer. Despite that, he felt Baltasar had a very good chance to become champion. Martinez Fort and many of the writers were aware of Brown's less-than-peak condition. Since his arrival Brown had been training at Martinez Fort's spacious gym in *La Plaza de San Agustin*. A friend of Brown's since 1930 when he made his own run through the lightweight ranks of New York, Martinez Fort acknowledged that Brown's time spent at the gym was trumped by his time spent inside the dark and narrow bars of *El Carme*.

But as the fight neared, some writers changed their tune. Despite his many vices, Brown's experience might again be too much for a challenger to overcome they wrote. His recent activity was a serious concern to some in the Sangchili camp.

Since his first meeting with Sangchili, Brown scored wins over the useful Luigi Quadrini in Madrid and looked to be in good form during a two-round blowout of Javier Torres in Barcelona. Torres, a featherweight, was coming off a seven-round loss to Freddie Miller and drew over ten with Kid Francis the previous November. Based on those performances, one reporter gave Brown a 90% chance of winning. Sangchili on the other hand was in the midst of what was then considered a layoff. His last match was the March 18th win over Brown.

BLACK INK

When the title was on the line, Brown had a way of winning despite his lack of proper preparation. There was something about show time that brought out in Brown the ability to get the job done. For him, dancing, drinking and breaking night was a successful pre-fight routine. Sangchili's camp knew that very well. While Baltasar did his part, training like a gladiator, someone on the promotion did what Jack Ortega did many years before in Panama.

A spy was planted in Brown's camp. It was someone who got close enough to the champion to have witnessed the training sessions and the after hour jaunts. The seed got close enough to note the foods Brown ate, check for any signs of injury, and even had an idea of the number of hours the champ slept.

With more access than usual, unfamiliar faces approached Brown daily. Some shook his hand with their right while their lefts felt his arms and shoulders or patted his belly to gauge his condition. Wherever he went, a group of unknowns stood close by and observed his actions and provided the perfect camouflage for a plant to blend into. Unlike Abe The Newsboy, Brown had no idea there was a plant in his camp.

When writer Georges Peeters checked into the Hotel Regine the week of the fight, Brown, who was staying on the same floor, greeted him with open arms and invited him to tag along for dinner. Brown excitedly added that it was a great time to be in Valencia. He would take him to the best cafes and afterwards, they would go to hear the best flamenco singers in all of Spain.

Valencia was packed that week. Travelers made their way down and across from Barcelona and Madrid on caravans of buses that slowed traffic to a snarl on the *autopistas* and *autovias* of Valencia. They came by the thousands to see and hear Manual Azaña.

It was the first major appearance of the former prime minister since he was freed from prison after being acquitted of charges that included instigating an uprising. Hotels were booked to capacity and all the restaurants along the *gran vias* and the *carrers* near the *Plaza De Toros* sold their specialty rice and seafood dishes well past normal operating hours.

Taking advantage of the thousands of extra visitors; performers, including the best singers and dancers from nearby areas, converged on the city that week. Hoping to persuade some of the throng that assembled for the Azaña speech to stick around a few hours more and travel the two miles to the west from Mestalla Stadium to the bullring, Jules Avernin had the city and buses wallpapered with fliers of the fight. As a sweetener, Valencia's most popular fighter of the day, light heavyweight Jose Martinez De Alfara, was booked for the undercard.

While promoters took advantage of the influx of people in town, Brown took advantage of the extended hours and performances in the local cafes.

Without unpacking or changing out of his travel-weary clothes, Peeters joined Brown for what he thought would be a short night. He reminded the fighter that it would be prudent to rest up before the fight.

"Don't worry about that. My handlers told me Baltasar is in no shape to go 15 rounds."

Brown and Peeters caught up over a glass of fine red wine and a small meal. His stomach satisfied and his eyes tired, Peeters eagerly grabbed his coat when Brown said "let's go."

But he didn't mean back to the hotel. Instead they went to a night spot where a flamenco dancer performed. Seated in the front and ignoring the occasional taunt about his championship days being numbered, Brown excitedly watched the performance, his applause interrupted only when he reached for a drink.

Towards the end of the performance, around the time a champion boxer in training for a defense should have been in the REM state of sleep, an invitation was extended to Brown to join the dancer on stage. Encouraged by the audience and the alcohol in his veins, Brown got up and improvised his way through the dance and when it was time for the *cantos*, showed off his fluency in Valencian, the language spoken throughout Catalonia before it was forbidden during the Franco regime.

BLACK INK

After the performance the dancer joined them at the table and sat close to Brown while more sparkling cava was ordered. By then trainer Bobby Diamond had joined them and instead of halting the night's festivities like most trainers would have, he instead kept ordering another round and personally made sure Brown's glass was always filled to the top. When the patrons got up to go and the barkeep stopped pouring drinks, Brown relented and agreed it was time to go. Brown did the champagne stumble through the hotel lobby, bumped into a few walls, and passed out as soon as his head touched his pillow.

Around that same time, Baltasar suited up for his run just ahead of the traffic and daily hustle and bustle, when he could fill his lungs with air while it was at its freshest. He followed that with a light breakfast of toast, tomato spread, cheese, sausage, and fruit. Speaking from his own gym in Torrent, where he did most of his training, Baltasar expressed great respect for Brown but felt his preparation would be the difference.

Brown, for his part, made it to the all-white gym before lunch, shadowboxed under the portraits of past boxers, lashed out at the heavy and maize bags with combinations, and spoke with reporters. One of them wrote that Brown, a boxer who didn't like to train, was, since his bout with Quadrini in Madrid, in good condition for the rematch.

"Paris was too cold," Brown told the reporter. "They made me lose confidence in myself over there. But here in Spain, I've gotten the rest I need and found the ideal climate I needed to train properly."

Though he didn't reply when asked if it were true that his right hand was injured, Brown reminded the writer that Torres, a fighter who troubled Freddie Miller before losing and who had a considerable weight advantage over him, was handled with ease.

"I prefer facing an eager fighter who comes to fight," he said.

When reporters and spectators were around, the old champion still knew how to entertain the crowd. Those sessions were filled with a lot of movement, shadowboxing, bag work, and some flashy rope skipping but very little intensity and no strategic preparation. Brown, it seemed to some, intended to wing it.

Boxing was a welcome reprieve for many. Since the 1931 revolution up to the 1933 elections, the political climate had gone from simmering to unrest to violent. Demonstrations, strikes, riots, and murders of Catholic priests dominated Spanish headlines. In the eyes of many, Manuel Azaña and his about-to-be-formed Popular Front was the solution.

Arrested and imprisoned the previous October in Barcelona by the center-right government for aiding and abetting an uprising in Catalonia, he gained his freedom after being acquitted of all charges that January. The morning of the fight, the bespectacled Azaña spoke to the nearly 60,000 who filed through the doors of Mestalla and filled the field and every seat of the steep grandstand.

From a podium high above the masses, he tugged at the lapels of his tight black suit jacket and spoke of forming the Popular Front and warding off the fascist caudillos led by military generals including Francisco Franco.

At that same time, Brown, Sangchili and the undercard fighters weighed in for their respective matches. Despite the scent of rain in the air and the humidity, Brown was bone dry. His eyes were sunken and if not for the ashy skin that covered his body, Peeters would have thought a skeleton stepped on the scales that day.

If it were a skeleton, all they had to do was remove about two ribs to make weight. Instead, Brown had to spend the rest of the morning in a sauna.

He was 700 grams over the limit.

The champ was puzzled. His biggest concern throughout the week had been making sure his weight was on target. Twice a day he allowed Bobby Diamond to weigh him. Making weight was not an issue for this fight. About two hours and hundreds of punches thrown in the middle of hot vapor later, Brown weighed in again.

A tired, hungry, and weak Brown took a deep breath and stepped on the scales. A refreshed Sangchili, his belly filled with brunch, leaned over to get a better view of the scale. To everyone's surprise and relief, Brown made weight. The fight would go on.

Outside, most pedestrians took one look at the grey clouds that formed above the arena and decided to skip on the fight. As the caravans of buses made their way out of Valencia, Brown headed back to the hotel and hoped to squeeze in a meal and a nap before the fight.

While the threat of rain hovered above, fans dressed in rain gear took their seats under the agitated clouds. The show started with Pedro Ros stopping Clovis Sablons. One report estimated the crowd at about three thousand. That number started to shrink as Hilario Martinez and Ramon Badia made their way to the ring under a drizzle. By the time the first round started, a torrential downpour had the fighters shielding themselves from the rain as much as from each other's punches.

In the second round Badia got caught with a right hand he didn't see and, with his soaked handlers instructing him to stay down with a let's-get-out-of-here wave of the hand, Badia didn't bother to get up.

Sharing that sentiment, the majority of spectators got out of there too and filed out of the arena by the hundreds.

The third fight got underway before a few dozen fans. Vicente Riambau and Primo Rubio boxed literally underwater for a round and a half before the referee called a halt to the action. By order of the Governor of Valencia, the rest of the card was called off and rescheduled for the following Saturday.

After the rain died down Brown was spotted with glass aloft, toasting and drinking the night away while munching on fried calamari. The following five days were spent in similar fashion. The relief Brown's camp felt when the fight was called off made Peeters think they would use the five days to recuperate Brown's strength. Instead, with Bobby by his side, the champ spent more time seated on a bar stool in *La Cerveceria Fenick* with his fedora leaning to the side than he did working out in his black gym tights and white tank top.

Early in the week the promotion took a major hit. That same Saturday in Madrid, Marcel Thil was to defend his middleweight championship against the wide-swinging-hands-down but hard-to-hit Ignacio Ara. Thil and Ara were familiar foes and some considered the fight something of a rubber match. Ara, despite losing the official decision, was generally believed to have gotten the better of Thil in one of their matches.

Splitting newspaper space and radio time with the Madrid show was bad for business. Then the loss of one of the star attractions to the rival promotion had them worried about breaking even.

Jose Martinez Valero was his real name. Alfara, the area of Valencia where he came from, was tacked onto the back of his name as if he were a character from *Carlito's Way*. Much like the character from the movie, wherever he went, his people followed. Once Martinez De Alfara announced his decision to pull out of the card and accepted a match on the Madrid show, quite a few people showed up for refunds.

The promoters prepared for a financial loss.

Brown was promised 50,000 pesetas. Sangchili, who was promised a percentage of the gate, ended up not getting paid.

The morning of June 1st, Brown weighed himself in the hotel room. He was on target. Throughout the week he checked his weight repeatedly. With confidence, he headed over to the official weigh-in. A sizeable crowd that included reporters, fans, the president of the boxing federation Francisco Cortijos and one of his vice presidents, Mr. To, gathered to witness Brown step on the scales. With the events of the previous week fresh in their minds, everyone in the room held their breath and silently waited.

The limit was 53kgs 534g. Sangchili weighed in moments earlier at 52kgs 650g.

Wearing only a white robe, Brown tipped the scale at 53kgs 900g.

He was more than half a pound overweight.

"Can't be," he said. "I just weighed myself at the hotel."

"We need a different scale," Bobby Diamond proclaimed. "Like the ones they use in Panama!"

Everyone began speaking at once. "Sabotage," Bobby whispered to Brown in French. They demanded another scale. The scale was checked thoroughly by a certified technician, Cortijos insisted. Someone suggested a nearby pharmacy.

A conga-line of boxers, boxing officials and fans followed the dark-skinned boxer in the white robe through the streets of downtown Valencia. Curious onlookers inquired what the fuss was about. Many of them tagged along.

When the mob descended upon the store, the startled pharmaceutical staff manned their stations behind the counter and braced themselves for a Black Friday type of sales day. Their surprise turned to disappointment once it was explained what they were there for. A scale, though not the type they used in Panama, was placed in the middle of the store.

Brown was still overweight.

"This one is off too," Brown declared to the increasingly agitated group. "By 200 grams."

Off to another pharmacy they went. The crowd behind Brown grew at each intersection in both size and annoyance. One of the officials reminded the fighter that the weigh-in had to be completed by a certain time. Brown, by virtue of being over the limit, risked losing his championship on a Valencian side street.

Not only was he battling against "dishonest" scales, he was racing against the clock too. So Brown power walked and the mob behind him, to keep up, power walked as well. Up and down the streets they went in search of a pharmacy.

The scene was repeated at the second pharmacy. Brown dropped a few grams but was still overweight. "This scale is off too," Bobby proclaimed. He insisted on another scale and threatened to pull out.

The third and final stop was at a blue-and-scarlet-colored sport pharmacy owned by the president of *Club Gimnastico*. Located in *Plaza de la Virgen*, about a mile and a half away from where they started, the president of the soccer club, Galileo Montoro Gomez, allowed the procession inside of the pharmacy that bore the colors of the *fútbol* team. He pulled out the same scale the players used to check their weights and ceremoniously asked Brown to step on.

Brown, stripped down to a loincloth, held his breath and stepped on the scale as lightly as he could. 53kgs 450g. The fight would go on as long as Sangchili didn't gain any weight during the colossal march through Valencia. It was just a formality since Sangchili originally made weight with room to spare, but because of the circus act that transpired, the official weighing-in ceremony was over *here* instead of back *there*. 52kgs 050g was Sangchili's new, and official, weight.

Brown's antics left some of the officials fuming. They were offended by the inferences of dishonesty. They called the champ superstitious, paranoid and unprofessional. Brown had worn out his welcome in Spain.

A crowd described as "average sized" by *El Mundo Deportivo* and as "disappointing" by Madrid paper *El Sol* flowed into the 10,500-seat brick arena that resembles the Colosseum in Rome. *El Sol* suspected the defection of Martinez de Alfara was the main cause of the low turnout with recent uninspired showings by Brown another possible reason. *El Mundo Deportivo* went one step further and described the first match between the two as having been suspect. "*Pelea amistosa*" they called it - horseplay, play fighting, friendly fighting - anything but a real fight. They suspected Brown would show up in usual winning form with the title on the line.

Opening the show was a brawl between Felix Gomez and Manuel Arlandis. Gomez started aggressively with Arlandis, also spelled Orlandis in the same write-up, covering up. A right to the jaw dropped Arlandis for a count of two in the fourth round. A follow-up assault buckled his knees. But Arlandis fought back and lashed out a left that instantly closed one of his opponent's eyes.

The fight degenerated into a dirty brawl after that with Arlandis being disqualified for dropping Gomez with a head butt.

A listless Brown arrived at the arena and settled into his dressing room with the usual smile but lacking the usual bounce in his step.

BLACK INK

While he slipped out of his street clothes and into his ring attire to shadowbox, his right knee buckled.

Bobby wrapped the knee heavily in bandages while Riambau and Rubio picked up where they left off the previous Sunday. They went the distance with hometown fighter Rubio declared the winner.

Hilario Martinez boxed again on this card in a much-anticipated fight. But he fell short on points to Pedro Isasti.

In the audience a band warmed up.

In the dressing room, the fighters did too.

When the fighters made their way through the green swinging gates the bulls normally rushed through, it was about 11 PM. The band played when Sangchili walked towards the ring. When Brown's purple-with-violet-trim robe was visible to the few thousand fans in the red and yellow stands, he too was cheered though not nearly as loudly as Sangchili was.

After the fighters posed for the pre-fight photos, the crowd cheered long and loud muffling the sound of the first bell. It was a slow round with few exchanges, usually initiated by Sangchili. Sangchili managed to slip underneath the long punches of his opponent only to be wrapped up in a clinch.

"Go to the body," were the instructions Sangchili received between rounds. With the instructions ringing in his head, he bobbed and weaved like Jack Dempsey did on the big screen and unleashed a volley of hooks at the midsection.

Brown wasn't given a chance to hold this time. Too many punches forced him into a shell with his chin tucked deep into his skinny but muscular chest. Brown attempted to deflect the body blows with his elbows. It worked.

But Sangchili was world-class too and in one instance, he faked a left to the body. Brown predictably lowered the elbow to deflect it and briefly exposed his forehead. That brief moment was the window Sangchili had been waiting for. .

Instead of going to the body, he threw the punch upstairs and landed a left squarely on the temple with the force of someone who's been waiting all his life to throw that punch. Stunned, badly, Brown immediately abandoned his post along the ropes. He used his legs to get away from Sangchili who was on him like a rising shadow, still punching. Brown's clinching drew boos from the crowd and warnings from the referee.

Midway through the third round, the champion timed with perfection a right uppercut just as the challenger bored. It landed flush in the middle of Sangchili's hairy chest. Baltasar stopped for an instant, bobbed and weaved - the weave accompanied by a one-two to the champion's face.

After that round, Brown told friends, Bobby gave him something other than water to drink.

"Take this, it'll pick you up."

By round four, Brown could not move the way he would have liked. His right knee started to buckle. A change in tactics was necessary but, instead of tactical instructions, his trainer made him sip from a champagne bottle wrapped in a towel.

Forced to stand his ground, Brown grabbed and punched back. He was, however, unable to keep up with Sangchili's pace. Sangchili pulled ahead and by round ten, it was clear Sangchili would win. Brown sensed it too but could do nothing about it. His body faltered and he was unable to tap into that reserve like he'd done so many times before. He felt sensations he'd never felt before in the ring. As he felt the title slip away, tears dripped from his eyes.

The last three rounds saw Brown bravely withstand the fierce attack from that little Dempsey who tore into him the way Dempsey tore into Carpentier and Willard. The crowd's roar was heard outside the arena. Realizing something big was about to happen, hundreds of people rushed the gates and shoved their way ringside.

While he withered away, almost defenseless, he looked out into the crowd where the delighted faces cheered and roared ecstatically, encouraging Sangchili to throw more.

"Screaming for his blood," Jean Cocteau recalled Brown telling him some years afterwards.

The band played and the people cheered and it did not matter that the official announcement was barely heard. Fans entered the ring and hoisted the new champion into the air and passed him around until order was somewhat restored.

In a locker room filled with people uncertain of what to say, Brown suspected foul play. He couldn't feel his legs. He felt dizzy but not the kind of dizziness he'd felt before from punches. He complained of a strange taste in his mouth. No matter how much he spat, the taste remained. His camp suggested he ate something or, worse, his food may have been poisoned either at the hotel or at one of the cabarets.

When Peeters went to shake Brown's hand, Brown grabbed him by the wrist and pulled him close to him. He whispered in his ear.

"I think I was poisoned by my own corner."

He would tell Jean Cocteau the very same thing years later.

After the fight smug faces delighted in calling him "ex" champ. Boxing is a sport for real men, he was told. A part of him was glad he lost. He thought it would be easier now to walk away from the sport and the many cruel spirits it attracted.

The next day an *El Mundo Deportivo* headline informed readers that Spain had its first world champion. Baltasar Sangchili triumphed despite an indifferent public. The few thousand who attended, and the few hundred who bum-rushed the doors at the end, would never forget it.

Brown fired all of his handlers.

Bobby Diamond immediately found work in the Sangchili camp as a masseuse for the new champion. Quizzed about the allegations of foul play, he shrugged them off and said Brown "is a drunkard."

Redemption

Brown wanted one more payday. A match against old rival Pete Sanstol in Norway was scheduled. Billed as Pete's last fight, the hometown crowd came out in force once again, this time to bid farewell. Brown remained a curiosity to fans. They turned out by the hundreds to watch him train. He displayed his still acrobatic moves in a series of spirited sparring sessions. When the night covered the skies, Brown did his roadwork. From bar to bar he ran and inside, the different combinations he worked on included orange juice, seltzer, and vodka.

As it turned out, that might have been all the training he needed. Descriptions of the fight gave an impression of a friendly affair that concluded with neither boxer being sure about what round it was.

Before the final bell rang for the Sanstol fight, Brown decided it would be the last bell of his career. As far as he was concerned, he was divorced from boxing.

At a tavern after the fight, Brown was asked if he ever engaged in a fixed match. Between sobs and sips of his drink, he insisted he never had. And never would.

Breaking from the sport cold turkey initially didn't seem to faze the champion. He received a six-month offer to dance and sing at the recently renovated National Scala in Copenhagen. But his celebrity faded and when the contract expired, there was no offer to extend his stay.

He returned to Paris with no intention to box. He found work as a tap dancer and sometimes sax player at the narrow *Caprice Vennois* owned by openly gay singer, actress and model, Suzy Solidor.

As time went by, empty seats shared the room with customers who went not to see him but to talk with friends over a drink. Instead it was Brown who watched them. As they got lost in their conversations, Brown danced to the beat of irony.

"I find myself needing to dance at the Caprice to make a living," he lamented. As he danced, inside his arms, to the bone, he still felt his speed and reflexes were championship caliber. But the sport disgusted him.

"I'm repulsed by it." Two-faced managers who were "always willing to work with" the opposing side to their personal benefit and "disloyal trainers" who made their livings off the flesh they "clung to like ticks to a dog," were his complaints. At the Caprice, he mentioned entertaining people who only a few years earlier sought his company. As he stomped out the final few steps of his act, he told his friends that the situation he found himself in did not embarrass him since "I am a broken man."

On most nights he followed his performances with a lonely smoke at the bar. Occasionally someone engaged the former champ though the topic of boxing was off limits. Actor Marcel Khill became a frequent visitor. At times, he brought Jean Cocteau with him.

Brown spent a great part of his days clutching his *lampara China*. That's what he called his small, elaborate, hand-crafted-in-China opium lamp. Still warm from the last puffs, that lamp - and that drug - did for him what his vaunted straight right used to – it bailed him out.

Before his shows, when he needed a pick-me-up, and after his shows when he needed another, his trusted lamp and the sweet-smelling smoke it emitted were always there for him.

While Brown spent his nights and days behind a veil of white smoke, Sangchili found out, like Brown did many years before him, that being champion of the world wasn't quite what it was cracked up to be. Despite receiving offers to box in the United States, Sangchili instead remained in Europe where he boxed featherweights in non-title matches throughout Spain, Algeria, and Morocco.

Meanwhile in New York, Sixto Escobar had the backing of the NBA and New Yorker Lou Salica possessed the California State version of the world title. Sangchili, backed by the IBU, would join them in New York in 1936 to participate in a tournament to crown a divisional king.

On the ship with him were Diamond, his manager Jules Avernin, and Italian lightweight Enrico Venturi.

"What is your occupation?" the immigration officer asked.

"I'm a boxer," replied the world-ranked lightweight.

"What is the purpose of your trip?"

"To look at all the pretty girls," Venturi replied with a smile.

The stone-faced official wasn't amused. They placed Venturi in detention awaiting further investigation.

When the very same official returned to the line, Sangchili was readying himself for the questions.

"Occupation," the official asked.

When he replied "boxer" the official announced, "We have another funny guy" and proceeded to place Baltasar in the cell alongside the now-beside-himself Venturi who asked hysterically, "You too?"

There was more to it according to Immigration Commissioner Rudolf Reimer. He explained to the United Press that Sangchili had no commitments lined up when he arrived. If he had signed contracts, he said, they would have let him into the country. He had none.

"In reality, he has come to see if he can get a fight. Under these conditions, I have no other choice than to refuse entry," Reimer said.

The matter was quickly settled when Burston presented signed contracts for several lucrative bouts. Commissioner Reimer was satisfied but Sangchili wouldn't be. He would only see a fraction of the money mentioned in the contracts. Those big paydays were contingent on him winning all of his fights.

The first fight was a tune-up bout at the Ridgewood Grove Arena near the Brooklyn-Queens border. After that Sangchili appeared in a semifinal match under the John Henry Lewis-Bob Goodwin light heavyweight fight at Madison Square Garden.

Then came the big fight. His opponent was the Ray Arcel- trained Tony Marino - kid brother of former bantamweight title challenger Tommy Ryan. Marino was a slick boxer who was coming off a win over Salica but lacked what the scribes back then called "important" punching power.

The match took place at the Dyckman Oval in New York's Dyckman neighborhood. The ring was set up where the New York

BLACK INK

Cubans chased down fly balls. Working Sangchili's corner that night was Bobby Diamond.

Sangchili floored Marino in the first round. Marino, more agile, stayed away just enough to win the second, third, and fourth rounds. Sangchili took over in the fifth and nearly scored another knockdown. In the seventh, the "Little Hercules" dropped Marino for a second time and added three more times in the eighth round.

When Marino answered the bell for round 14, he was a battered, bloody fighter who trailed on the scorecards. Halfway through round Marino threw a right hand to the head of Sangchili. Sangchili stopped cold. His hands dropped to his sides.

Marino, said ringside reporter Teddy Sanchez, was perhaps the "most surprised person in the arena." A follow-up combo landed and Sangchili crashed. The left side of his body was stiff as a plank as the referee counted him out.

He was carried to his dressing room where moments later, he cried and passed out. When he came to, the left side of his body was numb. Dr. Bliss, the ringside physician, explained what happened. The blow to the temple area struck a bone or a nerve that caused a muscle contraction that caused temporary paralysis.

Sangchili believed he was poisoned. Perhaps it was something in his pre-fight meal or perhaps it was the same thing that happened to Kid Tunero. Tunero, a star middleweight who once beat a prime Ezzard Charles, said that just before the final round of his match with Jock McAvoy, his handler, like always, wiped his face with a towel. The towel, he said, had an odd smell. That was the last thing he remembered.

Sangchili was not sure what happened. None of it made sense to him.

Bobby Diamond was once again suspected of treachery. Similar accusations about Diamond were made by other fighters. Theo Medina had to be restrained from choking Diamond after his loss to Ray Fitton in England. He demanded to know what the trainer gave him to make him sick. Diamond allegedly confessed with a laugh and told him he gave him the same thing he gave his "little black" champion - rat poison.

Another champion expressed his suspicions too, though he was a possible beneficiary. During round 13 of his title fight against Chamroen Songkirat, Robert Cohen recalled being exhausted and unable to feel his legs. Raymond Charles Gaston instructed Diamond to give him the water between rounds. Instantly rejuvenated, Cohen went on to win the fight.

"I never asked what was in the water he gave me," he wrote. "It worked but I just know it was something I wasn't supposed to be drinking."

Cohen's future was bright. A defense against unbeaten South African Willie Toweel in Johannesburg followed. He floored the popular Toweel three times in the second round and once more in the tenth. Then out came a vial of unknown liquid.

The fight was scored a draw but Cohen didn't remember much about the ending. After the fight, he vomited violently in the dressing room. Once so promising, Cohen never won another fight.

Sangchili immediately fired Diamond and his manager Jules Avernin and partnered with Bertys Remy. Marino lost to Escobar and then lost to Sangchili in a ten round rematch in Pittsburgh. Following a few wins, Marino's family and friends noticed subtle behavioral changes in Marino. The talk of retirement came up but the doctors deemed him fit to compete.

His family thought otherwise. Something was wrong, they sensed. He suffered multiple knockdowns in his fights with Sangchili and Escobar. And when he stepped into the ring on the Brooklyn - Queens border against Indian Quintana, he was once more sent to the canvas repeatedly. After the final one, he lapsed into a coma for two days.

He paid the ultimate price.

The three knockdown rule was passed in New York shortly afterwards.

Hearing and seeing "ex" before "champion" bothered Brown. If only they knew, he thought whenever he heard or read that word.

BLACK INK

He was oblivious to the happenings in New York and boxing in general. He was immersed in the bipolar clutches of opium.

Read one of the many recollections of an opium fiend and you'll find they all describe the sensation the same way. The poppy makes even the wildest imaginations seem real. It puts the user in a super heroic world where everything feels right, at least for the moment. Then it's time for another hit.

During those private smoke-fests, Brown recounted how he felt the title was taken away from him. First by seemingly homophobic officials, then, by some concoction slipped into his water. When sober, Brown refused to talk boxing. The topic was not allowed. Under the influence, he confided feeling that he was still the rightful champion. Then he would stand and flawlessly perform the moves of his heyday.

"When I met Al Brown he was stalled in a paste of fatigue and disorder," Cocteau recollected.

Jean Cocteau was born in 1889 in the city of Maisons de Laffitte. He was an admittedly sickly child who started out as a photographer before having his poetry published. He met Brown in Montmartre, dancing and leading a small orchestra under the mirrored ceiling of the Caprice Viennois.

No fan of boxing, Cocteau was nevertheless familiar with the name Al Brown but knew very little about his ring career he wrote in *Voilà*. Something about the 35-year-old former boxer fixated the poet. Brown danced, sang and comported himself in a manner Cocteau described as elegant. They were introduced after the show.

Cocteau quickly realized Brown was "drowning in his disgust of the ring." A former abuser of the drug himself, he too had been intimate with seductive pipes though he never smoked "more than 10 pipes a day." Being high on the drug felt better than good health, he said.

The author of *Les Enfants Terrible,* Cocteau saw a younger version of himself in Brown. The dependency on his drug of choice, the way he clung to and relied on it like medicine, and the countless hook-ups with nameless individuals equally lost were all part of the road he traveled in his own younger days. Cocteau also knew the path out and would soon give Brown the directions.

Their affair reputedly ran the gamut from lovers to friends to business associates. Cocteau's amorous affairs were well publicized. He was the teenaged partner of actor Eduord De Max and later lived with poets John Le Roy and Jean Desbordes. In 1936 and 1937, he spent a lot of time with Brown. They marveled at their coincidences - the same birthday, same shirt size, same shoe size. What Brown liked about Cocteau was his willingness to bathe in the same bath water Brown had just used. "He doesn't change the water."

Little by little, Cocteau brought up the subject of boxing. At first, Brown wanted none of it. Cocteau insisted and one day while in Cocteau's room at the Hotel De Castilla, Brown let him in on all the details. From the early days as an amateur near Brown Square in Panama up to the day he quit and everything in between.

"I was poisoned," he confided. "By my own corner."

When Cocteau heard that story the thought of writing about it entered his mind. He decided redemption was better.

This was no typical comeback. Brown wasn't a boxer who refused to acknowledge the deterioration of his skills. He wasn't a boxer looking for checks to cash. The idea was Cocteau's. He convinced Brown to recapture what was wrongfully taken away from him.

"Promise me you'll regain your title," he told Brown.

"I'll help you."

Cocteau knew a little bit more than nothing about boxing. But in his friend's voice and eyes, he heard and saw a prisoner held captive without a cage.

Amid vehement criticisms that Brown shouldn't be fighting, and Cocteau shouldn't be managing, one of, if not the most, amazing comebacks in the history of boxing took place. The idea, conceived between puffs of an opium pipe, was dangerous as it was cockamamie.

"We can't have any of this." Cocteau put out the pipe.

About an hour later, he found Brown hunched over a different pipe.

A detox was necessary.

Funded by designer Coco Chanel, who considered Brown to be the only "honorable" person Cocteau kept company with those days, he checked into a hospital, possibly the *Charenton*. Without a pipe and nothing else to distract him, Brown began feeling every one of his muscles twitch within hours of checking in. Tears ran down his face even though he wasn't crying. Cold sweat accompanied the tremors that began on his first night. Kept awake by constant vomiting and diarrhea, he uncontrollably hit himself several times in the arms and legs.

It was several weeks of hot and cold flashes, insomnia, and weaning off drugs until his body expelled the poisons. Exhausted, he checked-out and headed to a desolate farm in Aubigny where a makeshift gym was set up for him. With the capable Bob Roberts supervising the training, Brown shook off the rust, burned off the extra ten pounds of weight and in between, fought off the boredom by shooting at chickens with a rifle.

Cocteau contacted Jeff Dickson.

"I'm not surprised," the promoter said.

Many thought it was a foolish idea. A poet with no experience in the boxing business managing a burned out druggie was a recipe for disaster; and possibly worse. While most of the boxing world averted their eyes, Dickson went ahead with his plans.

Around the same time, just as the Spaniards put down their civil war rifles, Dickson received word that Sangchili sought a return to European rings. Unable to return to Spain during their war, Sangchili made his way down to Mexico where he lost a decision to Juan Zurita, then headed over to Cuba and the Dominican Republic. Lacking fights and management, Sangchili soon found himself stranded on the Caribbean island.

He reached out to Dickson. The promoter paid Sangchili's way back to France and began to orchestrate simultaneous comebacks that would culminate in a rematch between the two.

As his comeback fight approached, Brown left behind the chickens in Aubigny for the Berlitz gym in Paris. In the days that lead up to his return, Brown impressed while he went through his paces at the gym. On September 9th, 1937, following an absence of two years, he stepped into the ring at the Salle Wagram to face the sturdy Andre Regis. A sellout crowd gathered about an hour before the doors opened.

Next-day reports didn't bother to mention the undercard details. It was all about Brown, who they said looked sad and almost apologetic when he climbed through the ropes to mostly cheers.

The cheers had not completely quieted down when Brown knocked out Regis. Brown glanced down towards the ringside seats and gave Cocteau a look that seemed to say you were right.

One week later, Sangchili ended his eight-month layoff. In the same arena, he stopped his opponent in three rounds. It was clear to the public the two were on a collision course. Talk in the sports bars compared their performances.

A week after Sangchili's return, Brown stepped in against a more capable foe. Maurice Huguenin was mostly on the losing side of his big fights. Every once in a while, he upset the cart and scored big wins over the likes of Young Perez, Eugene Huat, and Victor Ferrand.

In a fight reported by both the *NY Times* and the *Brooklyn Daily Eagle* as being for the vacant IBU featherweight title, Brown became a two division claimant when a jab he threw in the third round knocked Huguenin down for the count.

On October 8th Sangchili scored a win in Paris and a second round knockout in Geneva. He scored another win one week later and then, on October 28th again in Paris, outscored former champion Young Perez over ten rounds.

Around that time Cocteau wrote that reporters, the grizzled boxing scribes, often flashed angry glances at him and wrongfully predicted that Brown would get knocked out.

He was accused of intruding on the sport without having any expertise or knowledge and of having made a mockery of the game by bringing back a battered old champion, possibly his lover, and making him fight for his own perverted pleasure.

They watched as Brown, from the ring, and Cocteau, from ringside, glanced at each other and seemed to be involved in a cryptic conversation. When they quizzed Cocteau on boxing tactics and strategies, he was at a loss for answers.

Do you know the difference between a hook and a jab?

How are points awarded?

How many minutes in a round?

What's the difference between a speed bag and a heavy bag? Why use one over the other?

Instead of the correct answer, Cocteau laced his responses with philosophy. A reporter at the *Epitecto* wrote that the poet was playing monkey-see-monkey-do. One day he was a poet, the next an athlete, and the day after that, a philosopher. He asked Cocteau to take a good look at himself and ask if he was indeed right for the task at hand because, no one is built to do everything.

Some reporters suggested black magic was involved.

"I've been accused of sorcery," Cocteau wrote in his published letters. "I know nothing of the art I assure you."

With fan interest high for a Sangchili-Brown match, Dickson scheduled the next two fights for both against the same opponents. Sangchili boxed Perez, then Joseph Decico - Brown fought Decico and then Perez.

For Brown's November match with Decico, Cocteau was no longer welcomed ringside.

"Attempts were made to keep me from getting to my seat at ringside for his matches in an effort to keep me from applying, casting, my spell on the fighter who they figured boxed in a trance that I somehow controlled from ringside."

Cocteau continued, "Indeed he did look at me, signaling me to call for the ringside bookies by swiping across his forehead with his right glove. That was the signal he was ready to end the fight. And once my bet was placed, he lowered the boom, usually a left hook, which, at that point in his career was his best punch."

The two laughed while they headed back to the dressing room. They laughed some more when Cocteau went to collect the winnings from his bets.

"It was the only money I made from his fights, forgoing collecting the customary manager's share." Cocteau reiterated that he was never officially the manager of the champion and never collected the customary managerial cut of the purse.

Brown scored three knockdowns in the fifth round and huffed and puffed his way to a ten-round decision. And seated ringside was Cocteau because it was hard to bar entry into a prize fight to a man whose connections extended into the offices of Prime Minister Chautemps.

In December, with Cocteau awkwardly carrying his towel and bucket, Brown floored Young Perez with a right hand shot on the ear in round five. Perez, down in the previous round, complained it was a rabbit punch while the referee counted him out.

Sangchili spent the final months of the year at home in Spain and returned after the holidays for the final tune-up. While Brown sat out the beginning of 1938, Sangchili faced Decico on February 3rd. It was almost a disaster as he struggled against Joseph Decico, being held to a draw in ten rounds.

The stage was set for March 4th.

He spent less time with Cocteau, who was away in Montargis writing the play *Les Parents Terribles*. He finished late in February and headed back to Paris with his new lover, actor Jean Marais. Marais stood so close to Cocteau there wasn't room for anyone else. He accompanied Cocteau while the latter performed his managerial duties during the days before the fight. Marais was with them when they went to restaurants where Cocteau had the waiters pour champagne down the sink and then fill the bottles with tonic water. When a reporter or someone from the boxing fraternity showed up, Cocteau summoned to the waiter to bring the bottle. With everyone watching, Brown would gulp down the contents, say "ahh," then ask for another bottle.

BLACK INK

Brown battled flu-like symptoms the days leading up to the fight. Along with an assortment of hot drinks he received cupping therapy. The symptoms lingered until the morning of the fight. That, along with the "champagne" guzzling, had most thinking Brown's only chance to win was to score an early knockout.

Just before the fight, the IBU confirmed Sangchili was still the IBU champion. Partly because they didn't honor Marino's win - officially, because it was held overseas; unofficially because of suspicions - and partly because boxing organizations always did what they pleased.

The Palais des Sports was full when the first bell sounded. Brown, his hair long and straightened, his knees unwrapped, bounced around and unleashed stinging one-twos. Sangchili ducked down as low as his 5'1" stature allowed and evaded the majority. Enough bounced off his skull to keep him from trying to get in close.

Sangchili wanted to strike Brown's midsection. But he was kept back by the sharp punches Brown threw in the early rounds. Rushing in proved futile so Sangchili waited as Brown put the early rounds in the bank. Brown boxed with a "chaotic excitement" while Sangchili stalked with "calm hate," according to Cocteau.

As the rounds passed by, Sangchili began landing more. By the tenth, Brown had the look of a fighter who might not make it to the final bell. It became a race to the finish with Brown, his hair in disarray, weakening as that finish line approached.

Ringsiders glared at Jean Cocteau and reminded him it would be his fault if Brown were seriously hurt. Cocteau squirmed in his seat as Sangchili poured on the punches. Blood streamed down the side of Brown's face from a cut near his eye. In the 12th, Brown looked at Cocteau.

"I'll never forget the look he gave me," Cocteau wrote. "The same look a child gives his parent after he's scolded."

The last three rounds saw Brown, almost in a trancelike state, struggle to clinch and stand as Sangchili "savagely but without style" bounced mighty blow after mighty blow off the side of Brown's head. Brown's sweat was flung onto the ringsiders and his face contorted by pain.

The last round saw Sangchili attack while Brown retreated with the uncertain steps of a man walking in the dark. Brown was about to collapse when the final bell rang. Sangchili had run out of time.

Bob Roberts and his assistant, Odolini, rushed into the ring to grab hold of Brown before he collapsed and then hoisted him into the air. When the decision was announced, Brown was the winner and once again champion of the IBU. Too weary to walk out on his own, they placed the new champion on a stretcher and carried him back to his dressing room. A worried Cocteau pushed his way through the hysterical crowd and into the dressing room. The comeback was complete. Brown had redeemed himself.

Afterwards, Brown told Cocteau he suspected something, a type of sleeping agent, was rubbed into Sangchili's hair. He said he caught the scent of something foreign whenever Sangchili head butted his face, which happened with increased frequency during the late rounds.

Dickson immediately set the wheels in motion for Brown's next fight. Once beaten bantamweight from Merseyside, Peter Kane had created a stir in both England and Paris with a series of knockouts. In his first 44 bouts, 36 ended early. Decico and Huguenin each went out in the first. And Huat and Petit-Biquet also failed to make it to the final bell. The only blemish on Kane's record was a loss to Hall of Fame-bound Benny Lynch.

Brown had different ideas. He wanted one more fight and coming off of the grueling match with Sangchili, his plan called for something less brutal. Brown, at that point in his career, wanted nothing to do with Kane.

Instead, Brown signed for an April 13th bout against Valentin Angelmann and Kane attempted to avenge his only loss in a rematch against Benny Lynch. Angelmann had more than 200 fights when he faced off against Brown. He had challenged Frankie Genaro and Jackie Brown for the flyweight championship, holding Brown to a draw. He later won the IBU flyweight title, defended it once, then moved up to bantamweight. In 1936, after winning the IBU title, someone with the same name sent the French Federation a letter asking if they could find out if the great champion named Angelmann was his son. Separated during WWI, father and son reunited after 20 years apart.

A week before the bout, Cocteau wrote an open letter to Brown that appeared in *Paris-Soir*.

"You promised me to regain your title and I promised you to help yourself to the end in this amazing quest. It is done…Take advantage of your triumph. Do not imitate the celebrities who cling. After the wonder of this revenge, give to the world the example of a man who leaves the room for young people."

He pleaded for Brown to retire.

"One last match; Angelmann. Be wise and leave the scene. This is my last advice."

The letter was a surprise. Those who considered Brown crazy for coming back now thought he was crazy for retiring. Dickson pleaded with Brown to reconsider. Fine, he said. If Brown must retire, then why not retire as a champion, he wondered. He requested that Brown change the Angelmann match from 10 rounds to 15 and put the IBU bantamweight title on the line. Even though, he added, he was confident a match against Kane would gross one million francs.

The Panamanian's mind was made up. His response to Cocteau was published in several French newspapers. Following 48 hours of consideration, he decided that Cocteau was correct. He would heed his advice and retire. After "231 fights", it was time to go. The Angelmann bout would be his last.

Brown was reportedly seen drunk at a bar called "Rugby" the night before. When the bell rang for what was billed as "Funeral of a Champion" since it was his last fight, rumor had it that Brown was still buzzed.

His "farewell" fight was bittersweet. Cocteau slowly but surely, and willingly, was pulled away from Brown by Marais. And Brown entered the ring under the impression that every effort would be made to see Angelmann win.

For seven rounds he danced circles around his opponent and struck him as he pleased. The crowd grew discontented with the lack of action. In between rounds, Brown sipped champagne. Before the eighth round, Roberts refused to let him sip from the bottle. Why not, asked Brown. The fight's over this round anyway, he said.

About a minute later, Angelmann was stopped.

Publisher of *L'Auto*, Henri Desgrange, wrote an editorial loaded with questions for Cocteau.

Why are you depriving sportsmen of the opportunity to watch Brown in action?

It is true that you are responsible for bringing him back to the championship, but how are we to show our gratitude if he leaves?

Do you wish to sadden us?

Is it in Brown's best interest to retire?

What choice does he have left?

To start drinking champagne again?

If that's the case, then why deprive him of that at all?

Wouldn't it have been better in the first place to just leave him amid his bottles?

Do we have rights to him too?

Do you doubt his ability to last the distance? He did beat Sangchili and the punch he knocked Angelmann out with in the eighth round was not the punch of a tired fighter - do you believe he could not have boxed another four rounds?

And even if can no longer box more than ten, eight, or six rounds - wouldn't that be better for him than sitting around uncorking bottles?

Desgrange ended with a request. "Return him to us sir!"

"My advice was not an order," Cocteau responded. "Brown has no reason to receive orders from anyone. I brought him back to the ring and if he decides to stay there, I will be the first to applaud and purchase my ticket. My role as a poet ends when reality kicks in and the reality is the competence of the boxing professionals. Those who guess should bow to those who know. The important thing is knowing whether Brown wishes to continue living the difficult life of a boxer. I advised him to quit the ring because he wanted to. I supported him before. You should support him too. I'm done. It's your turn."

Cocteau later stated his public plea to Brown was the fighter's idea. The Angelmann fight was one more payday and also a commercial for his next act. Cocteau arranged for Brown to perform at the *Cirque Medrano*. Before he stepped into the ring against Angelmann, the posters were already made.

"Here's the event- following his triumphant match- Al Brown- the Black Marvel- with his orchestra and partner – watch him dance- in his sporting attire- amid eccentric acrobats"

In a hastily arranged number, he appeared on stage dressed in his boxing robe, an oversized white cap dangling from the side of his head. He shadowboxed and skipped rope in a makeshift ring before a decidedly different type of crowd. Gone were the jeers and the vulgar insults. In their place was a jovial, if indifferent, crowd who came to watch the swinging, hanging, stair-climbing acrobats. They applauded politely when Brown, in a tux, returned to the stage and danced while Freddie Taylor conducted the band.

When the contract with the Medrano ran out, Brown found similar work with a traveling *Cirque Amar*. When that contract expired during the fall of 1938, the organizers saw no reason to renew the services of the shadowboxing tap dancer.

The life of a traveling circus act didn't agree with him though it proved a suitable distraction. Aside from a visit or two, Cocteau was out of his life almost as quickly as he entered. It was as if he were never there.

In his place was someone with a money-making idea. All he needed was the financing. The can't-miss business idea was a cabaret/brothel in Toulouse named the *Kit Kat*. It quickly became a place where half the people inside were selling either drugs or a piece of their asses and the other half were buying one or the other and sometimes both. Occasionally the police came through, made everyone scramble for the exits and hurt business for the days that followed. It didn't take long for the club to close.

With the Germans close to violating the Munich Agreement and the Italians about to invade Albania, Brown was advised he'd be better off in New York than he would if he stayed in France. He sold what he could. The rest he left behind - his friends, horses, and house. When the Il De France turned west and picked up speed, he closed his eyes and resisted the urge to look back. A feeling came over him that told him he would never see Europe again.

Days after he arrived, he was at the gym asking for a fight. One month and a few pounds later, with the assistance of Pincho Gutierrez, he found himself in the ring against Puerto Rican featherweight Cristobal Jaramillo. Trained by Ray Arcel, Jaramillo had never been stopped in a career that saw him go head-to-head with Tony Marino, Petey Scalzo and Chalky Wright.

Before the match he paid a visit to the West Side dentist who protected the teeth of the top rated boxers with custom-made mouthpieces.

By then "He had no teeth," according to Dr. Jacobs. It was "the most difficult mouthpiece I had to make," said the man who made gum shields for champions Joe Louis, Harold Johnson, Fred Apostoli and Lew Jenkins, who Jacobs said broke out into a sweat he was so terrified of dentists.

His hands were in worse shape. They were curved - like talons - with calcium deposits clustered where all the breaks occurred that made it look like he had six or seven knuckles throughout his hands. Those hands carried his own equipment when he entered the Rockland Palace on W 155th St.

Brown fought through his rust and fatigue to score a fourth round stoppage over the durable Jaramillo in front of nearly three thousand fans. Two weeks later he headlined at the Palace again.

His opponent that night was the experienced but also past-his-prime Spaniard, Mariano Arilla. Managed by Gutierrez, he boasted wins over Angelmann and Frankie Genaro- who was disqualified for fighting like a billy goat. Arilla would later settle in Cuba and train several fighters including the excellent Sugar Ramos.

BLACK INK

Despite being matched with solid opposition they were small shows before small crowds with small purses. According to the *Afro American*, Brown looked impressive in his three-round destruction of Arilla. The final blow was a straight right that conjured up images of his youth and justified the tag of *Black Lightning* that European writers gave him. Despite bolstering his dossier with two decent wins in two weeks, the only record Brown added to next was his arrest record.

Twilight Years

On November 7th, 1939 a New York City detective from the alien squad arrested Brown at his home at 55 W 110th Street for overstaying his travel visa. The issue with the visa, which was valid from March through September, was settled easily enough much as it was some ten years earlier when he was picked up for the same offense.

What wasn't easy was getting relicensed to box in the state. The Arilla fight was his last boxing match in the United States. Rumors of his participation in an occasional smoker match circulated. Those matches, usually after closing hours in smoke-filled gyms, put little money in his pocket. But a fighter beginning to exhibit signs of being punch drunk didn't have too many options.

He spent his time in that part of the hood where the prostitutes, homeless, semi-homeless and the stray dogs dwelled. Barred from fighting, his mind too scrambled to hold a job, he once again looked to the dope dealers for therapy.

Heroin was the choice drug in New York. Once used in cough medicine by Bayer, it was then being used mainly by, according to the *Psychiatric Bulletin of the New York Hospitals,* "members of gangs who congregate on street corners particularly at night, and make insulting remarks to people who pass." Addicts, called "junkies" because many of them sold scrap metal and other junk found in trash to support their habit, either sniffed or injected the heroin into their veins.

Brown's voice, hoarsened over the years, was no longer used to sing or conduct interviews for the press. Instead, it could be heard as a whisper on the upper left side of Central Park and in the pubs at night, letting people know he could help them get a hit if they were looking.

Visits to the gym became less frequent. His days were spent using the drugs he pushed. Income and meals were inconsistent. For a while, he stayed with a friend in Hartford. Within months, he was back in Harlem making headlines.

BLACK INK

During the summer of 1940, newspapers reported that a crime spree occurred in the neighborhood. A July 14th headline read: "One Dead - Two wounded."

One of the wounded was Brown. It was originally reported as an altercation at a restaurant on 100th Street. A fight over a woman led to pushing and shoving. Then Bernard Creach, who lived two blocks away, pulled out a knife and slashed Brown in the chest.

Both were arrested.

None of the follow-up reports mentioned anything about a woman. Four weeks later, Magistrate Ambrose J. Haddock freed Brown and Bernard Creach, who by then was referred to as Brown's " companion."

Brown was arrested again a few months later.

In January of 1941 he stood before federal judge William Bondy and loudly said "Alfredo Brown" when asked to state his name.

After someone whispered something into the judge's ear, the judge looked at the disheveled man before him and asked, "Are you Al Brown the former boxing champion?"

Brown admitted he was and spent the next few minutes explaining his plight. He was champion and earned enough money in Paris to own $280,000 worth of property in what became occupied territory. Because of the Nazis he fled the continent and left behind his money and property with no way of regaining any of it. He went back to boxing and took beatings until a friend told him to take some heroin because "it won't hurt as much."

The judge offered him eight months in prison or rehab. Brown choose a term in an unnamed government sanitarium in Harlem where, he told the judge, friends could look after him. Whether he deserted or attended and was released early is unclear. What is known is that less than six months after speaking before Judge Bondy, Brown was gloved up in a ring in Panama awaiting the opening bell.

At the docks in Colón a crowd of none waited for the old boxer with the crooked hands and flat nose. The mayor wasn't there; the governor did not call; and no parades were planned. Within 24 hours

Brown voiced his intentions. On this trip, he was free to box as he pleased.

Within a few days he and his new managers - a group that included his brothers and a local businessman named Cambra, went before the commission in Panama City and applied for their licenses. Less than a month after his arrival, Brown's arthritic knees buckled as he climbed through the ropes for his first match on home soil in 18 years.

On July 14th, 1941 a supportive and curious crowd watched the virtually one-handed fighter as he labored through seven rounds against Leocadio Torres, before finding the sweet spot in the eighth round with a left hook. Two weeks later he turned in a relatively impressive win in front of three thousand, stopping a writer and photographer who moonlit as a boxer under the name Battling Nelson. Next, he pleaded with the commission to allow him to challenge for the national title.

A national championship as a professional was the one thing that had up to this point eluded him. Bypassed during his youth, in 1941 it meant almost as much as winning a world title to him. As local promoters worked out the details for his challenge of Kid Fortune, Brown gulped down anything that intoxicated.

While his career had some direction, outside of the ring he was increasingly uncomfortable. The years abroad had left him in an in-between state - neither from here nor from there. His behavior had become too American or European for the tastes of his neighbors.

Whispers about his lifestyle grew louder and circled around until they were no longer behind his back. The disapproving stares were everywhere. Unlike Harlem and Montmartre, Colón had fewer places to escape to. To make the stares and the comments about him more palatable, Brown found refuge in cocaine.

Hot, humid, and high was how he spent his days. He rarely went out in public and his gym sessions were fewer and shorter. The thing he worked on most was conserving energy.

Leading up to the Kid Fortune fight, he was in an agitated state. More pumped up than he had been for the previous two encounters,

BLACK INK

Brown launched ferocious left hooks and had Fortune out on his feet at the end of the first round.

The shocked crowd called for the referee to stop it when the badly dazed Fortune stumbled out for the next round. Not wanting to hit him, Brown simply shoved him and Fortune dropped to the canvas. Brown had finally won a national title as a professional. He was the Panamanian featherweight champion.

Fans and writers called for the suspension of Fortune's handlers and Brown called for a match against Young Hurtado, the lightweight champion of Panama. He previously mentioned that he preferred fighting out-of-towners. Since there weren't any, he boxed against locals.

Young Hurtado, who considered Brown too damaged, never accepted the challenge. Brown's options were thin. In October he fought a Peruvian lightweight who was passing through and lost a ten round decision. It was a hard fight that saw Brown floor Eduardo Carrasco twice in the opening round. By the fifth, it was Brown who was in trouble. Carrasco, who looked up to and later became friends with Brown, appeared to step off the accelerator and allowed the fatigued former champion to last the distance. It was his first loss in Panama.

On December 16th, 1941, the United States Immigration and Naturalization Service processed Brown's narcotics violation and banned his re-entry into the country. Within months, he found himself before a Panamanian judge facing similar charges.

In March, Brown lost another ten-round decision to Carrasco. He still had the national championship since both fights were above the 126-pound featherweight limit. One month after his 40th birthday, he defended the Panamanian title against old foe Leocadio Torres. Set for 15 rounds, the fight was in jeopardy of being canceled.

The week of the Torres fight, the Superior Court (*Tribunal Superior del Primer Distrito Judicial*) cleared Brown of all charges of drug trafficking. The reason cited was lack of any evidence. The only link the courts found was the testimony of a fellow boxer who, upon being arrested, informed the authorities that Brown was his supplier. Since no other link was confirmed, Brown was cleared. The fight with Torres went on as scheduled.

No longer able to throw the right hand with full force, he relied on his jab and movement. It was enough to get him through the fifteen rounds. Torres was equally ineffective and pursued with little success. The crowd, progressively smaller since his arrival, met the decision - a draw- with scattered applause.

The promoter in Panama City had seen enough. The fans had seen enough. The novelty of ex-champion no longer stirred up interest. He had one more fight. In a place in Colón where most nights musicians played their instruments.

On December 4th, 1942, they cleared the stage of Club Tropical of its mics and speakers and built a makeshift ring where Brown would throw the last of his jabs. Panama's, and Latin America's, first ever boxing champion boxed his last fight around the corner from where he boxed his first one decades before and for not much more money.

The faces were familiar. Their expressions were not. Thirteen years earlier, Brown said they used to tap on store windows until he waved whenever he passed by. When he walked in the streets, hands grabbed at him from all angles and tugged at him, pulled him towards where they were going. The star-struck expression in their eyes was gone. So were the looks of awe he got when he started out.

In the opposite corner was a familiar foe. Kid Fortune. When the bell rang for his last hurrah, he was introduced as Kid Téofilo. The referee, named "Colon" Al Brown, signaled to the timekeeper to ring the bell. Ten rounds of jabs, clutches, and feints later, Brown was awarded the decision.

It was the 129th victory of his career against 19 losses. There were a few no decision fights and a couple of draws scattered throughout boxing rings in Panama, France, Italy, Spain, Algeria, Tunisia, England, Wales, Cuba, Switzerland, Belgium, Norway, Morocco, Canada, and the United States. In each canvas-covered ring, he displayed his art. With each work of art he left a piece of himself in the ring. When he climbed out of the ring for the last time, there was almost nothing left.

BLACK INK

In 1943, a Baltimore newspaper published an article updating readers on the whereabouts of Brown. He went from a poor thirteen-year-old in Colon to racing horses and managing a nightclub in France. He was married to a white woman, the paper wrote, and had a six-year-old son. His property, the wife and the son "disappeared" during the German occupation of France, it claimed.

That same year, Jeff Dickson flew missions over Germany during the war. He listed apartment 3503 in the Waldorf-Astoria as his residence when he re-enlisted. He never returned from one of his missions. Somewhere over the rocky terrain of Germany, in an air battle with the Luftwaffe, Dickson was last seen. He and his plane were never found.

A few months after Brown fled France, Marcel Khill was dead and Eugene Bullard lay wounded on a battlefield in Orleans. He too fled Paris months after Brown did, taking his daughter with him to the south of France. He joined the 51st Infantry and defended Orleans from the occupying troops. He lifted himself off the ground and was still bleeding when he made his way out of the battle field. He escaped to Spain and by the summer of 1940, he was in a Harlem hospital recuperating from his battle wounds. He never fully recovered. He worked as a salesman and later pushed buttons as an elevator operator in Rockefeller Center.

Brown found work at the "Happy Landing" bar in Colon. That lasted a couple of months. Some reported he opened a bar of his own and called it the *Cantina Campeon Al Brown*. Wherever he worked, wherever he went, the questions were the same.

What happened to all your money?

Why didn't you send any to your mother?

How come she had to clean *fulana y fulano's* clothes while you lived it up?

How could they take that much money without you realizing?

He packed his bag and moved to Panama City. He was given a job with the Panama City police. To help catch the pickpockets and the petty thieves, he was given a loaded gun. Some say he didn't like the job. He left, they said, because he wasn't fond of harassing poor people with few alternatives.

Others say he was fired. Fired for being a punch-drunk quick-draw cop with a short fuse. If you looked at him the wrong way, you'd find yourself face-to-face with the muzzle of his revolver, they said. If you made a comment about him, or if he thought you did, he'd place his overhand right on his open holster and stick a badge clutched in his left in your face while he asked you to repeat what you just said.

He became a loner and, according to Arroyo, literally had only one real friend during those years. A barber originally from Mexico who cut his hair for free and let him crash on the couch inside his barbershop. I never judged him, the barber told Arroyo many years later. He was always just the champ to me.

A bit overweight and with a mustache that hid his scarred lip, he walked the streets with a toothbrush in his shirt pocket looking for anyone to talk with. To talk about his career and the great battles he had. Some looked at the ailing old man before them and shrugged it off as some figment of his imagination.

The barber, Genio Escobar, a former boxer himself from the days the first boxing clubs opened in Mexico, said Brown was the "nicest champion I had ever met, and, believe me, I've met them all."

Escobar also managed boxers. One of them, flyweight Simon Vergara, was offered a handsome purse for a fight in Havana.

"I can't go," he told Brown and asked if Brown would be willing.

"You can keep ten percent for yourself."

No one had to twist Brown's arm to go. He had nothing tying him down and was anxious to reunite with Kid Chocolate in Cuba. On May 27th, 1946, they boarded Pan American Airways flight 302 to Camaguey, Cuba via Miami. Brown flew under the name "Téofilo Brown" and was listed as manager of boxer Simon Vergara.

Feeling rejuvenated once his shoes touched foreign soil, one of the first things Brown did was look for Kid.

Like Brown, the riches were long gone. Kid Chocolate lived in a housing project on the outskirts of Havana. In that part of the city the streets had lot numbers and all of the apartments looked the same. But it wasn't difficult for Brown to find his old friend.

The Kid's ribs and collarbones stuck out as much as the knuckles on his famed fists. On a street with no name, two of the greatest champions shook battered hands and embraced while no one watched.

Gone were the crowds and the cheers. Kid, like Panama, still had the occasional fans come up to him. Some were sincerely pleased to meet them. They wanted to know who was the best they'd fought and who was the fastest and who hit the hardest and did they ever meet Joe Louis. Some named their sons after them and others bought them a pack of cigarettes or a bottle of rum and thanked them for the memories.

Others were only initially excited to see them.

I remember when…

I watched you the day…

You were my favorite…

But as soon as they walked away, their tunes changed.

Look at how he turned out…

Kid Berg fucked him up…

What a waste…

On June 15th, Vergara was stopped in the third round and returned to Panama. Brown stayed in Cuba. The two former champions spent the afternoons seated in wooden chairs on a patch of dirt where grass should have been. They drank, they smoked, and they talked.

While Brown and Kid Chocolate drank from Bacardi bottles that said "Santiago de Cuba" on the front, Brown looked for a way out of Cuba. He made up his mind not to return to Panama and preferred Harlem over Paris. It was a place he could blend in more anonymously than the others and a place where the majority of the neighbors couldn't care less what the guy down the hall did.

Like he did twenty-three years before, he worked in the galley aboard a ship from Cuba to New York. When he arrived, he once again washed dishes in restaurants on the side streets along Sugar

Hill. And again, he spent some nights in Central Park. Desperate, he showed up at the Salem Crescent Athletic Club and asked to spar. Most of the pros refused. Brown didn't give up.

He showed up with more regularity than he did when he was an active fighter in his prime. He gave pointers to the young fighters when they cared to listen. Most of the time, Brown was left alone. The trainers had grown tired of telling him no.

He did a poor Panama Al Brown impersonation as he shadow-boxed and hit the bags wearing a white wife beater and slacks. Eventually he sparred up-and-coming fighters in the gym. They gave him a dollar and a beating per round. Brown sparred many rounds those days. Perhaps as many as he had when he was champion. After each session, he stumbled out of the ring and with unfocused eyes and an unsteady hand, he collected his money.

He was mocked and battered by fighters who would never approach his level. Still, he never said a word when they ridiculed him. With a dignity only champions possess, he held his head high above the snickers and comments and exited the gym in Harlem the same way he exited the rings around the world when they called him "n****r" and "f****t."

It went on for close to two years.

Then he stopped showing up at the gyms.

Right before the Ray Robinson-Steve Belloise fight, Ted Carroll of the New York Age reported that Brown lay sick in a bed at a charity ward in City Hospital on Welfare Island.

"Brown's ability was such that even the gay life he led could not prevent him from winning the championship," he wrote.

Carroll didn't elaborate on his condition other than to say Brown was seriously ill. Later it was revealed he suffered a stroke and was partially paralyzed on his right side. He was visited by Lew Burston and Marcel Cerdan, who went with contender and sparring partner Jean Walczack.

Cerdan, who boxed on the undercard of Brown's fight with Valentin Angelmann, had just lost the middleweight title to Jake LaMotta. I told you you'd be champion, he reminded Cerdan. You can win it back, he encouraged.

Two months after visiting Brown on that island of hospitals now called Roosevelt, Cerdan died in a plane crash while returning to America for a rematch against LaMotta.

Brown walked with a limp when he was released and used whatever he could lean on as a kickstand. That's the condition he was in when Peeters met him in Small's Paradise. Dressed in a blue tuxedo he hadn't worn in ten years, Brown greeted his old friend and asked if he remembered that night in Tunis when he told him about how he got started in boxing.

"What a long time ago that all is!" Brown said. "Now I am an old man." For the first time in all the years Peeters knew him, Brown admitted his age.

"I'm nearly 48," he sighed. "Ah, if I could only get back to Paris and see my friends. Life is too hard for me here," he said between coughs.

Of his finances he said he didn't have enough to pay his way back to Paris. "I have practically nothing. I've sold all my clothes. I only kept three suits and this tuxedo that I wore at the *Bal des Petits Lits Blancs* in 1938." His hand was broken he said and his business went bankrupt because he did not keep up with collecting from those who drank on credit.

He and Peeters sipped the last drops of scotch from their glasses and walked out together. They stopped in front of where Mayfield's Beauty Shoppe and later an ice cream shop stood, shook hands and said their final goodbyes. Peeters went left. Brown went right.

The Final Round

The winter season of 1950 - 1951 was an especially cold one. Several single-digit temperatures combined for a daily average below freezing in January. A few months after he met Peeters in the basement of Small's Paradise, a policeman poked with his nightstick at the homeless man who slept alongside a building near Times Square.

The homeless man didn't get up. He didn't say anything either. In fact, he didn't move or even twitch. The police threw the body in a cruiser and took it down to the station house where they threw him into a cell to sober up. A few hours passed and the body was still in the same motionless heap. An ambulance was called.

Brown was taken to Bellevue. When Brown came to, he had the hospital notify Lew Burston. Together with *Ring Magazine* editor Nat Fleischer, they had him transferred to Sea View hospital in Staten Island.

On January 12th, 1951 a fundraising dance was organized in Manhattan by former champion Barney Ross and Pedro Montanez, who was back and forth between his apartment in New York and his house on *Avenida Jose De Diego* in Cayey. During his final days, he dictated to a nurse a letter he wanted sent to Burston. He was losing this fight, he said. When Cocteau heard Brown was on his death bed, he recorded a message and sent it to him. It arrived just in time.

On April 11th, 1951, just as U.S. President Harry Truman prepared to relieve General Douglas MacArthur of his command in Korea, Panama Al Brown died. With the tape player to his ear according to Cocteau.

The medical superintendent at Sea View, Dr. Irving Klein, confirmed Brown had died of an advanced stage of tuberculosis. He was penniless with no friends or relatives the doctor said.

Fleischer and Burston made the funeral arrangements.

The night of his death, three unknown men showed up at the hospital. They were relatives they claimed and asked for the body.

BLACK INK

The hospital turned over the remains in a pine box that the three loaded onto the back of a white van.

The van weaved its way through the complex of Spanish mission-styled buildings, through the wooded area that led to the main entrance on Breille Avenue, and headed north.

That night, the three never-identified men drove the van to all the Harlem bars Brown frequented. They parked in front, swung open the rear doors and propped the opened casket on the rear bumper so all could have one last peek at the champion. They drank a final round with the champ and then they closed the casket and the van doors and drove to the next place. The following day they did the same, all the while collecting for his funeral costs.

When they were finished, the van made its way back to Staten Island and through the wooded entrance to Sea View Hospital. They parked at the entrance, carried the coffin out of the van and drove away.

He was buried in Resurrection Cemetery in Long Island City about two miles from where he defeated Gregorio Vidal. It was a modest ceremony that consisted mostly of the Harlem boxing and bar scene. A short time later, a Panamanian sports editor raised $750 to have him exhumed and placed on the SS Ancon and shipped to Panama.

In a small ceremony, Brown was laid to rest in the national cemetery, Amador Guerrero in tomb number 3165.

In New York, his tombstone read – Al Brown 1902-1951.

In Panama it reads - *Alfonso Téofilo Brown, gloria nacional del boxeo.*

They could have written that he was the first boxing champion from Latin America and that he lived an epic life. And, like Jean Cocteau wrote, they could have written that he was a poem.

Written in black ink.

References

Arroyo, Eduardo: *Panama Al Brown, 1902-1951*. Alianza Editorial, 1988. Print.

Benson, Peter: *Battling Siki: A Tale of Ring Fixes, Race, and Murder in the 1920s*. University of Arkansas Press, 2006. Print.

Brassai: *The Secret Paris of the '30s*. Thames and Hudson, 2001. Print.

Brown, Frederick: *An Impersonation of Angels: A Biography of Jean Cocteau*. The Viking Press, 1968. Print.

Cocteau, Jean and Phelps, Robert, (compiler): *Professional Secrets: An Autobiography of Jean Cocteau*. Farrar, Strauss & Giroux, 1970. Print.

Canal Zone Governor: *Annual Report of the Governor of the Panama Canal*. Various publishers- various years.

Flanner, Janet: *Paris Was Yesterday, 1925-1939*. Mariner Books, 1988. Print.

Hollandersky, Abe: *The Life Story of Abe The Newsboy Hero of a Thousand Fights*. Abe The Newsboy, 1952. Print.

Hughes, Brian, MBE: *For King and Country*. Empire Publications, LTD, 2001. Print.

Hughes, Brian, MBE: *Jock McAvoy: Portrait of a Fighting Legend*. Empire Publications, 2002. Print.

Mahr Van Hardeveld, Rose: *Make the Dirt Fly!*. Pan Press, 1957. Print.

Menendez, Elio and Ortega, Victor J: *Kid Chocolate: El Boxeo Soy Yo*. Editorial Orbe, 1980. Print.

Mustelier, Evelio: *Kid Tunero Viente anos de ring y fuera*. Editorial Playor, 1957. Print.

Peeters, Georges: *Monstre sacres du ring*. La table ronde, 1959. Print.

Shack, William: *Harlem in Montmartre: A Paris Jazz Story Between the Great Wars*. University of California Press, 2001. Print.

BLACK INK

Stovall, Tyler: *Paris Noir: African Americans in the City of Light*. Houghton Mifflin, 1996. Print.

Tamagne, Florence: *A History of Homosexuality in Europe: Berlin, London, Paris 1919-1939*. Algora, 2004. Print.

Various Newspapers containing fight previews, reports, and interviews between 1923- 1951 were used including:
ABC (Spain)
Associated Press (USA)
Associated Negro Press (USA)
El Mundo Deportivo (Spain)
El Mercantil Valenciano (Spain)
L'Auto (France)
L'Echo (France)
L'Oran (Algeria)
London Mail (England)
Daily Mirror (England)
Echo (Wales)
The Afro American Weekly (USA)
NY Amsterdam News (USA)
The Brooklyn Daily Eagle (USA)
NY Times (USA)
Montreal Gazette (Canada)
Ottawa Citizen (Canada)
Panama Star and Herald (Panama)
Pittsburgh Courier (USA)
Chicago Tribune (USA)
La Estrella de Panama (Panama)

Websites used included boxrec, a database of records with links to primary sources; boxeo 1930s BlogSpot- a site filled with profiles of many Spanish boxers of the past; BAVCC- Le Bureau des Archives des victims de conflits contemporains- includes information on victims of wars and conflicts including the Holocaust; politique-auschwitz BlogSpot; servicehistorique.sga.defense.gouv.fr; and the website of France's national library, BNR.

Other resources used were those found in the Hank Kaplan collection at Brooklyn College and all of the resources and microfilms of historical newspapers of both the United States and Panama which are available at the Schomburg Center for Research in Harlem.

Boxing Record

1922

Mar-19 Jose Moreno   Colon, Panama W 6
Apr-22 Montalbo Kid   Colon, Panama W KO 2
May-21 Battling Miller   Colon, Panama W TKO 5
July-29 Ernie Rijfkogel   Colon, Panama W KO 4
Aug-09 Kid Pelkey Panama City, Panama W TKO 4
Oct-07 Young Jeff Clark   Colon, Panama W TKO 6
Dec-09 Sailor Patchett Colon, Panama   Draw 15
   Panamanian flyweight title

1923

Feb-11   Pedro Troncoso   Colon, Panama W 6
Aug-22   Johnny Breslin New York, USA   Draw 4
Sept-22 Tommy Martin New York, USA W TKO 1
Oct-06   Bobby Risden New York, USA   Draw 6
Oct-13   Bernie Hyams New York, USA   W KO 3
Dec-12   Willie Darcy   New York, USA W 12
Dec-17   Willie LaMorte Trenton, New Jersey, USA ND 8

1924

Apr-12   Willie Farley   New York, USA   W KO 1
May-03   Bobby Burns   New York, USA   W KO 7
May-24   Joe Colletti New York, USA W 12
June-07 Willie LaMorte New York, USA   W KO 2
June-28 Allie Kaufmann   New York, USA   W KO 1

Aug-09 George McNally New York, USA W TKO 4
Aug-30 Joey Russell New York, USA W 10
Sept -13 Jimmy Moreno New York, USA W KO 1
Sept-27 Billy Marlowe New York, USA W 10
Oct-25 Frankie Ash New York, USA W KO 1
Nov-11 Tommy Milton New York, USA W 15
Dec-06 Jimmy Russo New York, USA L 10

1925

Jan-03 Jimmy Russo New York, USA W 10
Feb-07 Terry Miller New York, USA W 10
Feb-19 Davey Abad Brooklyn, NY, USA W 6
May-16 Dominick Petrone New York, USA W 6
June-11 Frankie Murray Atlantic City, NJ, USA L DQ 1
June-27 Johnny Breslin New York, USA W 10
Aug-22 Eddie Flank New York, USA W 10
Sept-09 Davey Adelman Atlantic City, NJ, USA W 10
Sept-21 Joey Ross Jersey City, NJ, USA ND 10
Oct-3 Bobby Green New York, USA W 10
Oct-16 Johnny Breslin New York, USA W 10
Nov-14 Marty Gold New York, USA W 10
Dec-12 Tommy Hughes New York, USA W 10

1926

Feb-06 Dominick Petrone New York, USA L 10
Mar-20 Eddie O'Dowd New York, USA W 12
Apr-10 Willie O'Connell Brooklyn, NY, USA Draw 6
Apr-23 Abe Goldstein New York, USA L 10
May-21 Teddy Silva New York, USA W KO 3
June-05 Jacques Pettibon New York, USA W KO 4
June-26 Billy Marlowe New York, USA W KO 4
July-08 Pete Zivic New York, USA W 10
Aug-05 Harry Forbes Albany, NY, USA W 12

BLACK INK

Sept-02 Joe Ryder   New York, USA   W DQ 4
Nov-10 Antoine Merlo Paris, France   W KO 3
Dec-01 Roger Fabregues Paris, France   W KO 1
Dec-14 Henri Scillie Paris, France   Draw 12

1927

Jan-25 Edouard Mascart Paris, France   W TKO 5
Mar-08 Kid Socks   Paris, France   W KO 5
Apr-02 Eugene Criqui Paris, France   W 10
May-10 Young Ciclone Paris, France   W 10
Oct-18 Albert Ryall Paris, France   W KO 2
Nov-22 Henri Scillie Paris, France L 12
Dec-10 Andre Routis   Paris, France   L 10
Dec-18 Henri Scillie Paris, Paris, France   Draw 10

1928

Mar-23 Benny Schwartz   New York, USA   W 10
Apr-10 Steve Nugent   Toledo, Ohio, USA   W DQ 2
Apr-27 Eddie O'Dowd Toledo, Ohio, USA   ND 10
June-21 Billy Shaw   New York, New York, USA   W KO 1
Sept-13 Kid Francis New York, USA   W 12
    Vacant NBA bantamweight title
      Stripped of NBA title Oct. 15 by new NBA president
Nov-17 Johnny Cuthbert   Paris, France   Draw 12
Dec-18 Harry Corbett Paris, France   W 12

1929

Jan-29 Gustave Humery Paris, France   W KO 1
Mar-23 Domenico Bernasconi   Madrid, Spain W 10
Apr-09 Joe Cadman Paris, France   W KO 3
June-18 Gregorio Vidal Long Island City, Queens, New York, USA W 15

vacant NYSAC World bantamweight title

July-03   Vic Burrone   Newark, NJ, USA   W 10
July-16   Vernon Cormier   Portland, Maine, USA   W KO 4
July-26   Battling Battalino   Hartford, Conn, USA   L 10
Aug-28   Knud Larsen   Copenhagen, Denmark   W 12

1930

Jan-25   Pinky Silverberg   Havana, Cuba   W 10
Feb-08   Johnny Erickson   New York, USA   W DQ 4
   NYSAC World bantamweight title
   NBA World bantamweight title

Feb-18   Johnny Canzoneri Allentown, Pa, USA   W 10
Mar-14   Tommy Paul   Buffalo, New York, USA   Draw 6
Apr-15   KO Morgan   Toledo, Ohio, USA   W DQ 7
Apr-21   Al Gillette   New Bedford, Mass, USA   W KO 9
June-05   Milton Cohen   Waterbury, Conn, USA   W KO 1
June-16   Johnny McCoy West Springfield, Mass, USA   W TKO 6
June-18   Benny Brostoff   Bayonne, NJ, USA   W TKO 2
June-24   Mickey Doyle   Scranton, Pennsylvania, USA   W 10
July-04   Calvin Reed   Baltimore, Md, USA   W KO 4
July-23   Domenico Bernasconi   Brooklyn, NY, USA   W 10
Aug-29   Johnny Vacca   Bridgeport, Conn, USA   W TKO 3
Oct-04   Eugene Huat   Paris, France   W 15
   IBU World bantamweight title
Oct-22   Jose Girones   Barcelona, Spain   Draw 10
Nov -08 Nic Bensa   Paris, France   W 10

1931

Feb-11   Nic Bensa   Paris, France   W 10
Mar-09   Billy Farrell Manchester, UK   W TKO 3
Mar-23   Douglas Parker   Newcastle, UK W TKO 11

BLACK INK

Apr-13 Jack Garland   Manchester, UK   W 15
Apr-15 Roger Simende   Paris, France   W KO 3
Apr-30 Julien Verbist Paris, France   W KO 8
May -21 Teddy Baldock   London, UK   W TKO 12
June-15 Johnny Cuthbert London, UK   L DQ 8
Aug-25 Pete Sanstol   Montreal, Canada W 15
   NBA World bantamweight title
NYSAC World bantamweight title
Sept-21 Ginger Jones   Mountain Ash, Wales, UK W KO 9
Oct-27 Eugene Huat   Montreal, Canada W 15
   NBA World bantamweight title
Nov-18 Art Chapdelaine Quebec City, Canada W KO 7
Dec-15 Newsboy Brown   Los Angeles, Ca, USA   L 10

1932

Jan-04 Speedy Dado   Los Angeles, Ca, USA   L 10
Mar-14 Golf Ball Bernard New Bedford, Mass, USA W 10
May-18 Dominique Di Cea   Paris, France   W 10
May-28 Luigi Quadrini Cardiff, Wales, UK   W RTD 6
May -31 Francois Machtens Paris, France   W 10
June-13 Nel Tarleton   Liverpool, UK   Draw 15
June-18 Eugene Huat   Paris, France   W 10
June-25 Vittorio Tamagnini Milan, Italy L 10
July-10 Kid Francis   Marseille, France W 15
   IBU World bantamweight title
Aug-17 Roland LeCuyer Montreal, Canada W TKO 6
Sept-19 Emile Pladner   Toronto, Canada W KO 1
   NBA World bantamweight title
Sept-26 Mose Butch   Pittsburgh, Pa, USA   W 10
Oct-18 Francois Machtens Antwerp, Belgium W 10
Oct-23 Nicolas Petit-Biquet Brussels, Belgium W 10
Nov-14 Emile Pladner   Paris, France   W KO 2
Dec-01 Dick Burke   Sheffield, UK   W 12
Dec-03 Henri Scillie   Brussels, Belgium Draw 10

Dec-08 Francois Machtens   Paris, France   W 10

1933

Feb-09   Henri Poutrain   Paris, France   W 10
Mar-05   Johnny Peters   London, UK   W 15
Mar-19   Domenico Bernasconi   Milan, Italy   W 12
   IBU World bantamweight title
Apr-30   Tommy Hyams   London, UK   W KO 9
May-07   Arthur Boddington   Royton, UK   W RTD 3
May-13   Dick Burke   Cleethorpes, UK   W TKO 12
June-12 Dave Crowley   London, UK   W 10
July-03 Johnny King   Manchester, UK   W 15
   IBU World bantamweight title
Sept-30 Georges LePerson   Algiers, Algeria   W 10
Nov-12   Alfredo Magnolfi   Casablanca, Morocco   W 10
Dec-08   Luigi Quadrini   Oran, Algeria   W 10

1934

Feb-19   Young Perez   Paris, France   W 15
   IBU World bantamweight title
Apr-07   Maurice Dubois   Geneva, Switzerland   W TKO 2
Apr-16   Kid Francis   Paris, France   W 10
May-17   Gustave Humery   Paris, France   L DQ 6
June-30 Johnny Edwards   Zurich, Switzerland   L 10
Nov-01   Young Perez   Tunis, Tunisia   W KO 10
   IBU World bantamweight title
Dec-09   Francois Machtens   Lille, France   W 10
Dec-24   Freddie Miller   Paris, France   L 10

1935

Mar-02   Henri Barras   Paris, France   W 10
Mar-09   Gustavo Ansini   Paris, France   Draw 10

BLACK INK

Mar-18 Baltasar Sangchili Valencia, Spain L 10
Apr-12 Luigi Quadrini Madrid, Spain W 10
Apr-24 Javier Torres Barcelona, Spain W TKO 2
June-01 Baltasar Sangchili Valenciana, Spain L 15
    IBU World bantamweight title
Sept-13 Pete Sanstol Oslo, Norway L 10

1937

Sept-09 Andre Regis Paris, France W KO 1
Sept-23 Maurice Huguenin Paris, France W KO 3
    Vacant IBU World featherweight title
Oct-08 Francis Augier Geneva, Switzerland W KO 2
Nov-25 Joseph Decico Paris, France W 10
Dec-22 Young Perez Paris, France W KO 5

1938

Mar-04 Baltasar Sangchili Paris, France W 15
    IBU World bantamweight title
Apr-13 Valentin Angelmann Paris, France W KO 8

1939

Apr-22 Cristobal Jaramillo New York, NY, USA W TKO 4
May-06 Mariano Arilla New York, NY, USA W KO 3

1941

July-14 Leocadio Torres Panama City, Panama W KO 8
July-26 Battling Nelson Panama City, Panama W KO 4
Sept-07 Kid Fortune Panama City, Panama W KO 2
    Panamanian featherweight title
Oct-26 Eduardo Carrasco Panama City, Panama L 10

1942

Mar-08 Eduardo Carrasco   Panama City, Panama   L 10
Aug-30 Leocadio Torres   Panama City, Panama   Draw 15
    Panamanian featherweight title
Dec-04 Kid Fortune   Colon, Panama   W 10

Index

A

Abad, Davey, *65*, *73*, *88*
Alexi, Joe, *81*
Alfara, Jose Martinez De, *189*, *193*, *195*
Ali, Muhammad, *63*
Angelmann, Valentin, *211*, *212*, *213*, *214*, *215*, *226*
Ara, Ignacio, *89*, *193*
Arcel, Ray, *45*, *47*, *201*, *215*
Archibald, Joey, *200*
Arguello, Alexis, *109*
Arilla, Mariano, *215*
Armstrong, Louis, *75*, *116*
Arroyo, Eduardo, *60*
Ash, Frankie, *58*, *87*, *151*
Attell, Abe, *42*
Avernin, Jules, *200*

B

Badia, Ramon, *192*
Baker, Josephine, *81*
Baldock, Teddy, *78*, *91*, *100*, *114*, *135*, *136*
Baldwin, Chris, *76*
Balin, Mireille, *174*
Ballerino, Mike, *49*, *57*
Bancroft, Hubert Howe, *10*
Battalino, Battling, *112*, *130*, *131*
Bell, Ansel, *46*, *58*
Bell, Archie, *87*, *92*, *106*, *119*
Bellevue, *227*
Belloise, Mike, *224*
Belloise, Steve, *225*
Benaim, Gilbert, *169*, *170*, *171*
Bentley, Gladys, *61*
Berg, Jackie "Kid", *85*, *123*, *131*, *137*
Berlin, Irving, *16*
Bernasconi, Domenico, *78*, *104*, *122*, *123*, *125*, *147*, *161*, *162*
Bettinson, Arthur, *133*
Bimstein, Whitey, *70*, *180*
Black Bill, *89*, *109*, *125*, *142*, *143*
Blake, George, *105*
Bowker, Joe, *134*
Boyles Thirty Acres, *41*
Brennan, Bill, *41*
Breslin, Johnny, *49*, *50*, *53*, *69*
Brown, Jimmy, *63*, *71*, *74*
Buchenwald, *176*
Budinich, John, *5*, *23*
Buff, Johnny, *87*
Buffer, Michael, *86*

Bullard, Eugene, *75, 76, 158, 173, 222*
Buonaugurio, Guy, *147*
Burah, Gabriel, *182*
Burke, Dick, *v, 156, 157*
Burston, Lew, *168, 169, 172, 183, 226, 227*
Burton, Gene, *226*
Butch, Mose, *142*

C

Callura, Jackie, *120*
Canzoneri, Tony, *123*
Caprice Vennois, *199*
Carbone, Paul, *148*
Carnera, Primo, *161*
Carpentier, George, *31, 55, 56, 72, 81, 125, 175, 176, 186, 197*
Carrasco, Eduardo, *220*
Carroll, Ted, *2, 225*
Casanova, Baby, *179*
Cerdan, Marcel, *102, 226*
Chanel, Coco, *206*
Chautemps, PM, *209*
Chavez, Julio Cesar, *109*
Chip, George, *18*
Chocolate, Kid, *89, 94, 105, 106, 107, 115, 119, 120, 121, 123, 130, 131, 135, 138, 143, 223, 224, 226*
Ciclone, Young, *82, 83, 128*
Clark, Jeff, *17, 26, 29, 34*

Cocteau, Jean, *7, 204, 205, 206, 207, 208, 209, 210, 211, 212, 213, 214, 228*
Cocteau, *7, 145, 197, 198, 200, 204, 228*
Cohen, Robert, *203*
Colletti, Joe, *87*
Corbett, Harry, *79, 99, 100*
Cortijos, Francisco, *193*
Cotton Club, *37*
Coulon, Johnny, *122*
Crawford, Jamal, *119*
Criqui, Eugene, *80, 81, 102, 131, 160*
Cros, Charles, *75*
Crouse, Buck, *18, 19, 20*
Crow, Jim, *15*
Cuthbert, Johnny, *100, 137, 172*

D

Dado, Speedy, *87, 141, 142*
Datto, Johnny, *41*
Dawson, Hook, *27*
Dawson, James P., *72, 93, 98*
De Max, Eduord, *205*
De Niro, Robert, *1*
Decico, Joseph, *183, 184, 208, 209, 211*
DeLa Lastra, Abel, *116*
Dempsey, Jack, *17, 25, 30, 41, 45, 47, 70, 92, 186, 196*
Desbordes, Jean, *205*
Desgrange, Henri, *213*
DeVos, Rene, *167*

BLACK INK

Di Cea, Dominique, *136*
Diamond, Bobby, *56, 137, 158, 159, 160, 164, 165, 183, 190, 191, 193, 198, 202*
Dickson, Jeff, *71, 76, 77, 99, 123, 171, 175, 206, 222*
Dillon, Jack, *18*
Dixon, George, *42, 73, 92, 134*
Docusen, Bernard, *39*
Dollings, Dai, *45, 47, 48, 49, 51, 53, 59, 60, 132, 140*
Donahue, Tom, *88, 91, 92, 93, 94, 96*
Dorazio, Gus, *65*
Douglas, John, *132*
Driscoll, Jim, *48, 134*
Dundee, Johnny, *45, 48, 79*
Dupas, Ralph, *39*
Duran, Roberto, *5, 54, 109*
Durant, Milton, *28*
Dyckman Oval, *201*

E

Ebbet's Field, *122, 123*
Edmond's Cellar, *61*
Edwards, Johnny, *178*
Ellington, Duke, *36*
Erickson, Johnny, *87, 108, 119, 120*
Erne, Frank, *74*
Escobar, Genio, *223*
Escobar, Sixto, *109, 120, 179, 181*

F

Fahy, Tom, *60*
Farrell, Billy, *133*
Father Divine, *65*
Ferdinand, Franz, *22*
Fernandez, Ignacio, *131*
Fields, Jackie, *112*
Finlay, Carlos, *14*
Firpo, Luis, *5, 41, 57*
Fleetwood Walker, *39*
Fleischer, Nat, *227*
Flix, Carlos, *125, 187*
Flowers, Tiger, *57, 64*
Flynn, Leo P, *29, 44, 45, 46, 47, 48, 49, 51, 56, 60, 63, 64*
Forbes, Harry, *73*
Foreman, Al, *123*
Fortune, Kid, *219*
Foster, Edward C., *114*
Foul Proof Taylor, *51*
Francis, Kid, *78, 87, 91, 92, 98, 104, 108, 147, 148, 150, 174, 175, 176, 187*

G

Galileo Montoro Gomez, *194*
Gamble, Tom, *137*
Gandon, Pierre, *153*
Gans, Joe, *16, 25, 38, 44, 54, 137*
Gaston, Charles Raymond, *56*
Gavilan, Kid, *109*
Genaro, Frankie, *57, 60, 66, 73, 151, 167, 174, 211, 215*

Gibbons, Young Mike Risden, *27, 30, 44*
Gil, Pres. Emilio, *114*
Gillette, Al, *121*
Girones, Jose, *125, 126, 127, 128, 129*
Glick, Joe, *85*
Godfrey, George, *41, 156*
Goldstein, Abe, *70*
Goodrich, Al, *19, 30, 69*
Goodwin, Bob, *201*
Gould, Alan, *156*
Graham, Bushy, *73, 91, 92, 98, 111, 131*
Graziano, Rocky, *183*
Greb, Harry, *70, 86, 122*
Grupp's Gymnasium, *44, 45, 53, 82*
Guiralechea, Segundo, *22*
Gutierrez, Luis Pincho, *89, 106, 115, 121, 215*

H

Hearns, Thomas, *54*
Hemmingway, Ernest, *75, 76*
Henderson, Fletcher, *36*
Henderson, Smack, *116*
Herman, Babe, *122*
Herman, Pete, *122*
Herrera, Aurelio, *42*
Hindenburg, Pres., *179*
Hine, Hie, *153*
Hollandersky, Abe, *17*
Holtzer, Maurice, *128, 167, 184*

Houck, Leo, *18*
Huat, Eugene, *123, 125, 126, 139, 140, 141, 147, 151, 174, 181, 207, 211*
Hughes, Ed, *69, 92, 105, 107, 108, 122, 123, 125*
Hughes, Langston, *36, 55, 75*
Huguenin, Maurice, *207*
Humery, Gustave, *81, 100, 102, 108, 171, 172, 176, 177, 184*
Humphries, Joe, *51*
Hurston, Zora Neal, *36*
Hurtado, Young, *220*

I

Isaac, Stanley, *114*

J

Jack, Beau, *64*
Jackson, Michael, *127*
Jacobs, Joe, *178*
Jaramillo, Cristobal, *215*
Johnson, Jack, *16, 22, 23, 37, 38, 40, 67, 133*
Johnson, Len, *132*
Jones, Ginger, *140*

K

Kane, Peter, *212*
Khill, Marcel, *200, 222*
Kid Norfolk, *16, 17, 18, 19, 25, 27, 29, 35, 38, 42, 46, 54, 55*
Kid, Dixie, *75, 76, 186*

BLACK INK

King, Johnny, *163*
King's Hall, *133, 134*
Klein, Irving, *227*
KO Morgan, *120*

L

LaBarba, Fidel, *72, 91, 92, 98,
105, 131, 147*
Ladoumégue, Jules, *129*
Lake, Bugler Harry, *78, 79*
LaMotta, Jake, *226*
Landfield, Herman, *112*
Lang, Clubber, 1
Langford, Sam, *17, 26, 29, 44,
133, 137*
Lardner, John, *135*
Larsen, Knud, *106, 112, 113,
114, 127, 128*
Le Roy, John, *205*
Lee, Canada, *89*
Leonard, Benny, *45*
Leperson, Georges, *169*
Levan, Larry, *2,3*
Lewis, Harry, *74*
Lewis, John H, *201*
Livingstone, Jack, *28*
Loayza, Stanislaus, *41, 69*
Louis, Joe, *181*
Lumiansky, *88, 89, 90, 92, 93,
94, 98, 99, 100, 101, 103,
104, 105, 106, 107, 111, 112,
115, 117, 118, 121, 130, 131,
132, 134, 136, 137, 138, 139,
141, 143, 144, 148, 150, 151,
154, 155, 156, 157, 158, 159,*
*160, 162, 163, 164, 165, 166,
167, 168, 169, 170, 171, 172,
173, 175*
Lynch, Joe, *122*

M

MacArthur, Gen. Douglas,
227
Mack, Georgie, *148*
Madame Bey's, *51*
Madison Square Garden, *72,
87, 89, 92, 98, 106, 120, 147,
151, 201*
Malibran, Frederico, *153*
Mann Tower, Horace, *180*
Marino, Tony, *201, 202, 203,
210, 215*
Marshall, Lloyd, *67*
Martin, Pete, *180*
Martinez Fort, *187*
Mascart, E, *79, 80, 100, 128*
McGovern, Terry, *42, 92*
McGraw, Phil, *57*
McLarnin, Jimmy, *69, 72, 89*
McMahon, Eddie, *63, 66, 115,
162*
McMahon, Jess, *87*
McVae, Sam, *17, 26, 28, 29, 44*
Medina, Theo, *202*
Mendes, Jimmy, *99*
Merlo, Antoine, *77*
Mestalla Stadium, *189*
Miller, Bill, *64, 102*
Miller, Freddie, *184*
Mitchel, Georges, *102, 183*

Montanez, Pedro, *6, 180, 183, 184, 226, 227*
Monzon, Carlos, *109*
Moore, Archie, *67*
Moran, Owen, *134*
Moulin Rouge, *82*
Muldoon, William, *110*
Mussolini, *161*

N

National Sporting Club, *133*
Nelson, Battling, *42, 219*
Nugent, Bruce, *61*

O

O'Brien, Philadelphia Jack, *23*
Ortega, Jack, *17, 18, 19, 20, 188*

P

Palais des Sports, *210*
Palermo, Blinky, *22, 64*
Palmer, Pedlar, *134*
Parra, Routier, *88*
Patchett, Sailor, *30, 31*
Pattenden, Kid, *87*
Paul, Tommy, *120*
Peerless Quartet, *16*
Peeters, Georges, *30, 188*
Pep, Willie, *83*
Perez, Benjamin Kid, *174*
Perez, Victor Young, *151, 174, 181, 182, 183, 187, 207, 209*
Petrone, Dominick, *70, 73, 87, 91*

Picasso, Pablo, *82*
Pigallé, *82, 99*
Pincus, Nat, *65*
Plaza de Toros, *167*
Polo Grounds, *51*
Prehn, Paul, *96, 113*

Q

Quadrini, Luigi, *128, 144, 187, 190*

R

Reed, Calvin, *122*
Reimer, R, *201*
Remy. Bertys, *203*
Renault, Jack, *41*
Riambau, Vicente, *192, 196*
Rickard, Tex, *38, 56, 63, 66, 73, 85, 92, 97, 98*
Rivers, Mexican Joe, *42*
Riviere, Edouard, *135*
Riviere, Georges, *135*
Roberts, Bob, *206, 211*
Robeson, Paul, *55*
Roderick, Ernie, *102*
Rodriguez, Angel, *41*
Rodriguez, Blas, *114, 117*
Romero-Rojas, Quintin, *56*
Roosevelt, Pres. Teddy, *17, 226*
Ros, Pedro, *192*
Rosenberg, Charley Phil, *48*
Ross, Barney, *227*
Roth, Gustave, *79*

Routis, Andre, *79, 85, 86, 88, 100, 112, 130, 137*
Routis, André, *78, 85, 87*
Rubio, Primo, *192*
Russo, Jimmy, *65*
Ryall, Alberto, *83*

S

Sabatino, Attilio, *180*
Sablons, Clovis, *192*
Saguero, Relampago, *180*
Salica, Lou, *200*
Sanga, Guiseppe, *153*
Sangchili, Baltasar, *174, 185, 186, 187, 188, 189, 190, 197, 198, 201*
Sanstol, Pete, *87, 119, 139, 151, 181, 199, 200*
Sarron, Petey, *87, 119*
Saxton, Johnny, *64*
Scalfaro, Joey, *106*
Schemann, Rene, *163, 166, 167, 168*
Schmeling, Max, *51, 122, 143, 178*
Schwartz, Benny, *87*
Schwartz, Corporal Izzy, *55, 58, 88, 91*
Scillie, Henri, *78, 83, 85*
Shakespeare, William, *98*
Sharkey, Jack, *123*
Shaw, Billy, *89*
Shea, Eddie, *147*
Shibe Park, *107*

Siki, Battling, *55, 56, 63, 67, 69, 70, 79, 81, 82, 174*
Silverberg, Pinky, *119*
Simende, Roger, *135, 167*
Slattery, Jimmy, *72*
Small's Paradise, *36, 226, 227*
Smith, Ada Bricktop, *75, 123*
Smith, Harry, *153*
Smith, Solly, *42*
Snaz, *1*
Solidor, Suzy, *199*
Songkirat, Chamroen, *203*
Sparks, James, *149*
Spirito, Francois, *148, 149, 150*
Sriber, Charles, *131*
Stillman's, *44, 45*
Strand Gym, *25, 26, 28, 29, 88*
Sugar Hill, *225*
Sugar Ray Robinson Robinson, *37, 65, 226*
Suggs, Chick, *73, 88*
Sweatman, Wilbur, *36*

T

Tarante, Jimmy, *153*
Tarleton, Nel, *100, 147*
Tate, Bill, *28*
Taylor, Charles "Bud", *91, 92*
Thil, Marcel, *100, 132, 154, 175, 193*
Thomas, Saint, *65*
Thompson, Yg Jack, *112*
Thurman, Wallace, *36*
Torres, Leocadio, *219*

Troncoso, Pedro, *31, 118*
Truman, Pres. Harry, *227*
Tunney, Gene, *70, 97, 98, 113, 135*
Tyson, Mike, *20*

U

Uzabeaga, Carlos, *80*
Uzcudon, Paulino, *114*

V

Vaccarelli, Tony, *48*
Valdez, Pres., *29*
Valentino, Rudolph, *180*
Venturi, Enrico, *200*
Vergara, Simon, *223, 224*
Vicentini, Luis, *56*
Vidal, Gregorio, *89, 106, 107, 108, 110, 119, 156, 180, 228*
Villa, Pancho, *41, 48, 55, 58, 68, 87, 89*
Villepontoux, J, *71, 74, 76, 79, 137*
Vincent, Armand, *180*
Volante, Dom, *100, 163*

W

Walczack, Jean, *226*
Walker, Mickey, *72, 122*
Wallace, Coley, *64*
Wilkinson, Enrique, *22*
Willard, Jess, *23, 24, 41, 121, 197*
Williams, Kid, *57, 92, 122*
Wills, Harry, *17, 29, 38, 44, 45, 57*
Wilson, Pres. Woodrow, *22*
Wolgast, Ad, *42*
Wolgast, Midget, *57, 120, 200*
Wright, Chalky, *215, 224*

Z

Zenti, Kid, *153*
Zivic, Fritzie, *113*
Zivic, Pete, *87*
Zorilla, Santiago, *88, 110*
Zurita, Juan, *200, 206*

Bob Roberts and Al Brown. Photo by Henri Manuel. Paris, 1938.

www.ingramcontent.com/pod-product-compliance
Lightning Source LLC
Chambersburg PA
CBHW032022230426
43671CB00005B/166